Engaging with Empowerment

I dedicate this book to my father, the late Prof. Amulya K.N. Reddy, who taught me to care about injustice in the world, and to think clearly and analytically; to my mother, Vimala Reddy, for her love and support; and to my aunt, Sudha V. Reddy, who, as Chair of the Karnataka Social Welfare Board, introduced me, when I was just a child, to the problems poor women face in our society.

I also dedicate this book to the many mentors who encouraged my capacity to straddle the worlds of action and analysis, and pushed me beyond the limits I might have set for myself: Noshir H. Antia, J.P. Naik, Devaki Jain, Sheela Patel, Anil Bordia, and Sharada Jain.

Above all, I dedicate this book to those scores of incredible women in Bombay's slums and Karnataka's remote villages, who revealed to me, through our collective struggle, that empowerment is both a journey and a destination. I remain humbled by their courage and grateful for their wisdom.

Engaging with Empowerment

an intellectual and experiential journey

SRILATHA BATLIWALA

women
UNLIMITED
an associate of
kali for women

Engagine with Empowerment:
an intellectual and experiential journey
was first published in India in 2013
by
Women Unlimited
(an associate of Kali for Women)
7/10, First Floor
Sarvapriya Vihar
New Delhi – 110 016
www.womenunlimited.net

ISBN: 978-81-88965-78-6

Cover design: Neelima Rao

Typeset at Tulika Print Communication Services, New Delhi,
and printed at Raj Press, R-3 Inderpuri, New Delhi 110 012

Contents

Foreword

THIS inspiring book takes us on a journey through a lifetime of thought and action that has touched and transformed the lives of countless women in India and beyond. Exploring the trajectories of her own engagement with the politics of transformation in the fields of activism and action (in which she has become so pivotal a figure), Srilatha Batliwala gives us, with this collection, a book that is beautifully written: evocative and moving in places, sharply analytical in others, rich with ideas, a treasure trove of tools for thought. It offers us enormous insight into the sparks that can ignite processes of change, the contours of feminist leadership, and the dynamics of power and empowerment.

The book begins with an engaging tale of the author's coming of age as someone for whom the imperative to act in the world was stronger than exploring ideas for ideas' sake. Srilatha talks of the sense of personal responsibility she grew up with, a sense that the world was wrong and needed to be put right, and her conviction that she had to be 'out there, in the trenches, so to speak, if I was a worthy person'. Narrating the story of an upbringing in which she was taught to act, periodically take a step back to reflect and analyse, and then act again, she describes how the experience of reflection and action shaped her own praxis. In doing so, she shows that ultimately the best test of a theory is not its elegance, but the extent to which it can make sense of lived realities. In her account of how she put theories to the test, we never lose sight of those realities, nor of the people who are so much a part of them. As Srilatha puts it,

> I always carried in my head, the faces, voices and perspectives of the
> hundreds and thousands of real women I had worked with over the
> years; I had a sense of the sort of questions they would ask of a theory or

conceptual framework, the kind of holes they would poke in it from the perspective of their experience and location.

Unfolding through a series of pieces written at different points in the course of her engagement with power and empowerment, the book offers many lessons for contemporary feminist activism. The first section contains three chapters that open up the questions to which Srilatha subsequently came to devote so much energy; these evocative pieces are also a testament to quite how much we can learn from stepping out of the familiarity of our everyday lives and engaging with people in entirely different circumstances. What struck me while reading them is the importance of her travels—which took her into myriad conversations with different women in different places—in shaping Srilatha's expanded vision of the possible, and enriching the quality of her analysis.

Srilatha's writing effortlessly weaves conceptualisation and critique with a vivid sense of, and commitment to, the possibilities for positive change. The second section brings together writings on empowerment that trace a path through familiar terrain, and offers us new perspectives on some of today's challenges. Unafraid to sound the alarm, her courage and honesty shine through in her critique of the co-option of the transformatory promise of the term 'empowerment'. Srilatha and Deepa Dhanraj's exposé of micro-credit schemes in India, 'Gender Myths that Instrumentalise Women: A View from the Frontline', came at a time when the development establishment was still so wildly in love with micro-credit that it was positively heretical to bring some of the practices associated with it into the spotlight. The facts they brought to our attention came with an analysis that called for renewed caution about development's tendency to bank on 'magic bullet solutions'.

It is this willingness to tackle development's most sacred cows that marks out Srilatha's work as especially important. Elsewhere in this and the following section, we see her taking on the evisceration of 'empowerment' and the trite platitudes that surround development's talk about 'leadership'. What she gives us is a reading of these terms that is deeply imbued with a concern about the notions of privilege and justice. Her definition is one that emphasises the power, politics, and, above all, the process of empowerment:

> Empowerment is not a goal, but a foundational process that enables marginalised women to construct their own political agendas and form movements and struggles for achieving fundamental and lasting transformation in gender and social power structures.

I can think of no better definition of empowerment; with these words, Srilatha gets to the heart of the matter, and is uncompromising about what it means to be 'empowered', and how that might contribute to achieving a more just and equal world.

Srilatha talks of how, when she first encountered it, the term had an almost visceral effect on her. She recalls

> ...the immediate reaction the term created within me—a profound sense of resonance, of having found the *perfect word*, the *perfect concept* for what I believed I was doing in my everyday work with women.

No one could have imagined that this of all words would lend itself to the kind of appropriation we have witnessed over the last decade. The term has been co-opted by banks and global corporations as part of the instrumentalisation of women for development, and deployed in the creation of new consumers. This new 'empowerment' promises women as the means to development, so that families, communities and nations can thrive in an unchallenged, intensely unequal neo-liberal order. It is still about transformation, still about power; however, the story is a very different one, transformed into one about buying and selling power, where the power to consume and to facilitate consumption is the desired goal.

Rural Indian women have been enlisted in marketing products for major multinational corporations in the name of 'empowerment'—they 'empower' themselves with their small profits, and as those who consume the goods, they create capillaries into the most remote areas to enable other women to 'empower' themselves through their purchases. In the name of 'empowerment', self-help groups offer women opportunities to borrow themselves into debts that are difficult to shift, especially when the money flows out of their fingers towards those who will not bear the responsibility for repayment.

The hallmark of the 'new model citizen' produced by this instrumentalised version of empowerment—or 'empowerment lite'—is that they keep women fully occupied. As Srilatha and Deepa Dhanraj observe in 'Gender Myths that Instrumentalise Women':

> The neo-liberal rules for the new woman citizen ... are quite clear: improve your household's economic condition, participate in local community development (if you have time), help build and run local (apolitical) institutions like the self-help group; by then, you should have no political or physical energy left to challenge this paradigm.[1]

The last two sections of the book deal with what it takes to challenge the neo-liberal paradigm and build a new, more just, social and economic order. Entitled 'Beyond Empowerment' and 'Assessing Empowerment', they take us into areas of Srilatha's work that are contiguous with her earlier concerns, but represent a branching out into a bigger picture informed by an ever more complex analysis of what it takes to make change happen. In shifting her focus from empowerment to other processes critical to gender equality, she never takes her eye off the critique that she developed of the appropriation and distortion of the notion of empowerment. But in doing so, she gives us something new: a more profound focus on developing both the structures and the agency to build a solid foundation to transform power relations.

Her reflections on movement-building come from deep experience, and from an acute insight into the politics of constructing counter-hegemonic institutions. Again, she is uncompromising in her honesty, stating that some of the barriers to transformation exist as much within feminist-led organisations as outside them. For all of us who have experienced the angst she writes about when reflecting on the lack of good role models of feminist leadership, as well as those of us who have been fortunate to learn from leaders who are truly democratic and enabling, her writing comes as a breath of fresh air. Her emphasis is, as always, on power: on the use of power to close and to open space, on authoritarianism and the unwillingness to surrender power, and on what it takes to create a genuinely different

---

[1] See Ch. 10 in this book.

style of leadership that resonates more closely with feminist values and aspirations.

Locating movement-building within a larger terrain of shifting fashions in the development industry calls for an engagement with the discourse of rights. In one of the most powerful pieces in the book, 'When Rights Go Wrong', Srilatha is again incisive and unflinching in her critique. Her call for the appropriate contextualisation of global rights framings still requires a response from transnational feminist activism, even now, when we are witnessing a rapid slipping away of the gains made in the international arena at a time when the universalism of human rights seemed to hold the promise of overarching normative principles that could offer feminists scope to articulate a set of common goals. This piece takes us to the most painful contradictions of the rights discourse, and to a set of truths that cry out for closer consideration.

Highlighting the cul-de-sacs and dead ends that aid institutions have pursued, Srilatha speaks of how mainstream development's magic bullets represent feminist ideas 'divested of the complex transformative strategies within which they were originally embedded', but now have been 'reduced to formulas, rituals and mantras'.

The 'simplistic recipes' that donors and governments have come up with, she reflects in her introduction to the third part of the book, are 'so that they don't have to deal with the fact that it is—and has always been—about fundamental shifts in power, privilege, and the control of resources and agenda-setting'. In the last chapter, she ends with a resonant piece of advice from Sundaramma, a women's leader from rural Karnataka:

> Work with us, not for us; don't tell us what to do to change our lives but share your knowledge and skills so we can figure out how to do it; you cannot do much for us economically, but help us eradicate the poverty of our ideas and dreams—show us new ways of understanding the world. Help us be heard by those who don't listen to us. And when we find the path we wish to tread, first, walk in front of us; then, when we are stronger, walk beside us; and finally, when we are truly strong, walk behind us, so that if we should stumble and fall, you will be there to help us get up and walk again.

Srilatha's work embodies the essence of Sundaramma's words. As a resource with which to contemplate what it takes to make these shifts, this book is unparalleled. Reading it, I was transported by the stories that Srilatha tells of the worlds of the women she has worked with at the grassroots level, and moved by her passion and conviction. I was lent new insights through her analysis and offered valuable new resources for my thinking and practice. Most of all, this collection re-stoked the fire that animates my own activism. It is my privilege to commend it to readers as that rare combination: a book that nourishes the heart as well as the mind.

ANDREA CORNWALL

Professor of Anthropology & Development
University of Sussex

Introduction

I cannot recall exactly when or where I first came across the term *empowerment;* maybe some time in the early 1980s when I was working in Bombay and became involved with a handful of others in mobilising and organising women living in the pavement slums[1] of that city. What I *do* recall is the immediate reaction the term evoked within me—a profound resonance, of having found the *perfect word,* the *perfect concept* for what I believed I was doing in my everyday work with women. I knew that I was *not* working for any of the social change goals that were popular at the time, viz., 'women's welfare', or 'upliftment', or even 'development'. I knew I was working for their *empowerment.*

Why did I feel so strongly about this? Especially since I don't think I could have defined the term very clearly then, or even explained exactly why it was the best descriptor for what we were doing in the field with poor urban women. I think it was because I understood intuitively that the core word *'power'* within the term shifted the conceptual and strategic meaning of what we were doing. We were wrestling with the way power operated in this particular context, particularly in the lives of women, and this set our work apart from any welfare or development interventions. Having been exposed to Marxist theory from an early age by my socialist father,[2] I

---

[1] These are hutments built directly on the pavements or footpaths at the side of city roads, and are hence smaller and more precarious than the structures in other kinds of slums, where the poor built their shelters on once-open lands, which grew into the informal settlements that were later termed 'slums'. Pavement slums are far more vulnerable to the elements and enjoyed little political protection, unlike other slums, and hence were targeted for clearance by city authorities on a regular basis.

[2] My father, the late Professor Amulya K.N. Reddy, was a staunch socialist all his life, and had given me the *Communist Manifesto* as a fifteenth birthday present!

recognised that, in essence, the core goal of our work was to change the relations of power between the seemingly impoverished and marginalised women living in Bombay's pavement dwellings, and the city that both despised and exploited them.

However, I also knew that I was engaging with *women's empowerment*, and therefore in uprooting and shifting control over something deeper than Marx's land, labour and capital. My father had introduced me to Marxist analysis; and I had an eccentric and brilliant English literature lecturer[3] who introduced me to the writings of feminist theorists like Simone de Beauvoir, Betty Friedan, Germaine Greer and Shulamith Firestone, while I was in college between 1969 and 1972. He completely ignored the fact that he was supposed to be teaching us Shakespeare and the medieval poets, and spent all his time outside the classroom with a hand-picked group that he felt should be reading the important works of the time, which included these great feminist thinkers. Although I may not have readily used the term 'patriarchy' in this early stage of my activism, I was familiar with the concept and realised that by focusing on women, we were going beyond class relations to that unique form of discrimination based on gender that was both ideological and structural. I also sensed that we were exploring the difference between power and poverty—that women had power, and particularly the power to change, even if they were poor.

Thus began my personal journey in the world of empowerment—a journey that was both intellectual and experiential—understanding and unpacking it conceptually, as well as operationalising it with real women in real situations of social, economic and political exclusion.

I have always been interested in abstract ideas and concepts—I remember being intrigued by the idea of caste when my primary school classmates in the small town of Karaikudi in the heart of Tamil Nadu asked me about my caste. I recall being fascinated by the idea of race, nationality and citizenship when, a few years later, my parents took me to the United States and sent me to the neighbourhood public school which had a student population that was 95 per cent

---

[3] T.G. Vaidyanathan, or 'TGV', as he was known to his favourites.

Black (or 'African American', as the politically correct term now is). This was when I realised that I was not black, not white, not American, not Christian, but something called Indian, and of a race that was neither black nor white. My agnostic father and deeply religious Hindu mother would answer my questions about my religious identity with, 'You were born in a Hindu family, but you can choose whether or not you want to be a Hindu.'

What were all these categories about? Why did they exist? My progressive father[4] was more than happy to answer my questions and his answers were more than explanatory, they were fused with values—of equality, non-discrimination, social justice and human rights. This early interest in social structures and hierarchies soon blossomed into a conviction that I had to do something to change things, to bring about the better, more egalitarian and inclusive society that I believed was not only possible, but essential for the future of humanity.

After my Bachelor's in English Literature, I embarked on a postgraduate degree in social work at the Tata Institute of Social Sciences in Bombay, where not only were my interests piqued and honed, but my skills and knowledge for doing work to bring about social change also developed and sharpened. Of course, we didn't come across the term 'empowerment' then, but I was introduced to the work of the great community organiser Saul Alinsky, and the popular Brazilian educator Paolo Freire. It was here that I first encountered the life-long struggle between my natural love for theories and concepts and research, and my conviction that these were unethical indulgences when so much had to be changed in the real world. I felt strongly that doing research and academic work alone was somehow morally suspect when there were so few people out there taking on the real-world challenges of injustice and poverty and discrimination; I had to be out there, in the trenches, so to speak.

Despite my attraction to social change theories, my instinct in

---

[4] The late Professor Amulya Kumar Narayana Reddy (1930–2006), was founder of ASTRA (Application of Science and Technology to Rural Advancement) at the Indian Institute of Science, and of the International Energy Initiative, and an internationally acclaimed guru of energy for sustainable development.

those early working years when I was doing grassroots work with poor women was to first explore these ideas in practice, rather than in theory. My father's influence in affirming this approach as not only valid, but also possibly the better way, was great. In a discussion about how best to understand complex social phenomena, his advice to me was:

> If you want to understand these things, don't read a lot of books or theories. First act. But always *analyse* your actions—step back periodically and assess what they're telling you. *Then* read the theory. Your reading will then help you make more sense of your actions, and your action experience will help you make more sense of the theory. This is the best way to keep theory in its place, and to act effectively.

These words of wisdom became my guiding mantra. In some ways, I've been a life-long schizophrenic—unable to decide whether I wanted to be an activist or a researcher, a thinker or a doer; so I've simply done both, sometimes simultaneously. Rather than fragmenting my thinking or my action, however, these dual tendencies have influenced and enriched each other. When I was engaged in social change action, I was always analytical; and when I was involved in research or theorisation, I questioned how this would strengthen or inform action. If I was located in a social change organisation, I pushed fellow activists to think more conceptually and analytically; and if I was in a research or academic setting, I challenged academics to subject their ideas to the test of reality.

There was another critical benefit of this synergy: because I began life as an activist and believed that even the most sophisticated theory was worthless if it did not guide or strengthen action in the real world, I was never tempted by armchair intellectualism, or by the arid, disconnected discourse of academia. I always carried in my head the faces, voices and perspectives of the countless women I had worked with over the years; I had a sense of the sort of questions they would ask of a theory or conceptual framework, the kinds of holes they would poke in it from the perspective of their experience and location.

Almost as soon as I began working with the pavement dweller women, I detected the flaws in the Saul Alinsky approach: in Indian slums or villages, the 'community' itself is deeply divided and hierarchical, not unified by common interests, as in Alinsky's world. I saw that approaching and winning the confidence of the community's leadership—which Alinsky commends as the first step in community organising—was very problematic in our context, since the leaders themselves were an integral part of the structure of exploitation, directly involved in the control of the information, resources and access that we were seeking to change. The leaders were also invariably men, deeply threatened by the idea of women gaining access to resources they didn't control, or organising themselves and challenging the hegemony of leaders or the male supremacy on which these communities were based. Essentially, the leaders were part of the problem, part of a systemic inequality, and therefore not ideal candidates for creating democratic solutions that benefitted the poorest, especially the women. There went theory number one!

For precisely the same reasons, Freire's 'liberation theology', articulated so powerfully in *The Pedagogy of the Oppressed*, did not work. It had initially made so much sense, when I realised that the kind of consciousness-raising work we had been doing with women living in the slums was incredibly similar to the 'conscientisation' process that Freire described: getting people to analyse their own reality, identify what they wanted to change, and strategise how to bring about that change. But Freire had ignored gender and spoke of the oppressed as though they were all men—or at least as though oppression did not include patriarchal oppression by community men of community women.

Another interesting development was a very early and unconscious experiment with democratising knowledge and knowledge generation—what I later learnt was called 'epistemology' in the academy, the science of knowledge. Since my intellectual bent was tempered by a focus on action, I was able to grasp complex ideas and translate them into simpler, more accessible terms, or locate them in the everyday world that the communities I worked in occupied. For instance, I could take Marx's idea of the 'expropriation of surplus value' and explain it to women in a way that helped them to quickly see how their highly underpaid occupation of recycling waste created huge economic benefits for the city in terms of savings on the large-scale waste disposal system it would otherwise need.

Over the decades, this preoccupation with democratising knowledge and bottom-up knowledge generation followed two separate but interconnected trajectories. On the one hand, I continually tried to 'demystify' complex ideas and concepts and make them accessible and useful to the women I worked with, as well as to my activist peers, and on the other, I began to use what I had learnt from my own and others' grassroots activism to frame new concepts and theories, or to create and publish 'grassroots research' that could contest dominant discourses.[5]

This was very empowering in and of itself, because it involved breaking the academic stranglehold on the production of theory and research, and bridging the worlds of theory and practice. On the ground, however, it was an uphill task convincing activists that action without a theory of change and periodic analysis was futile and possibly dangerous, because one may simply be reacting to circumstances rather than working strategically and politically for longer-term transformation. Activists were in general indifferent, sceptical, or openly hostile to anything 'academic', including doing their own research. By taking this position, they often surrendered to external academics and professional researchers their right to participate in theory-building or researching the very issues they worked on through their own frameworks. This actually meant surrendering the analysis and interpretation of their realities to others. Interestingly, this was a middle-class activist syndrome; marginalised people had no such biases. As soon as women understood the power of doing their own data-gathering and evidence-building, they seized upon these strategies, wasting no time in debating whether it was 'academic'.

For me, the power of bridging the worlds of theory and practice became a kind of obsession—I would read any interesting ideas I

---

[5] 'We the Invisible' (SPARC 1985), containing the results of the first ever census of pavement dwellers in south Bombay, conceived, designed and coordinated under my supervision, permanently changed the entire debate on the role and rights of people living in informal settlements in that city, and eventually government policy on their right to resettlement with security of tenure.

could lay my hands on and begin figuring out how to apply them to my work and explain them to the people I worked with. Building theory based on the learning from my own grassroots work and that of others was a similar preoccupation; my discoveries about it were very much related to the nature of the work I was currently involved in.

I got my first glimpses when I was involved in a community health project (1975–83); others revealed themselves when I worked with women pavement dwellers (1984–88), and still others when I was organising and building the rural Dalit and tribal women's movement in my home state of Karnataka (1988–92). It was also related to the sectors and issues I was working on at different times. While working in community health, a spectrum of discriminations related to food, access to medical care, and the gender-biased health beliefs and practices of communities manifested themselves. I saw how infant boys were breast-fed often and for as long as two years, rushed to the doctor when sick, avidly given the oral rehydration therapy we taught mothers to give babies with diarrhoea, and fed the best foods as they grew older.

The first three papers I wrote examining the gendered impact of poverty and discrimination were written in the early 1980s, and reflect the deep grounding created by my eight years of work (1975–83) at the Foundation for Research in Community Health in Mumbai and coastal Maharashtra, and in mobilising the poorest urban women. The first of these has great significance in my evolution as a feminist thinker, researcher and writer. Without this early research and writing, the clarity and conviction that I brought to my later work on women's empowerment would simply not have been possible.

The rural energy piece was the first tentative application of my rising feminist consciousness, and also the result of my first major research insight—that 'eureka' moment when the data shares a special secret with you and no one else. I was visiting my parents at a time when my father and his team of researchers at the ASTRA initiative of the Indian Institute of Science (Bangalore) had just finished tabulating the data from their six-village eco-system study in Tumkur district (Ravindranath et al. 1981). The study attempted to assess and quantify all sources of energy in the village eco-system, including human energy, and all its end-uses for both productive and reproductive purposes. The data had been collected by a group of well-meaning, socially conscious but non-gender-sensitive researchers, and so although they had in their hands the first 'scientific' proof the world had ever seen that women did more work than men, they were quite unaware of this fact until I saw the data and exploded with excitement. I quickly connected the data to the growing body of evidence of gender differentials in nutrition and health status that was available at the time.

Although the ASTRA study did not collect nutrition intake data, I connected its data on women's average daily energy output to other studies on energy intake, and demonstrated that there was yet another dimension to the persistent problem of under-nutrition among poor rural women, viz., the amount of back-breaking labour they did in a given day, draining their already limited supply of calories. At almost the same time, there were studies by feminists like Veena Shatrughna at the National Institute of Nutrition (Hyderabad), showing that this persistent nutrition gap—aggravated by overwork—was creating a whole generation of young rural women who were shorter in early adulthood than their grandmothers, whose heights had shrunk with aging and a lifetime of under-nutrition. The ASTRA study provided solid statistical evidence in support of feminist contention that there was a gendered division of labour in the country, and that this division was the root cause of a host of disadvantages suffered by women, ranging from poor health, to exclusion from social and political life.

Despite this, I am struck now by how muted and cautious my feminist voice was in this piece, as if I was at pains to submerge the stark reality of women's work burdens and lack of food by clubbing them with children, or with the even more generalised category of the 'rural poor'. I read the paper now and think how differently I would have written it even a year or a decade later—how much more determined the gender perspective would have been! Nevertheless, it has stood the test of time. Thanks largely to the integrity and quality of the data collected by the ASTRA team, it is to date one of a handful of papers of its kind in the world, and continues to be cited, especially in the context of debates and policy advocacy on gender and energy.[6]

My article on women and cooking energy, published about a year and a half later, built upon some of those earlier arguments. Although it was not quite as path-breaking, it created an impact with the way it brought together usually disparate clusters of information (cooking energy, indoor air pollution, nutrition data, health data, time and work studies). It was also the first feminist analysis of data that had just become available on women's exposure to toxic emissions from biogas cooking fuels.

The final contribution of this first phase of my work was on women's access to food, which extended the discussion on women and cooking energy by analysing the appalling food deprivation suffered by women, which had become normalised in poor Indian households. With this, I was more confident about bridging the worlds of research and activism, in being able to research and wield data while at the same time offering an analysis that was deeply informed by my field experience.

These skills were further honed and new insights emerged when I worked with women living in the slums of Bombay, and I saw how displacement and migration, combined with women's reproductive roles, placed a disproportionate burden of survival upon them. Even when they arrived as economic refugees in the city with nothing but their strong bodies and the will to work, they were expected to create some kind of home, find water and fuel, cook the food, and take care of the children.

> We live on the footpath, and I work as a domestic in four houses to earn money. I have no choice but to leave my 8-year-old daughter in charge while I'm away; but if something bad happens to her, I will be blamed as a negligent mother. They will say that my daughter got spoiled because of me.

I saw that shelter and land tenure were deeply gendered. One woman said to me,

---

[6] For instance, I was interviewed in December 2011 by an international research group preparing a position paper on Gender and Energy for the Danish government, and found that they had not only read this early paper, but cited it as having continued relevance in the current global energy crisis context!

If you are a man, you can sleep or defecate anywhere; but we women have to build a shelter, even if it is just our sarees tied to bamboo poles; we have to remain modest even if we are living here on the pavement, in full view of the world. It is we who painstakingly change these makeshift shelters into homes, and when they come and demolish them, it is we who lose everything and must start all over again.

These women also shifted my entire perception of what constitutes a women's issue and what does not. When asked by feminists from an autonomous women's group about the 'women's issues' in the community, they said: housing, water, toilets, electricity, ration cards. 'But aren't these community issues?' the interviewer said. 'Don't you have problems like domestic violence, sexual harassment, things like that?' 'Oh yes,' they said, 'but those are not women's issues, they are community issues—they have to be solved by the whole community, not by us. But shelter, water, toilets, rations—those are women's problems, they have to be solved by us.'

In the remote and backward districts of north Karnataka—in Bidar and Bijapur—I learnt how cultural practices like *banamati* (casting a spell so that someone is 'possessed') were more potent methods of breaking the growing power of Dalit women's collectives than direct threats or violence. I also witnessed how women used this weapon in reverse, to break the stranglehold of demeaning customs like begging for wages they have earned. It is in this context that the great women's collective leader, Sundaramma, taught me what our role as external catalysts was at different stages of the empowerment process.

For me, grassroots women's experiences, voices, analyses and strategies were as vital as sources of learning about empowerment as were the ideas and theories of the world's great philosophers, political scientists, historians, economists and sociologists. I am convinced that neither source would have sufficed on its own—some nuance or dimension or layer would have remained undiscovered. I believe that this is the reason why the classes I taught at the Kennedy School of Government—a teacher without a doctorate or any formal academic credentials to my name—were crowded to capacity, sometimes without standing room. I believe the students knew they were hearing something unique and different: insights from real-world struggles illuminated through the concepts and frameworks of brilliant minds from multiple disciplines.

* * *

This volume is organised in three sections, comprising my personal journey in engaging with the concept and practice of empowerment. Part 1, 'Engaging with Empowerment', contains five chapters that lay out my attempts at conceptualising empowerment and analysing its eventual cooption and depoliticisation. Part 2, 'Beyond Empowerment', contains two pieces that comprise my research, analysis and conceptualisation of processes—like movement-building and feminist leadership—that represent my intellectual and practical journey to a new set of issues and challenges beyond empowerment. In Part III, 'Assessing Empowerment', I offer readers several chapters in which I grapple with the complex question of how to assess or measure empowerment, or prove that women had been empowered by any particular intervention. Each section carries an introduction in which I share with readers the context in which each piece was conceived and written.

The task of compiling these writings into one volume has taken me on a poignant journey of reflection, of looking at myself as an activist and thinker at different periods of my life. More importantly, it has helped me to look back at the evolution of the ideas and practices of gender-based discrimination, and of empowerment, feminism and women's struggles for justice, in a much larger arena, of which my own writing covers but a small part. I hope this will stand as some sort of chronicle—albeit within the narrow limits of one woman's work—of the rich and amazing history of women's struggle for empowerment and justice in India and across the world.

Reference

N. H. Ravindranath et al. 1981. 'An Indian village agricultural ecosystem—Case study of Ungra village, Part I: Main observations', *Biomass*, 1 (1), pp. 61–76.

I. Conceptualising Women's Empowerment

Introduction

THIS section contains a series of articles and documents written between 1993 and 2008, as I unpacked, conceptualised, implemented, and then revisited the idea of women's empowerment. Each was a benchmark in its own way, for reasons described below.

Chapter 1: Why I am a Feminist

I begin this section with a set of op-ed pieces from the late 1980s, written for a wonderful but all too short-lived newspaper called the *Indian Post*, because while they're not strictly about women's empowerment, they address a set of issues that are at its foundation, and demonstrate my growing clarity. These include one of my favourites, 'Why I am a Feminist', which articulates my personal understanding of feminism, and establishes the rationale for why I became interested and involved in women's empowerment.

There is a wonderful story behind this piece: the impulse to write it was triggered by a conversation with a senior woman academic during a long commute on Bombay's roads to my alma mater, the Tata Institute of Social Sciences, where I was teaching several women's studies courses at the time. My academic colleague was engaged in a past-time that continues to be very popular: dissing feminism and feminists with appropriate contempt. What made it worse was the insufferable smugness with which she distorted facts; for instance, she called feminism *a narrow and limited ideology*, which cared only about women getting even with men, and no one and nothing else!

It did not occur to her that without the struggles of a set of women who were undoubtedly feminist in their thinking (even if the label did not exist in their times), her position as a senior professor in a prestigious academic institution, the privileged higher education that gave her access to that position, and her complacent sense of her own power might never have existed. Little did she realise that far from being a Western import, she was dismissing, or even worse, negating, the struggles of a host of our very own feminist ancestors: from Mirabai and Akkamaha Devi in the medieval period, to Pandita Ramabai, Ahalyabai Holkar, Savitribai Phule and Begum Rokeya Shekawat Kabir of the late nineteenth and early twentieth century; the thousands of women who participated in India's struggle for freedom; and the multitude in our times who continue to break the barriers of discrimination, exclusion and tradition.

And so I sat down and wrote this piece in a fit of rage, but with great passion. It sought to remind all such women that they had no right to dismiss what feminism—whether indigenous or imported— had done to change our lives and our opportunities in such fundamental ways. I also wanted to tell these women why, unlike them, I took great pride in claiming the label 'feminist'.

In the other essays in this chapter—'Legislation Alone is not Enough' and 'For Women, it is Never a Matter of Choice'—I explore several other important development debates that were emerging in India at the time; for example, whether one can eradicate poverty and social evils through legislation, and whether the increasingly popular notion of 'people's participation' was in fact not another top-down strategy, with external do-gooders deciding what people would/could participate in. I conclude this chapter with an essay that explores what was, for feminists and women's rights advocates in the country, possibly the most dramatic event of our times: the sati by Roop Kanwar in a small village in Rajasthan.[1] This was a defining moment for India's powerful and extensive women's movement. Sati had been banned by the Moghuls and then by British colonial legislation in 1826, so its recurrence at the tail end of the twentieth century (1987) came as a shock to the entire country, and forced complacent urban middle-class eyes to open to the ugly plight of the majority of women in India. For those of us engaged in the struggle for gender equality, the Sati raised all sorts of questions about the meaning of choice and consent in women's lived realities.

---

[1] A province in India's northwest.

These essays are benchmarks in my development for many reasons: the views they express represent my growing clarity as a feminist activist and analyst. They also provided an opportunity, for the first time, to articulate these views to a more general public, rather than to other development-walas or activists. I will always be indebted to my dear friend Ammu Joseph, who was working as Assistant Editor at the *Indian Post* at the time, for encouraging me to write regularly for the *Post's* op-ed page.

Chapter 2: The Mahila Samakhya Strategy for Empowerment

This essay was actually written first in Kannada for the 150-strong team of grassroots women activists (called 'sahayoginis') who then comprised the Mahila Samakhya team in Karnataka state, because they were always involved in debates about the 'MS way', with some very questionable practices being justified as a part of this!

More importantly, however, the essay represents the clarity that emerged from a unique experience which had no precedent and no sequel in my life: founding and operationalising the Mahila Samakhya (hereafter, MS) Programme in Karnataka. This was undoubtedly the greatest challenge—and possibly the greatest achievement—of my entire life. Sometime in 1986, I was summoned by Anil Bordia, then Secretary Education, Government of India, to New Delhi, to help design a programme for women's education based on the new National Education Policy adopted by the government earlier that year. Since I was at the time working at the Society for the Promotion of Area Resource Centres (SPARC), and organising and mobilising women living on Bombay's pavements, I was mystified; my only connection to education was that we were using feminist popular education methods in our organising work. But Bordia reassured me that I was just the right person for the job! I arrived a few days later at Mr Bordia's enormous office in New Delhi's Shastri Bhavan to find a woman I'd never met before already ensconced in the other seat: Vimala Ramachandran. Vimala had been active in Jagori, but her full-time job was lecturer at one of Delhi's many women's colleges. Bordia then proceeded to inform the two of us that he wanted us to take the lead in designing a programme that would enable the government to operationalise the very innovative but abstract notion of 'Education for Women's Empowerment' articulated in the New Education Policy of 1986. Vimala and I were bewildered and rather dumbstruck, and asked Bordia, each in our own way—'Why US??'—especially when the country was full of far more eminent feminists, not to mention veteran adult educators and educational experts.

Bordia's response was classic, and typical of a bureaucrat who was known for thinking—and acting—outside the box. He said:

> I don't want old wine in a new bottle. I don't want any of the usual people who've been involved either with adult education or women's groups. I want people who can approach the problem with fresh eyes, fresh ideas—I want you to travel around the country, visit the most innovative women's projects; I want you to talk to grassroots women and ask them how to make education relevant for them, and come up with something completely new!

And so began my life's greatest intellectual adventure. Over the next few months, Vimala and I travelled and talked with scores of people, from grassroots women to leading women's rights activists and non-formal education innovators. Influenced by the insights and successes of the organising models used by organisations like SPARC (which I myself co-founded and worked at) and the Women's Development Programme in Rajasthan, we drafted the conceptual and strategic template for the now famous Mahila Samakhya Programme, published in what came to be called 'The Green Book', thanks to its verdant cover!

It was my original intention to share with readers the opening chapter of the 'Green Book'—the conceptual framework for the Government of India's Education Department's soon-to-be launched Mahila Samakhya Programme of Education for Women's Empowerment. But instead, I will share an article I wrote in Kannada for the Sahayoginis (or village-level activists) of Mahila Samakhya Karnataka, because I believe it is more to the point. This article attempts to capture the essence of the 'Mahila Samakhya Approach', and hence illustrates my understanding of empowerment as both a concept and a practice, at least as it had evolved up to that point in time (1992). While the opening chapter of the Green Book was still largely hypothetical, this essay is informed by a wealth of experience, since it came after the implementation of the MS Programme in over 700 villages of five districts of Karnataka, which had already mobilised well over 50,000 of the poorest Dalit and tribal women into strong and articulate village-level collectives called 'sanghas'. This remains the proudest achievement of my life, this experience that taught me more about empowerment than a thousand political treatises or hundreds of hours in a research library ever could. And I am equally proud to share this essay, which synthesised the understanding of empowerment that this profound experience had created in my mind and my heart.

What the essay does reveal, however, is the rather limited understanding of power that some of us had at that time, as something that arose purely from control over resources. This is very different from the far more nuanced and expanded grasp of the various dimensions and forms of power that are articulated in my later articles on feminist leadership, and feminist movements and organisations (Part III, this volume). But at the time, this represented more clarity about power and empowerment than most activists working on empowerment had, and this understanding of power informed what had already emerged as one of the most effective and dynamic women's empowerment programmes in the entire world, viz., Mahila Samakhya! So even this limited view of power, translated into an organising strategy, had enabled hundreds of different interventions and thousands of acts of resistance, assertion and empowerment by grassroots women in all parts of the country where Mahila Samakhya was being implemented.

Chapter 3: Defining Women's Empowerment

This is the essay that soon became the hallmark of my work on conceptualising women's empowerment. The original version of this essay was entitled 'Empowerment of Women in South Asia: Concepts and Practices', and was the result of a year-long process (spread over 1992 and 1993) of talking with key activists and leaders in four South Asian countries (Bangladesh, India, Nepal and Sri Lanka) about how they understood the concept of empowerment and how they implemented it in practice. Pakistan was to have been included among the countries visited, but had to be omitted because of the usual visa problems; however, Pakistani women contributed their bit to the final framework since a handful participated in a workshop held in Nepal to discuss the first draft of the essay.

The entire process was jointly initiated by the Asia South Pacific Bureau of Adult Education[2] (ASPBAE) and the South Asian regional office of the United Nations' Food and Agriculture Organization (FAO). The FAO might seem a strange entity to invest in studying women's empowerment, and indeed it was! In reality, this institutional collaboration was the result of Kamla Bhasin, one of India's great feminists, being located in the FAO. The idea itself—to build greater clarity on the meaning of women's empowerment by studying the practices of projects across the South Asian region that espoused the goal of empowering women—was Kamla's brainchild, and she mobilised most of the resources for the project from the FAO's Freedom from Hunger Campaign budget.

Kamla and many other feminists felt that on the one hand, 'empowerment' had become a buzzword among donors and many of their NGO partners, with little serious understanding of its implications, and on the other, there were some incredibly powerful and innovative women's empowerment experiences on the ground across the South Asian region. So the idea behind the project was to assess whether NGOs across the region had merely jumped on the empowerment bandwagon, encouraged or even compelled by their donors. Were they substituting the word 'empowerment' for a set of interventions—like savings and credit and income generation programmes—that were still based on older ideas of women's upliftment, welfare or development? Or were they really doing things differently as a result of adopting the empowerment approach? The purpose was to assess what the idea of empowerment had really changed, and should change; and to explore how we could create greater conceptual and strategic clarity for those who wished to adopt the women's empowerment approach.

To my great good fortune, Kamla convinced her fellow travellers in this enterprise that I was the right person to do it! She had visited

---

[2] A member of the International Council of Adult Education, and one of the last remaining bastions of Freirian popular education.

the Mahila Samakhya programme offices in Bangalore when I was the State Programme Director, and had perhaps seen how I was straddling the worlds of theory and practice in my attempt to push the programme beyond conventional boundaries. So at exactly the point when I was transitioning out of Mahila Samakhya Karnataka, Kamla visited me in Bangalore and proposed the idea of undertaking a study of the major women's empowerment projects in South Asia, and developing a sort of position paper with a clear definition of empowerment and the action strategies that it required. I was hooked even before she completed her pitch! There was nothing in the world that could have fascinated me more at the time than this exciting project; nothing that I was more ready to jump into, after four solid years of translating the concept of empowerment into concrete action in hundreds of villages across Karnataka through the Mahila Samakhya Programme that I had had the honour of founding and launching.

And so I set off, spending time in Nepal, Bangladesh and Sri Lanka (after giving up the struggle to get a visa for Pakistan!), talking to scores of project leaders, activists and grassroots women. There were many remarkable moments during this journey of discovery: the bizarre conversation, for instance, with a male head of a women's empowerment NGO in Nepal, who stated, somewhat condescendingly, that women's empowerment was an old-fashioned concept, and that his organisation was now engaged in 'gender empowerment'. But when I quizzed him on the exact meaning of this absurd term, he faltered, and could only repeat that they now worked with both men and women! Similarly, in Bangladesh, when visiting several Grameen Bank village-level savings groups, I asked the women who the Bank belonged to, and they said, with one voice: Yunus bhai! And in Sri Lanka, in conversation[3] with both Tamil and Sinhala women caught in that country's long-standing ethnic conflict and civil war, I discovered how women's empowerment had been instrumentalised by chauvinist leaders on both sides to mobilise women's support for their cause.

---

[3] Facilitated by the wonderful Kumudini Samuel of the Women and Media Collective.

The most unforgettable moment during the women's empowerment study was waking up in Dhaka on 6 December 1992 to hear that Hindu fundamentalist mobs had destroyed Babar's mosque in the town of Ayodhya. I was staying with my sister and Bangladeshi brother-in-law during the visit to the Bangladesh projects, and had barely been to one of the six organisations I was to visit when this terrible event occurred. My brother-in-law's family refused to allow me out of the house—they were terrified that my driving around the countryside would lead to my being discovered for an Indian and a Hindu by irate mobs bent on reprisal. Finally, after almost six days of seclusion, a loyal driver and stout guard were entrusted with my care, and I was allowed to complete my visits. But to be a Hindu Indian in a largely Muslim country at a time like that was a surreal experience—it was a window into the perception of India and Hindu fundamentalism that few of us ever get to look through. And the affection, care and protection I was offered by my Bangladeshi family, friends and colleagues only made me feel even more ashamed of what had happened back home.

The essay that follows, however, is not based only on the South Asian projects covered in this initial phase, but also on the several Asia-Pacific country experiences[4] included in the second phase of the ASPBAE study, conducted in 1994. I have included this, rather than the 1993 South Asian version of the essay, because it is a bit more comprehensive, and represents a further evolution in my own understanding of empowerment; it includes, for instance, the notion of force or violence (and the threat of violence) as one of the means used to police and co-opt subordinated people into supporting the power structure, or to subvert challenges to it. This is the version that has also travelled most widely around the world, being translated into dozens of languages. I continue to meet people, even in the present decade, who say to me: 'Oh, so you're *that* Batliwala! Your empowerment paper—we have translated it into [Bahasa, Zulu, Swahili, Tagalog, Uzbek, Russian, Czech, Portuguese, Spanish,

---

[4] Including Thailand, Indonesia, Philippines, Hong Kong (before it became part of the People's Republic of China), Japan, Fiji and New Zealand.

Sinhala, etc., etc.] and still use it for training our activists.'

Reading this essay today with the wisdom of hindsight, and knowing what I know now, especially about power, there is an inevitable sense of its limitations. There are so many dimensions of power that it did not address or analyse, especially power in the private and intimate sphere, as Veneklasen and Miller (2002) describe it, and the various realms in which power operates, all of which has greatly influenced my thinking and understanding of empowerment in the past decade or so. Its concept of gender is also limited to the male-female binary, which LGBTQI movements and queer theorists have rendered so completely obsolete! But I am also aware, having interacted with a number of people who have since advanced our understanding of power from a gender perspective—such as Naila Kabeer, Andrea Cornwall, or Veneklasen and Miller themselves—that these advances were possible partly because of this earlier articulation. By creating one of the earliest conceptual frameworks on gender power and empowerment, we enabled others to see the missing dimensions, or bring to it vital new concepts of power from the work of philosophers like Michel Foucault to which I, as an activist, had had no access.

And this, indeed, is a key part of the essay's incredible success: it was written by an activist-scholar, not an academic scholar, and was informed by the work, ideas and thinking of other feminists engaged in change processes with real women living in real communities on the ground. We had encountered power relations and the capacity of power structures to absorb or push back challenges in very direct ways, along with the women we had sought to organise. Perhaps that is why this conceptual framework has remained so robust, despite its gaps and shortcomings. The essay remains a remarkably relevant approach to power in the context of gender relations.

Chapter 4: Challenging Ritualised Caste Oppression: The Tegampura Story

I decided to include this piece because it so beautifully and powerfully illustrates what happened as a result of the Mahila Samakhya 'approach' described earlier in Chapter 2. This is the only time when I have tried to actually write about what empowerment looks like in action, and that too in a specific context, among a specific group of marginalised Dalit women, facing a very particular form of oppression. This essay takes the discussion of empowerment out of the abstract and into reality. It was written for the newsletter brought out by WEDO (the Women's Environment and Development Organization), of which I was Chair at the time, in response to the question, 'What Does Women's Empowerment Really Look Like?' The essay was designed to bring WEDO partners and newsletter readers 'back to the basics' about what we were really working for when we talked about gender justice and social justice.

Chapter 5: The Transformation of Political Culture: The Mahila Samakhya (Karnataka) Experience

This essay, prepared and presented at the Indian Association of Women's Studies conference in Jaipur (December 1995), was never published in a journal or a book, but remains one of my personal favourites. I believe it contains an important and original piece of analysis. It uses empirical data from the Mahila Samakhya Karnataka programme's work with women elected to local councils to make a case for a broader strategy of engagement by the progressive women's movement with women holding public office. It is an argument and an approach that I have not seen advocated in quite this way, even with all the mobilisation by feminist groups around the Women's Reservation Bill over the past decade.

The essay is also poignant in many ways because it was written after I had left Mahila Samakhya, and felt both relief and an acute sense of loss. It was written about two years into practising my policy of staying away from the programme and the staff, so that the new leadership did not feel threatened or cramped by my presence, but also after knowing how badly that leadership had failed the programme and the staff. Barely a year after my departure, there was a strike, a lockout, a horribly authoritarian and oppressive style of functioning by the State Programme Director, and a reversal of almost all the principles and values that we had tried to practice in the way the programme was led, managed and implemented. So for me, this was the deeply painful backdrop and parallel to the central hypothesis of the essay itself, viz., that women's personal experiences of power tend to lead to their using it in very oppressive ways when they gain access to it.

In fact, I finally got a chance to talk to my successor about why things went so wrong when she took over Mahila Samakhya Karnataka; about why she, who had enjoyed the benefits of the shared power model I had created, reversed it so harshly when she was in charge. Her response is a very interesting postscript to the analysis in the essay itself:

> It's all very well for you to talk about sharing power, about how giving power to others makes you more powerful too. You can do this because you have always been powerful—you have always felt powerful, even when you were a child. You walk into a room, and even if no one knows who you are, they will think, 'that woman is somebody important for sure!' When I walk into a room, no one will even notice. I cannot afford to share power—I had to *make* people respect me, to enforce my authority. If I did not, they would have ignored me completely.

Chapter 6: Taking the Power out of Empowerment

This essay resulted from an earlier one, entitled 'The Changing Context and Meaning of Women's Empowerment', written for a volume that revisited the great debates that dominated the population discourse of India in the 1980s and 1990s—*Handbook of Population and Development in India*, edited by my old friend A. K. Shiva Kumar with his colleagues Pradeep Panda and Rajani Ved at the Indian Institute for Human Development, published in 2010. The goal of the book was to assess how the context had changed—or had stayed the same—at the end of the first decade of the twenty-first century, especially given the shift of India's 'population problem' into our 'demographic dividend'. The entire project was catalysed and supported by the MacArthur Foundation's population programme in India, which had played a catalytic role in supporting some of the most innovative post-ICPD (International Conference on Population and Development) work on alternative approaches to population control, including an individual grants programme that virtually built the field of sexual and reproductive rights in the country.

My chapter in this book was filled with despair and anger at the way the women's empowerment approach—such as I had spelled out in Chapter 2 of this volume—had been depoliticised, degraded and instrumentalised in the Indian context, and attempted to analyse not only the reasons for this downslide, but also its potential costs. I shared this chapter with several colleagues around the globe who I knew were equally concerned about the co-option and de-politicisation of the empowerment discourse, and subsequently published a revised excerpt of it in *Open Democracy*, entitled 'Putting the Power Back Into Empowerment'. Andrea Cornwall, faculty at the Institute of Development Studies in Sussex and convenor of the Pathways of Women's Empowerment international research consortium, loved the piece. She was guest editing a forthcoming issue of the IDS journal *Development in Practice*, focused on 'Buzzwords and fuzzwords: Deconstructing development discourse', and asked me to do a slightly different version of the analysis for her issue, examining the evolution of empowerment in development discourse. My title for the article I subsequently wrote for *Development in Practice* was 'Taking the Power Out of Empowerment', and this is the one I have chosen to share in this volume because it is both more global in perspective than the earlier one, and far more incisively written.

This essay not only uses the Indian example to illustrate how and why empowerment was downsized in my own lifetime of applying the concept in practice with real women in very poor urban and rural communities, but also how the word itself travelled into other domains and became a personal power technique, rather than a transformative political process. I believe this analysis continues to remain largely valid, and needs to be addressed by feminist advocates and activists.

Reference

Lisa Veneklasen and Valerie Miller, 2002. *A New Weave of Power and Politics: An Action Guide for Advocacy and Citizen Participation* (Oklahoma City: World Neighbors).

1. Why I am a Feminist[1]

FOR years now, I have been repeatedly encountering women who are highly educated, professionally very successful, who take for granted a woman's right to develop her mind, skills and individuality while also enjoying the role of wife and mother, but who, at the same time, declare with vehemence, 'I am not a feminist!' These are women who demand and receive respect and equality at home and the workplace, who are utterly confident, who have achieved a sense of total personhood, and who would laugh at the idea that they are inferior in any way simply because of their gender. Yet, they vow they are not feminist. These are also women who did not weep at the birth of their daughters, who brook no eve-teasing or sexist jokes, who would not dream of seeking their identities purely as someone's wife, daughter or mother. They have taken for granted and exercised all the options and freedoms that exist for women only because feminism fought for and continues to battle for them every day, everywhere in the world. But they say that they are not feminists.

Who, then, is a feminist? Why do these women dissociate themselves so violently from feminism? Indeed, what do they believe feminism is—and from where did they get this information? After years of talking to such women, trying to understand their exaggerated reactions, I have drawn some conclusions.

Most of these women have never read feminist writings or writers, they have only read *about* them. And they read about them only in the mainstream Western and Indian media, which, with few exceptions, have distorted and sensationalised feminism by projecting in lurid detail vicious distortions of some of its symbolic forms: bra-burning, man-hating, anti-child, and the like. By simply choosing

---

[1] *The Indian Post*, 27 August 1988.

the most titillating, and therefore 'newsworthy' (read 'saleable'), bits and pieces, they have misrepresented feminism more effectively than the most ardent misogynist. And, of course, the symbolic acts of protest of feminists—whether of *suffragettes* chaining themselves to gates, or some latter-day women's libbers burning their *brassieres*— are usually reported without a context, without a framework for understanding what these actions represent.

What amazes me is that it is more than fifteen years since the last bra was burnt, but that image still clings like a leech in public consciousness, sucking away people's ability to see beyond or after it. They are smugly and self-righteously convinced that feminists want to divide the world in two, do away with children altogether, and overtake men in every activity. This leaves me with the sneaking suspicion that people—and especially the 'I am not a feminist' women— don't *want* to see beyond these crude and *naïve* images. And they don't want to see because they are intelligent enough to suspect that there is much more to feminism than that. I think they sense the profound and fundamental questions that feminism raises, *and they are afraid*. This is because more than most issues, feminism demands a confluence, a harmony, between the personal and the political. They might have to question their own lives and relationships—and that certainly won't do!

The major problem with Indian women who are 'not feminists' is that they know nothing of feminism or the women's movements in our own country. Our own media portrays morchas and rallies against dowry deaths, eve-teasing and rape, but never the deep, searching questions and analysis of women's condition, the struggle to evolve a manifesto for a just society for *all* human beings, to break down the tyranny and rigid roles and behavioural demands on both *men and women*, the growing attempts to reach out to and understand the perceptions of masses of poor women in the rural and urban areas. Some clarifications are, therefore, in order.

Feminism has never been against *men*, but against the discrimination or subordination of any person merely because of their gender. But like any other ideology and movement, there are tendencies and differences of opinion and strategy within feminism. Just as there are a score of left and right-wing parties, each with its own deviations or interpretations of Marxism and capitalism, so also are there different streams in feminism. But no one strand or group can claim to be the real or true feminism, or speak for all.

There are, however, certain basic principles which the vast majority of feminists, both in India and abroad, *do* stand for: The right of all human beings—whether male or female—to an equal share in social and economic life; the right of each woman and man to self-determination and a realisation of their talents, strengths and aspirations, rather than rigid, gender-based roles and biologically-determined destinies; the sharing of responsibility for domestic work and child-rearing by both parents and support services for these; the need for social and economic recognition and valuation of the work done by women, which has so far been invisible; and freedom from the exploitation and oppression of women because they are women, whether through rape, dowry demands, prostitution, wife-beating, or denial of control over their own reproductive systems. Apart from these, feminism has always opposed violence, war and militarism, and supported all movements that promote social and economic justice for the poor or downtrodden in every society.

None of this sounds terrible to me. In fact, I cannot see how any person of principle, possessing common humanity, would wish to dissociate his/herself from such a healthy, well-rounded and humane ideology—unless, of course, the person is firmly committed to the notion that the world cannot survive unless half of its people are enslaved.

But I believe that the world cannot survive if half its people *are* enslaved.

Which is why *I am a feminist.*

Legislation Alone is Not Enough[2]

An emerging trend in the development field is the attempt by voluntary agencies and activist groups to seek judicial redress for various socio-economic ills. Increasingly, such groups have gone to

---

[2] *The Indian Post*, 28 July 1987.

court for a host of social causes and issues hitherto absent in the legal arena. One recent example was the *Pavement Dwellers Case* (Olga Tellis and Others vs Bombay Municipal Corporation), a legal battle begun in 1981 to stop the demolition of 'unauthorised' homes without providing alternative space or shelter to their inhabitants. Similarly, scores of cases have begun to appear in the higher courts of the land, on issues as varied as bride-burning and bonded labour, maintenance for divorced women and industrial accidents.

All these indicate both the failure and the success of broader struggles for social change. For instance, the fight for women's emancipation would seem to have made little headway when more brides are being burnt and dowry demands are increasing. But the presence of so many voices to cry foul and take legal action is still a signal that such change is indeed occurring, and quite perceptibly.

Even more significant than the growing legal battles over social causes, however, is the number of such struggles that are now taking the shape of bills seeking passage into our jurisprudence. Several recent ones come to mind (among others): the Code of conduct for Voluntary Agencies, the Child Labour Bill, and the National Campaign for Housing Rights. Each one addresses, directly or indirectly, key poverty problems in the country.

The Code of Conduct, although condemned by many as a draconian attempt by pro-government elements to control and manipulate the voluntary sector for their own political ends, was nevertheless aimed at those agencies who do little while continuing to swallow large amounts of funds, all in the name of alleviating poverty.

The Child Labour Bill was considered an anomaly, given the fact that our Constitution bans the employment of children. However, recognising that grinding poverty and a desire for profit have ensured the continuance of this practice, the Bill sought to force employers and the government to provide healthcare, nutrition, education, vocational training, and decent working hours and conditions to child workers.

The National Campaign for Housing Rights was launched to coincide with the International Year of Shelter, 1987. Although it is still debated throughout the country, the campaign hopes to culminate in a Bill that makes Housing a Fundamental Right guaranteed to every citizen.

These efforts have been analysed individually, but not for what they represent as a whole.

India has always prided itself on having some of the most advanced and progressive social legislation in the world. Our Constitution guarantees equality regardless of caste, creed or gender. Our laws prohibit untouchability, the giving or receiving of dowry, the employment of child labour and child marriage. Bonded labour has been freed. We had universal adult franchise when many 'developed' nations denied their women the vote. Unfortunately, however, most of these acts and provisions have remained on paper, remote from those they sought to liberate.

What is more, most of this legislation was essentially conceived, debated and enacted by reform-minded or enlightened members of the ruling elite. Consequently, it contained many questionable assumptions: that the law is accessible to all; that the provisions were appropriate to their beneficiaries; that the dispensers of these laws would be impervious to the social and political biases around them.

But the legal movements being witnessed today are fundamentally different:

- They originate from groups that are actively working with and committed to the cause of those affected by social, economic and political exploitation—oppressed women, working children, dalits, pavement dwellers, bonded labour, the rural and urban poor, and other marginalised groups. Thus, the content and nature of the legislations they seek are much more sensitive and responsive to socio-political realities.
- The decision to draft a bill in the first place is taken with a specific group of people affected by a given problem—the Child Labour Bill, for instance, arose in this manner. Consequently, these bills reflect an awareness of specific life-situations and first-hand experiences, rather than the idealistic notions of high-minded reformers.
- More and more demands for new legislation are coming up as a

result of the increasing use of courts to fight social battles. A combination of success (as in bride-burning convictions) and failures (as in the pavement dwellers' case) have created a clearer recognition of the limitations, class biases and gaps in the existing laws, as well as the powerful demonstration-effect of successful litigation.

Consequently, exposure to the law is no longer limited to legal circles and the educated classes. Voluntary agencies, activist groups, women's organisations—all these have suddenly thronged the legal corridors, filing cases, formulating and drafting bills, and even becoming lawyers themselves!

Finally, the most radical new dimension of this emerging trend is the attempt to bridge the gap between the mass of people and the law. This is being done in several ways: by creating legal awareness, spearing legal literacy, and demystifying the law for the poor; by enabling and encouraging the poor to seek legal redress; by providing them affordable and non-exploitative legal aid and representation; and most of all, by empowering people themselves to frame new and more relevant legislation, tackling issues for which, quite often, no laws exist. All these strategies are attempting to remove the fear of poor people—that the legal system invariably works against them—and to truly democratise the process of legislation itself.

Obviously, this praiseworthy trend is not without its own drawbacks. Bills that began by seeking popular debate and ratification have often flown into rarefied realms of intellectualism, unintelligible to the masses. But more importantly, all this drafting of bills leaves one central question unanswered: Can mere legislation ever strike at the roots of social injustice? Can better laws remove or transform the structural defects of an inequitable society? And can there ever be a bill against poverty?

For Women, it is Never a Matter of Choice[3]

In the feverish debate surrounding Roop Kanwar's recent sati, the question of 'voluntarism' has been one of the key issues dividing

[3] *The Indian Post*, 20 October 1987.

opinion. Surprisingly, it is not only proponents of religious rights and fundamentalism, but also some progressive women's groups that have taken the stand that if the young woman *chose* to end her life with her husband's, why should others interfere?

This question of individual choice is an intriguing one: Where does society's right to control and regulate individual action end, and the personal right to determine one's destiny begin?

Unfortunately, this is not just the stuff of philosophical or political debate; it is a grim paradox that every one of us has to grapple with, especially those who commit themselves to social reform or change. A century ago, the British ruler had no such difficulty in interfering with practices like sati or *thuggee*. To him, the goal was clear: A custom like sati was, in his view, inhumane, barbaric, and a not-so-subtle way of getting rid of widows and seizing what may have been their share of the family assets. The colonialist did not worry about the widow's right to choose sati, or any religious sanction for it.

But the British have long been gone, and the dilemma is now faced by the group of Indians who have taken on the mantle of social reform (although that word is no longer fashionable)—social workers, activists, feminists, and even revolutionaries who work at the grassroots. I have heard these two positions argued endlessly: The individual must subordinate his/her personal freedom of action to the larger social good vs. who decides or defines what is the 'larger social good'? Should the latter be based on the values, traditions and viewpoint of the majority in that society, or that of a handful of thinkers or ideologues? And what if the majority is steeped in the traditions and values of an older time—is their ability to determine social norms equal to or greater than that of people who have broken out of those moulds, questioned and analysed them, and understood the mechanisms of oppression which are often enshrined in age-old customs? And what place does basic humanity have in all this?

One sati has traumatised the entire nation and brought all these dilemmas to the fore; however, there are scores of unsung but equally dramatic social practices affecting women that no one raves and rants about. Take, for instance, the continuing practice of female infanticide in many parts of our country. The whole business of voluntarism, the individual's right to practice their beliefs, and 'the larger social good' is perfectly illustrated by this example.

Where female infanticide prevails, the concerned families or communities theoretically have the choice to not kill the first-born if it is female. But in practice, the socio-cultural and even economic pressures enforcing it are too strong. The resulting shortage of women, and customs like polyandry which develop as a consequence, take a tremendous toll on women. It does *not*, as many like to believe, give women greater power and status in these communities, but increases their burdens, placing them at the mercy of a large number of men. Female infanticide, therefore, is *not* for the greater good of such societies, unless we exclude women from the term 'society'.

Now, what of the reformer or revolutionary who enters this scenario? Does he/she say, 'it is voluntary ... who am I to interfere?' Or, should he/she not only challenge the practice, but actively work with people to create viable alternatives? In other words, to create *choice*?

It is essential, therefore, to examine what choice really means. The dictionaries define it variously as 'the act or power of choosing; worthy of being chosen; select, appropriate; alternative, preference ...'. All these seem to indicate that choice is a selection between *several feasible alternatives*—if not, it is Hobson's choice.

So when we speak of Roop Kanwar's action (or that of the tribesmen who leave a newborn baby on the mountainside) as voluntary, it implies that she chose this action from several alternatives available to her: a secure widowhood, remarriage, a job. It also means that she was aware that such alternatives existed. Most importantly, the voluntarism of her act would mean that she chose sati from among *socially approved and viable alternatives*.

And this last, to me, is the most critical factor of all. How many sanctioned and approved alternatives does this society offer women? How many of these apparent choices that women make are true choices?

First of all, more and more women cannot even choose to be born—that choice is being made for them by parents steeped in a tradition that demands the birth of sons, aided and abetted by amniocentesis-cum-abortion clinics. Once born, she cannot choose (especially if she has brothers to compete with) how much food, medical care or education she will receive. She cannot choose who she will marry, at what age, or whether she wants to marry at all. She cannot decide whether or when to have children, or even to use contraception if her husband and in-laws are opposed to it. She rarely determines the number of children she will bear, no matter how physically weak she is. She cannot choose the sex of her children, but will have to bear the blame every time she gives birth to a girl.

A poor woman cannot choose whether to fetch water, firewood for the *chula*, or fodder for the cattle. She cannot decide not to cook today because she is tired. She has no choice about working for wages, or the kind of work she will do—she must take whatever job an unskilled, uneducated woman can get, for however little it pays. On the other hand, a middle or upper-middle-class woman cannot choose to go out to work if her parents, husband, or in-laws raise objections and forbid it.

A woman cannot determine how much of her husband's earnings she needs for her household expenses—*he* chooses how much to give her, and she must make do; nor can she have a say in what her husband spends on liquor, gambling, or the cinema. I know that many would like to dismiss these statements as rabid exaggerations—I dearly wish they were! This is the miserable reality for the vast majority of India's women, if one only bothers to take a look.

Interestingly, not many women recognise the lack of choice in their lives. In a recent survey of 300 slum women working in various informal-sector jobs in Bombay, the question was asked as to whether each woman controlled her own income. The overwhelming majority claimed that they did. But upon further probing, the real nature of this 'control' became clear: because most of their menfolk were unemployed, irregularly employed, alcoholics, or otherwise unable or unwilling to provide regular income to the household, it was the *women's* wages that ensured the family's basic, daily needs. So what the women meant by 'control' was the fact that they could decide how much rations, vegetables, kerosene or oil was brought each day! They could not, for instance, retain part of their income to go to the movies, or buy a saree, or take the children on an outing. They earned their own daily bread, but they had no *choice*.

In this sense, Roop Kanwar's sati is as voluntary as the earth's rotation; indeed, as voluntary as the actions of millions of our women. She and her sisters are robbed of choice by blind tradition, and by a steady diet of unquestioning sacrifice, obedience and the self-denying goddesses of legend whom they are taught to revere. They are robbed by the forces of fundamentalism, by vote-seeking politicians, by a frightened government, by armchair ideologues. They are robbed, most of all, by those who are so morally and intellectually bankrupt that they talk of 'voluntarism'.

So if we really care, let us stop fulminating with righteous indignation or engaging in sterile debates. Let us soil our hands and work to give all our women what they do not have today—a choice!

2. The Mahila Samakhya Strategy for Empowerment

OVER the past three years,[1] in discussions among ourselves and with others, we have often spoken of 'our Mahila Samakhya Approach', 'our strategy' and 'our philosophy'. While doing so, we generally assume that this is different from other strategies, but are we really clear about this? What distinguishes 'our way' from other ways? What is, in fact, the essence of the Mahila Samakhya approach to mobilising and empowering women? In this chapter, we will try and explore this question.

What is empowerment?

In every society, there are powerful and powerless groups. This power is manifest in political, economic and social terms. Power is only another word for control over resources of various kinds—physical resources (like land), intellectual or mental resources (like information and knowledge), human resources (people, people's labour, women's power to reproduce the human race), and financial resources (money or access to money). Those who have power are thus in a position to make decisions to benefit themselves, and increase their control over resources.

The Mahila Samakhya philosophy believes that women in general, and poor women in particular, are powerless because they do not have any decision-making power or control over resources. Yet, the decisions made by others affect their lives every day. Even

---

* Translated from the Kannada article published in *Samakhya Samvada*, I (3), July 1992. The article was written for village-level activists of Mahila Samakhya Karnataka.

[1] Meaning since the launch of the Mahila Samakhya Programme in Karnataka state in early 1989.

the resources at their disposal—such as a little land, a nearby forest, their own labour and skill—are not within their control. We therefore believe that there can be no equality for women until they gain some control over their own lives, and over the resources they most need for survival.

This process of gaining control is what we call 'empowerment'. But when we speak of empowerment, or gaining control, it is often seen as something physical or literal—like getting the patta for a piece of land in my name and cultivating it myself, or earning more money. But in fact, this is a very limited understanding of empowerment. Power begins in the mind: it begins with my own self-image and confidence; with my faith in my own knowledge, skills and intelligence; with my understanding of my environment and the different actors within it; with my ability to turn weaknesses into strengths and make my circumstances work for me, instead of against me. This means a kind of mental revolution!

This is not possible unless I can begin to think differently. This is particularly essential for women, because from birth they are taught to believe that they know little and have poor understanding; that their opinions are of little value, that they have no power of any kind, and that men are superior to them in every way. In other words, they are taught not to question, but to simply obey what they are told. And everyone around them—including other women—are reinforcing this stereotype all the time. In fact, the rare or unique woman who rebels against this mould is labelled a 'bad' or 'undutiful' woman whom others should avoid and abuse.

At another level, our culture and tradition has encouraged the abdication of decision-making responsibility to those above you in the social hierarchy (Melinavaru). So, to solve their problems, the poor must look to the rich, the illiterate to the educated, the lower caste to the higher caste, the common people to the government, and women to men! Thus, we are taught to believe that it is someone else—not ourselves—who must solve our problems or show us the way. This custom also ensures that someone else retains control over us, and makes decisions for us. So if you are very poor and a woman, chances are that you have never been allowed to think for yourself or find your own solution.

The one chance the system allows for breaking this pattern is through education. The simple exposure and access to new knowledge that even bad schooling can occasionally provide can trigger off new ways of thinking. But since poor rural women are seen only as fit for marriage, child-bearing, labour and housework, their families don't send them to school. They are thus trapped in a small, isolated world, with a strictly enforced code of conduct and no opportunity to reach out to new ideas or beliefs. In this way, our society ensures that poor women remain passive and powerless, and under male domination.

Earlier, we spoke about a mental revolution—but this does not mean that the change remains at the level of the mind alone. After all, it is not sufficient for a woman to start thinking differently; the world around her has to see the differences too. So we believe that women have to begin exercising the new sense of power in their minds in concrete, practical ways, which the world around them will be forced to acknowledge and accept.

And this is where another important part of the Mahila Samakhya philosophy comes in: history has shown repeatedly that change in one individual does not necessarily result in the transformation of society at large. Yes, there have always been outstanding individuals like Kittor Channamma and Rani Laxmibai, but these individuals cannot bring about a lasting change for all women. What is more, a true revolution must change *everyone*, not just a few.

It is also a fact that it is difficult for a single woman living in a traditional environment to break out of it alone, because she will be isolated and cast out, as we saw earlier. But if a whole group of women bring about such a process together, it will be much more difficult for society to reject them. For example, one woman who is being beaten by her husband may find it difficult to tackle him, but if twenty other women in the village support her, then the whole situation changes.

However, this does not mean that the Mahila Samakhya philosophy is against men. On the contrary, we feel that in terms of control over resources, poor men and women are almost equally powerless. But we believe that once women begin their journey to change, they will find the most appropriate ways of taking their men along—sometimes willingly, and sometimes unwillingly!

Finally, Mahila Samakhya believes that this philosophy must not end up creating new pressures on women—Mahila Samakhya itself must not decide what women should and should not do, and what their priorities should be. We can only create an opportunity for women to decide themselves what changes they want to bring about in their lives, and how to do so. Very often, women will begin articulating their new strength and awareness by tackling issues that are part of the external environment—such as land, water, access to forests, and so on. They may neglect burning gender questions within their own families and households—like wife-beating or not sending their own daughters to school. While we have to keep up the process of questioning and self-examination, we cannot dictate to them. All we can do is ensure that they have made an *informed* decision, rather than one based on lack of awareness.

How is all this to be done? This philosophy sounds very powerful and inspiring, but how can such a far-reaching change be brought about? This is where we must look closely at the question of strategies.

From the very beginning, right at the sahayoginis' training stage itself, we emphasised the 'time and space' concept, and stressed the need to create an opportunity for women to gather and talk about whatever they like. We spoke of the need for women to feel that this is *their* process, not ours. How have we actually done this in the field?

First of all, we consciously decided that Mahila Samakhya should not go to women with 'something concrete' to offer, although many people told us we would not succeed otherwise. Why?

This was because this 'something concrete' (like a health camp, balwadi, a night class) itself becomes *our* priority. It may not necessarily be the woman's interest or her need. Second, we get stuck with a label or image which is difficult to change later, for example, 'those health people', 'that balwadi organisation', etc. Finally, we believe we should empower women to improve existing services or run their own facilities—and not do it *for* them, so that once again they are dependent on an external organisation.

So our very entry into the village is different. Our task is to get to know the women, befriend them, and above all, LISTEN to them. We try, from the beginning, to make women feel that we are there to listen, and not that we have come there with our own hidden agenda or priorities.

Thus, when Kamala, Saraswati and Nagamma entered Hullalli village (in Nanjangud Taluk), they found everyone busy shelling sunflower seeds. Nobody spoke to them or greeted them. So they sat down with the women and started shelling seeds too. Very soon, the women asked their names, where they were from, and how their parents allowed them to roam alone! An old lady, Nanjamma, asked, 'Aren't you afraid of coming alone like this to a village?' The sahayoginis answered, 'Why should we be afraid? You are all women like us—we cannot be harmed when we are with you!' Nanjamma spoke using many proverbs. The sahayoginis asked her to explain each one, and then its meaning was discussed. Three hours passed in an interesting and lively discussion.

'But why have you really come?'

'To see your village and meet the women.' The women laughed. 'There is nothing here to see!'

The sahayogonis returned to Hullalli several times before Mahila Samakhya was mentioned. But by that time a rapport had been established. The women were happy to see the smiling faces of the sahayoginis, and welcomed them warmly.

Mahila Samakhya is full of such stories. In Bidar, sahayogonis were introduced to new villages by women from AIKYA's sanghas, who had relatives in those places. In one village, the women would run away in fear every time the sahayogini arrived. In desperation, she asked two other sahayoginis to accompany her on her next visit. When they entered, the women hid in their houses. The sahayogini sat down under a tree and began singing songs and telling stories and jokes. Slowly, curiously, the women began gathering around them to listen. Within two hours, they had apologised for their earlier behaviour. They explained that in the past, many strangers had come to the village and cheated them, and so they were afraid. But they wanted the sahayoginis to come back and sing and tell them stories.

In Bijapur, people were quite suspicious when strangers came to their villages. They would ask questions like, 'Why have you come? Who sent you? Is someone paying you to come here?' Each sahayogini had to find her own way of dealing with this initial suspicion. In some of Channamma's villages, people said that many others like her had come, saying they wanted to help. They had collected money from the villagers by telling them they would get them bore wells, or Janatha houses, or electricity—but then they had disappeared and never returned. In such cases, the sahayogini asked the women to give her an opportunity to prove herself. She assured them that she would never ask them for money, but would help them to find out how they could get a bore well, a house, or electricity through their own efforts.

Another problem faced in Bijapur (and to some extent in other districts) was the women's demand that the sahayogini get them loans or some other economic benefit. Many sahayoginis were confused about how to handle this, and especially about how to answer the question: 'What will you give?' But soon, they learnt to answer confidently, '*Mahiti*! Courage! Strength!' It is true, though, that the women were often sceptical about this answer.

For this reason, this initial resistance had to be tackled carefully and skilfully. For instance, the Bijapur coordinator went with the sahayogini to one of the 'loan' demand villages. She led the women through a step-by-step analysis of the real-life experiences of people who have taken loans and then have been unable to repay. Even the goats, chickens, etc., which they had bought had often died, or become diseased. The 'debt spiral' was easily understood by the women, who had themselves experienced it, but had never analysed it in this way. This discussion was a breakthrough in this and many other villages. But the important principle underlying it is this: We must hold on to our strategy and philosophy, rather than giving way to such pressures.

In such a case, you may wonder, why should we not do what the women ask, since it is, after all, their demand? The answer is quite simple: the women's demand here is not the exercise of an informed choice, but a sort of reflex action. They have not been exposed to any other concepts of development excepting loans and welfare services, so naturally that is what they think they want. More importantly, there is one key question we have to ask ourselves at every step, and especially when confronted with such dilemmas: 'Will this empower women?' Getting women loans without their first understanding the whole credit system and structure, how to get loans themselves, and how to use the loan to launch a sustainable economic activity is NOT EMPOWERING! It is further enslaving!

However, in every district, in almost all the villages, the manner in which we initiate contact has set the tone of our continuing relationship with the women. And almost everywhere, women have expressed in different ways what Laxmibai of Allapur in Bidar told me three years ago:

> You are the first person who has listened to us. By giving value to our thoughts and words, you have helped us to value ourselves. We have found our own strength. Now, no one can take this away from us.

This initial strategy of ours allows women to feel central to the process from the very start. It also establishes the philosophy of 'time and space', because women begin to look forward to the sahayogini's visits as opportunities for them to speak about their own feelings, experiences and problems to someone who truly respects them.

From these individual contacts, we have to move to women gathering together as a collective. In other words, the time and space concept has to be experienced collectively. This is because parts of the philosophy have to be realised through the collective or sangha:

1. To think differently and look at women's situation differently;
2. To find the courage to change individually with the support of the group; and
3. To translate the 'mental revolution'—that is, the new self-esteem and confidence—into concrete actions which the world around has to see and acknowledge.

Over the past three years, the strategies for moving from individual contacts to collective gatherings have varied a great deal. It is important to understand that one strategy is as good as another as long as the goal is achieved.

In some places, the process has occurred very naturally. Women automatically come out of their houses and sit together when the sahayogini comes. Or, after five or six visits, the sahayogini says, 'I can't spend so much time with you when I have to go to so many houses. Instead, why don't we all sit together on my next visit; then we can spend more time together.' Not only do the women agree, but they also suggest a time when they are free, as well as a good place for meeting. And so we have the beginnings of a collective.

This is another important part of the Mahila Samakhya strategy: the transition from individual to group should occur *before* we begin speaking of a 'Sangha'. That is, women should *feel* they are a collective, rather than someone else telling them they are one. This is why we often stress that a sahayogini should not go into a new village and immediately start talking about forming a Sangha. Moreover, another type of sangha may exist in the village already— such as the Ryot sangha or mahila mandal—and it is important to allow women to *experience* the difference in our concept of a sangha before actually giving it the label.

A recent experience in Gulbarga will demonstrate the point. The sahayogini had started talking to the women about forming a sangha very soon after she made contact with them. The women asked, 'Will it be like the Akkamahadevi sangha?' Without thinking, she said, 'Yes, something similar.' But then she discovered that the Akkamahadevi sangha was in fact very different! Everyone had to have a bath before going to the sangha, and the main activity was the singing of bhajans and praying. The sahayogini realised her mistake, but it would require a lot of effort to correct it. It would have been far better not to have started talking about a sangha at such an early stage; instead, she could have merely said, 'Let's have a meeting'.

A key factor which determines the pace at which the collective forms is the skill of the sahayogini. If she is dull, nervous, doesn't have interesting things to share with the women, or is very dominating, the process takes a long time. This is a part of the strategy that has been stressed in training: if we go to women with long, sad faces, or sit and give them lectures on women's rights, we cannot mobilise them effectively. They have enough problems in their lives and do not need one more person to make them feel depressed. But they will respond quickly and warmly to someone who brings a happy face, a sense of humour, and something new and interesting into their daily drudgery.

Thus, our strategy involves a lot of creativity and innovation. We must have a fund of proverbs, songs, stories, games and exercises to facilitate the sangha-formation process. In other words, women must *enjoy* their time and space so much that they will not want to give it up for anything. But our strategy here is not just to entertain women. On the contrary, every story, proverb, song and game must be used to trigger off the 'mental revolution' we spoke of earlier. They must help women analyse their situation, the myths society propagates about them, and to see the great strength and capability which lies within them. They must also enable women to begin articulating hitherto unspoken feelings, opinions and ideas.

Quite often, however, factors other than the sahayogini's skill slow down the sangha-formation process. In many areas, the women's own male relatives have tried to prevent them from meeting; or higher-caste men or leaders have interfered, sensing the threat to their power. Sometimes the women themselves have refused to sit together with women of another group/caste/community, even though they may be equally poor. In one tribal village in Mysore and one village in Bidar, the women refused to talk to the sahayoginis because they were Christian.

How we handle such situations is vital: our strategies must demonstrate our commitment to both secularism and women's rights to have a forum of their own. And this is what our actions in the above examples tried to do: rather than withdrawing the Christian sahayogini, we sent a colleague with her for some time, and openly discussed the women's fears until they changed their attitudes. In Bidar, a special workshop was held for the men and youth who were harassing the women, after which the sanghas there were able to move ahead. And sanghas themselves were encouraged to keep on meeting in the face of threats from upper castes, with the District Coordinators, Resource Persons or sahayoginis from other areas joining the meetings for solidarity.

What happens after a reasonably stable core group of women have formed a collective? That is, after something we can call a sangha has been formed? Do we sit back and say our job is done? In fact, this is only the 'prarambha'—the next phase of our strategy now begins, and is linked to two parts of our philosophy, viz., empowering women with access to and control over resources, and the acknowledgement of women's new power by the world around them. Let us see how this is done.

When women begin meeting together, there are two distinct phases that can be seen: meeting only when the sahayogini comes, and meeting once a week, whether the sahayogini is there or not.

As women begin the process of collectively examining their situation, they invariably talk about the problems affecting their day-to-day existence. In Karnataka, we have found that these are usually problems like water scarcity, illness, lack of childcare, encroachment on or alienation of their land, housing, lighting, lack of a place for the sangha to meet in peace, etc. We in turn discuss the role of illiteracy, social stratification, and women's status in relationship to these problems. Women then identify some key issues they want to tackle as a sangha—for example, preparing or getting a bore well, starting a childcare centre for their children, having their own centre for meeting and programmes, and learning to read and write at least their names.

The next phase of our strategy now begins: the sahayogini stresses that women must first become aware of what resources are supposed to be available to them from their own Mandal Panchayats, Taluk and District development schemes. This is done by what we popularly call 'Office Bheti'. The sangha nominates various members to go in twos and threes along with their sahayoginis to local offices, and get information about what schemes are available to them and how to apply for them.

The office-visit process is itself full of learning experiences. For most women, it is the first time they are going out of the village on their own, without some male relative. At the offices themselves, they are sometimes treated badly or sent away with scant respect. So they have to go back, discuss what happened and why in their sangha meeting, plan a new strategy and go back.

In one case in Bidar, the women went to meet the Block Development Officer (BDO). The watchman, chaprassi, etc., tried to put them off by saying the BDO was not there. Finally, someone came out and said he was the BDO's PA, and that they would not be able to meet the BDO, who was on tour. As the women were walking away, dejected, someone on the road told them that the man posing as the PA was the BDO himself! The women discussed the whole incident and saw clearly that they were being treated this way because they were viewed as poor, ignorant villagers who could be made fools of.

The following week, the women went back with a new plan: if they were told the BDO was not available, they would simply say that they knew where the man's house was, and would camp there until he agreed to meet them. Not only did the ploy work, but the BDO was so daunted by the prospect of being gheraod in his home that he was extremely cordial and informative!

Another sangha in Bidar decided that the reason for their shoddy treatment in government offices was their shoddy clothing. They decided to invest in two 'sangha sarees', which would be worn by whichever woman was going for the office visit. They also decided that neatly combed hair, an erect posture, and a confident voice and body language were necessary to success. So several role plays and voice and posture exercises were practised before the visits. These tactics worked most effectively!

The office-visit strategy pays many dividends:

- it helps women establish their right to physical mobility and use the transportation system independently;
- it raises their confidence and self-esteem;
- it enables them to interact directly with officials and people's representatives without any intermediaries speaking on their behalf;
- it forces these bodies and institutions to deal directly with poor women and respond to their pressures and demands; and above all,
- it wins the respect and support of the men (even if gradually), as women are able to get resources or solve problems their men folk had been unable to do. And this, for women, is the most important empowerment of all.

While the office-visit is going on, various other activities may
begin simultaneously: a literate youngster or elder in the village may
be asked to spare an hour to teach women reading and writing every
night; women begin exploring how to get a small piece of land to
build a sangha 'mane' of their own; they identify a couple of women
who could be paid to look after toddlers while their mothers are at
work in the fields, and ask the sahayogini to organise some training
for them.

Our strategy, in all these areas, is to find the most empowering
way of facilitating women to achieve their goals. As we have said
earlier, in each and every situation, we do not do things *for* women—
such as setting up and running a crèche—but help them with
information, training, contacts and support so they can do it
themselves. For instance, there may be a six-month gap between the
women talking about wanting a crèche and one actually being started.
During this period, we help them go through a process of debating
who and how they will manage it, how many children will be
admitted, what their ages would be, how many hours it will function,
how a good crèche should be, etc. The same process must be gone
through for anything else, be it a sangha mane or a literacy class.

Why do we bother with such a complicated approach? Why not
simply do it ourselves? After all, we could do it much better and
faster than the women! But this is not our goal. Our goal is to empower
women to organise and manage their own services, so that these
resources are within their control—so, there we go back to our
philosophy.

At this point, we must examine what our strategy vis-à-vis money
is, since so many components of our programme involve giving
sanghas funds for various activities: the sangha honorarium,
construction funds for sangha manes, grants for childcare centres,
adult literacy, etc.

We said earlier that we do not speak of 'giving' anything when
we enter a village. So how do we introduce the subject of the sangha
honorarium and other grants? First of all, the sahayogoni must wait
until she is quite sure that a cohesive collective has formed, and
there is no question of women participating in the sangha only

because they think they will get some money. While there are no hard and fast rules for deciding this, some broad parameters have emerged from experience.

- the sangha has a stable core group of women who meet regularly, regardless of the sahayogini's presence;
- the sangha women have tackled some issues on their own, and have come to know local resources and institutions fairly well;
- they have raised their own funds for bus charges and other minor expenses related to office visits; and
- they have demonstrated their ability to solve internal conflicts on their own.

At this stage, the sahayoginis introduce the possibility of the sanghas getting some financial support from Mahila Samakhya. But there is one important factor here—the group has to first go through the process of applying to the Samakhya for the honorarium, registering themselves as an independent entity (as a society), opening a joint account in a local bank, nominating signatories to the account on a rotational basis, learning to sign their names, and formulating a system for keeping accounts and sanctioning expenditure. Until all the checks and balances have been worked out, no honorarium is transferred. A similar process occurs for sangha mane funds or other grants.

The point behind this strategy is that the relationship of the sanghas to Mahila Samakhya should simulate their relationship with any other institution. It also establishes their autonomy from us as an organisation. Why is this necessary?

And here we come to the next stage of our strategy: as each sangha grows in strength and independence, we have to devise mechanisms for them to begin linking with each other. The reason is once again linked to our philosophy, viz., a true revolution is for large numbers of women, not just a few. So we have to facilitate sanghas to link together and become a large movement, whose power and impact cannot be ignored.

If you think about it, the logic behind this is obvious: what is the point of each sangha, no matter how strong it is, struggling on its own against defects which are ingrained in the whole social structure?

Yes, they may get a bore well here, or a violent husband locked up there, but how can these small victories be transformed into a massive defeat of exploitation and oppression at large? How can the strength of some women become the power of all oppressed and downtrodden women? Only when the change is sustained by a large network of poor women, who represent not a few hundreds, but thousands!

And thus begins the process of sanghas, or their representatives, meeting regularly at clusters, taluk and district levels. Clusters (ten sanghas) and taluk-level workshops give women opportunities to locate common issues, interact as a mass with local officials who are invited to these meetings, form common agendas, and generally discover the power of an even larger collective. They also begin to overcome narrow village or caste identities and see themselves as part of a broader movement.

By this stage, of course, the sahayogini's role changes drastically. First of all, instead of ten or twelve villages, she networks with twenty-five or thirty; she becomes a resource person and advisor, rather than an organiser. Similarly, as the network of women's sanghas grows in strength and autonomy, the role of Mahila Samakhya itself will change. As an organisation, we will increasingly take a back seat, providing information resources, analysis, strategic advice, and other types of support to the sangha networks.

Another change will also take place in our role, a change which had already begun in many places: that is, instead of Mahila Samakhya sending sahayoginis to organise women in new villages, the older sanghas will themselves take on the task of mobilising women in other areas. This process has already begun in the older districts of Bidar, Bijapur and Mysore. More importantly, women have taken up this challenge on their own, without consulting us or asking for financial help. They are so excited by the changes they have experienced in the last few years, that they want their neighbours to experience it as well. For example, Layavva, a sangha leader in Bijapur, visits five surrounding villages regularly, encouraging the women to meet and talk about their problems, and relating the history of her own sangha and its achievements for women.

This is the stage we are at now—an important transitional stage. Our task now is to analyse in greater depth what has occurred so far, and what our future roles should be. Only then can we begin to formulate strategies for the next five years of the programme. But whatever happens in the next few years, one thing has been proved beyond doubt: the Mahila Samkhya strategy has unquestionably empowered and mobilised women into the beginnings of a major movement. Our strategy is powerful; but it will continue to succeed only if we do not lose sight of our basic philosophy and continue to ask ourselves the fundamental question: will this empower women?

3. Defining Women's Empowerment

The term 'empowerment' has become a stock-in-trade expression wherever in the world women's issues are discussed. It is one of the most loosely used terms in the development lexicon, meaning different things to different people—or, more dangerously, all things to all people. It is therefore worthwhile to define the term somewhat precisely, so that we achieve some clarity about its implications for women in the social, economic, political and educational arenas.

This is all the more important because throughout the developing world—and even in many so-called developed regions—large-scale programmes have been launched with the explicit objective of 'empowering' women, and several older women's development projects now call themselves women's empowerment programmes. Increasingly, funding of work on women's issues is linked to whether development organisations adopt empowerment as a stated goal, even if no one is very sure what this implies for methodology and field strategies.

For the Asia South Pacific Bureau of Adult Education (ASPBAE), as a movement dedicated to education for women's empowerment, it is obvious that empowering education could not be defined or formulated without first setting out a clear conceptual framework of empowerment itself. This is what this chapter attempts to do, drawing upon the framework that sprang from the South Asian study jointly undertaken in 1993 by the Food and Agriculture Organization's (FAO) Freedom from Hunger Campaign and ASPBAE.

What is power?[1]

The most conspicuous feature of the term 'empowerment' is that it contains within it the word **power**. Empowerment is therefore concerned with power, and particularly with changing the power relations between individuals and groups in society.

What, in fact, is **power**? Throughout the history of organised society, philosophers and scientists of every hue have attempted to define power. There is a formidable amount of literature on the question of power, but it is not possible for us, as social activists, to enter into philosophical debate: we are simply concerned with the '... consequences of the application of power ...' (Etzioni, cited in Olsen and Marger 1993: 18).

So for our purpose, **power can be defined as the degree of control over material, human and intellectual resources exercised by different sections of society.** These resources fall into four broad categories: **physical resources** (like land, water, forests); **human resources** (people, their bodies, their labour and skills); **intellectual resources** (knowledge, information, ideas); and **financial resources** (money, access to money). The control of one or more of these resources becomes a source of individual and social power.

Power is dynamic and relational, rather than absolute; it is exercised in the social, economic and political relations between individuals and groups. It is also unequally distributed, that is, some individuals and groups are powerful (having greater control over the sources of power) and some are less powerful or powerless (having little or no control). **The extent of power of an individual or group is in turn correlated to how many different kinds of resources they can access and control.** This control confers decision-making power, which is exercised in three basic ways: to make decisions, make others implement one's decisions, and finally, influence others' decisions without any direct intervention—which, in one sense, is the greatest power of all. Decision-making of these kinds is used to increase access to and control over resources.

---

[1] This entire section is extracted from 'Empowerment of Women in South Asia: Concepts and Practices', New Delhi, FAO/ASPBAE (Asia South Pacific Bureau of Adult Education), 1993.

Different degrees of power are sustained and perpetuated through social divisions such as gender, age, caste, class, ethnicity, race, North-South; and through institutions such as the family, religion, education, media, the law, etc.

At the beginning, a given power structure comes into being through differential controls over resources; it may initially use force, or the threat of force, to strengthen and establish itself. But once that phase is over, a far more subtle and potent weapon is used to sustain and perpetuate itself: the creation of a supporting ideology aimed at rationalising and justifying the status quo, and most importantly, at gaining the acceptance and participation of the powerless and less powerful sections in the perpetuation of the existing—and unequal—pattern of control over resources. *Our understanding of power, therefore, would be incomplete unless we recognise its partner, IDEOLOGY.*

Ideology is a complex structure of beliefs, values, attitudes, and ways of perceiving and analysing social reality—virtually, ways of thinking and perceiving. These are themselves generated by the creation of various religious or philosophical theories and explanations that legitimise inequality. *Ideologies are widely disseminated and enforced through social, economic, political and religious institutions, and structures such as the family, the education system, religion, the media, the economy, and the state, with its administrative, legislative and military wings.* The economic, political, legal and judicial institutions and structures set up and mediated by the state tend to reinforce the dominant ideology and the power of the dominant groups within it, even though their stated objectives and policies may be superficially egalitarian. But while ideology does a far effective job of sustaining an unequal power structure than crude, overt coercion and domination, we should not forget that it is always being reinforced by the threat of force, should anyone seek to rebel against the dominant system. This dynamic of power relations is illustrated in Figure 3.1.

The survival of the caste system in many countries of South Asia is an excellent illustration of the role of ideology in the survival of a power structure. Apart from economic sanctions, it was through religious indoctrination and the 'Varna' philosophy that 'upper' castes

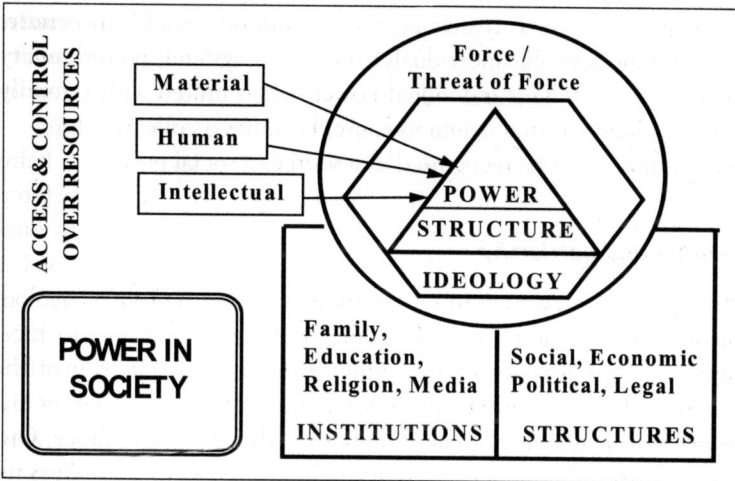

Figure 3.1

were able to co-opt and gain the participation of not only the 'middle' and `lower' castes in their own subordination, but even those whom they deemed casteless—the 'untouchables'. In a relatively short space of time, therefore, it was the latter who taught their children the ideology and rules of the caste system, rather than members of the dominant castes who benefited from it.

However, power, ideology, or the state is neither static nor monolithic. There is a continuous process of resistance and challenge by the less powerful and marginalised sections of society, resulting in varying degrees of change in the structures and relations of power. Thus, in the case of women, there is a popular saying: 'The first feminist was born on the day patriarchy was established'. When these challenges become strong and extensive enough, they can result in the total transformation of a power structure.

This analysis of power is almost entirely negative, in that it implies inequality, domination and exploitation. However, there is another kind of power—and other sources of power—which many of us recognise, more specifically at the individual level. This stems from physical and mental attributes as diverse as individual talents, skills, self-confidence, self-awareness and self-image, faith/spiritual strength, intelligence, communication skills, and so forth. The concepts of 'Shakti' (inner power) or 'honour' could, in certain circumstances, enable individuals to overcome systemic powerlessness to some extent. This individual power, when united with those of other individuals in a common cause, becomes a collective force—which must itself be recognised as a source of social power.

Gender and patriarchy

Where do women fit into our analysis of power and ideology? To answer this, we must tackle the concept of gender and the ideology and social system that feminists term 'patriarchy'. Patriarchy literally means `rule of the father' (patriarch in Greek), but in social terms, refers to the system of male dominance, that is, where descent is traced through the father; where the ownership, control and inheritance of all assets is in the hands of men; where males exercise the right to all major decision-making in the family, and hence maintain ultimate control over the family and its relations. Most of all, patriarchy establishes an unequal power equation between men and women, justifying the control of women by men in society in general, and the family in particular.

Patriarchy is almost universal in modern societies, but has, according to many scholars, definite historical roots.[2] What is more important, though, is the significant anthropological and historical evidence showing that more gender-egalitarian social formations existed in ancient times. This disproves the theory widely held by both men and women that there is a *natural* justification for patriarchy based on the biological/physiological differences between men and women.

The ideological foundation of patriarchy is the concept of *gender*. There is a good deal of confusion between 'gender' and 'sex', resulting in many people using the terms interchangeably, yet they are

---

[2] Patriarchy is by no means a universally accepted notion—many sociologists and anthropologists do not acknowledge its existence, and treat it as a spurious social theory. Even among those who accept it as a valid category of analysis, there is a great deal of debate about the origins and history of patriarchy, and whether its precursor was matriarchy or matriliny.

distinctly different categories. While sex refers to the biological and physiological differences between men and women, *gender is socially constructed, partly through the process of socialisation, and partly through positive and negative discrimination in the various institutions and structures of society* (religion, media, economic structures, law and legal systems, cultural beliefs and practices, education, healthcare, etc.)

Gender manifests itself in particular, rather than universal, forms, being defined and elaborated by other social categories like caste, ethnicity, class, race, religion, culture, the economic and political system, and geography. It is dynamic, rather than static, taking different forms in different times and regions. In contrast, *sex is biologically determined, universal and unchangeable,* in that a man or a woman is a man or a woman in any and every part of the globe.[3]

The construction of gender is achieved through the imparting of distinct qualities, attitudes, behaviour patterns and social roles, a process through which 'biological categories of male and female become social categories of men and women' (KRITI 1993: 12–13).

Socialisation is the process by which society trains its members to accept, and hence play, their socially determined roles, and begins from birth. Parents (especially mothers), teachers, peers, religious and cultural institutions, and the media are the main agents through which socialisation is accomplished, and gender differences constructed and sustained. Gender indoctrination and discrimination against women begins at birth.[4] And since women—themselves indoctrinated into the ideology of patriarchy—are the primary agents of socialisation in their capacity as mothers, they become active partners in the perpetuation of male dominance and control. Women thus become both victims and perpetrators in the patriarchal system.

Having understood power and its partner ideology, it now becomes possible to define empowerment much more clearly.

---

[3] This is generally true, although modern medical technology has created the means to change sexual characteristics.

[4] In many South Asian countries today, technologies like amniocentesis and sex pre-selection techniques allow discrimination against the girl child to manifest itself even prior to birth through female foeticide.

Definition of empowerment and women's empowerment

Box 3.1

Empowerment

Empowerment is the process—and the result of that process—whereby
- The powerless or less powerful members of a society gain greater access to and control over material and knowledge resources;
- Challenge the ideologies of discrimination and subordination; and
- Transform the institutions and structures through which unequal access and control over resources are sustained and perpetuated.

Women's empowerment is thus the process, and the outcome of the process, by which women gain greater control over material and intellectual resources, and challenge the ideology of patriarchy and gender-based discrimination of women in all the institutions and structures of society.

Box 3.2

The Goals of Women's Empowerment

1. To challenge and transform the ideology and practice of women's subordination;
2. To transform the structures, systems and institutions that have upheld and reinforced this discrimination—such as the family, caste, class, ethnicity, and the social, economic and political structures and institutions, including religion, education systems, the media, the law, top-down development models, etc.; and
3. To gain access to and control over material and knowledge resources.

The historical development of the concept of empowerment

The concept of women's empowerment was the outcome of several important critiques and debates generated by the women's movement throughout the world, and particularly in the Third World. Its source can be traced to the interaction between feminism and the concept and practice of 'Popular Education' that developed in Latin America in the 1970s. The latter itself arose from Paulo Freire's theory of conscientisation, but integrated the dimension of gender, which Freire had largely ignored. The popular education theory was also influenced by the work of Gramsci, which stressed the need for participatory and democratic functioning in institutions and society in order to create a more equitable and non-exploitative social order.

By introducing a hitherto absent gender dimension to theories of conscientisation and popular education, feminists incorporated gender subordination and the social construction of gender as a fundamental category of analysis in the practice of popular education. Feminist popular educators therefore evolved their own distinct approach, pushing mere consciousness-raising into the realm of radical action.

The feminist approach to popular education thus placed gender at the centre of conscientisation, and pushed it beyond mere awareness-building to organising the poor to actively struggle for change. This approach began to spread, much as the Freirian approach itself.

Meanwhile, the 1980s saw the rise of stringent feminist critiques of development strategies and grassroots interventions for having failed to make any significant dent in the status of women. This failure was mainly attributed to the approaches followed in such programmes—the welfare, poverty alleviation and managerial approaches, for example—which did not address the underlying structural factors perpetuating the oppression and exploitation of poor women because they had failed to distinguish between what Kate Young (1988) called the **'condition'** and **'position'** of women.

'Condition' is the material state in which poor women live—low wages, poor nutrition, lack of access to healthcare, education, training, etc.; whereas **'position' is the social and economic status of women as compared to men.** Young argues that it is precisely because most development interventions have focused on the former, that is, on improving the daily conditions of women's existence, that women's awareness of and ability to act on the underlying structures of subordination and inequality have been curtailed. While these approaches improve women's condition, their position remains largely unchanged.

Maxine Molyneux made a similar distinction between women's **'practical'** and **'strategic' interests** (1985; quoted in Walters 1991).

While women's practical needs—for food, health, water, fuel, childcare, education, improved technology, etc.—have to be met, they cannot be an end in themselves; mobilising and organising women to fulfil their long-term strategic interests is essential. This means:

> ... analysis of women's subordination and ... the formulation of an alternative, more satisfactory set of arrangements to those which exist ... such as the abolition of the sexual division of labour, the alleviation of the burden of domestic labour and child care, the removal of institutionalized forms of discrimination, the establishment of political equality, freedom of choice over childbearing and ... measures against male violence and control over women (ibid.).

Thus, by expanding the Freirian analysis and giving gender an integral place, feminists put forward the concept of women's empowerment. It is from these roots that the notion of empowerment grew. By the beginning of the 1990s, women's empowerment had come to replace most of the earlier terms used in development jargon. Unfortunately, while it soon became a trendy and widely used buzzword, the sharpness of the perspective from which it arose soon became diffused and diluted.

Essential elements of the women's empowerment process

- *Empowerment is a process*, although the result of the process may also be termed empowerment. More specifically, though, *the outcome of empowerment should manifest itself as a redistribution of power between individuals, genders, groups, classes, castes, races, ethnic groups or nations*. Empowerment means the transformation of structures of subordination, through radical changes in law, property rights, control over women's labour and bodies, and the institutions which reinforce and perpetuate male domination.
- *The process of empowerment is all-embracing, because it must address all structures of power*. Thus, there is no one single system or structure which can bring about empowerment through changes within itself; take, for instance, the claim that economic structures are the basis of powerlessness and inequality. This

would imply that in a situation where women are economically as strong, or stronger, than men, they would have equal status—but study after study has disproved this. Similarly, it is evident that improvements in physical status and access to basic resources like water, fuel, fodder, etc.—that is, the 'condition' of women—have not enabled women to become the equals of men. If that were so, then urban middle-class women should enjoy relative equality with their middle-class husbands, brothers and fathers—but we know this to be untrue.

- *The process of women's empowerment must begin in the mind, by changing women's consciousness.* This means changing a woman's beliefs about herself and her rights, capacities and potential; creating awareness of how gender as well as other socio-economic and political forces are acting on her; helping her to break free of the sense of inferiority which has been imprinted since earliest childhood; enabling her to acknowledge and rejoice in her strengths, knowledge, intelligence and skills. Above all, it means supporting her to recognise her innate right to self-determination, dignity and justice, and to realise that it is she, along with her sisters, who must assert that right, for no one who holds power will give it away willingly.
- *Power and rights have to be demanded by the powerless and the oppressed,* for it is they who have something to gain. However, because of ideological conditioning, the process of demanding justice does not necessarily begin spontaneously, or arise automatically from the very conditions of subjugation.
- *The process of empowerment must therefore be induced or stimulated by external forces,* more often than not. We have to transform women's consciousness by cutting through several layers—religion, mythology, social and cultural taboos and superstitions, behavioural training, seclusion, veiling, curtailment of physical mobility, distribution of work, dietary discrimination, and the rewards and punishments used to reinforce women's acceptance of and participation in their own oppression.
- Thus, external change agents have an important role to play in the process of empowerment—they encourage others to question the validity and credibility of the established order; they point

out who benefits from the subordination of women; they help legitimise women's articulation of the anger, rebellion and challenge simmering below the surface, which have been carefully suppressed. In short, the external change agent raises the consciousness of the oppressed, enables them to question the dominant ideology that has subjugated them, and assert their decision-making power.

- *Empowerment thus confers decision-making rights on each individual,* and aims at loosening the culturally enforced abdication of decision-making responsibility to those above us in the social hierarchy, by which the poor must look to the rich, the illiterate to the educated, the lay person to the priest, the 'lower' caste to the 'higher', the common citizen to the government—and women to men! In most cultures, a 'good' woman is one who surrenders all independence of thought and opinion to wiser male counsel. And since questioning is frowned upon, the vast majority of women grow up believing that this is the just and `natural' order of things.

- *Education is central to the process of empowerment,* since consciousness-raising is essentially a process of education. Education, in the context of empowerment, is a weapon of great potency, as it provides exposure and access to new ideas and ways of thinking, and triggers a demand for change. *Empowerment education seeks to build critical consciousness, analytical thinking, and the knowledge and skills to act for change.* The content and characteristics of empowerment education are discussed in greater detail in Chapter 4.

- *The process of empowerment must take place collectively.* History has repeatedly shown that change in one individual does not necessarily lead to a change for all others in the same situation. There have always been outstanding women who have risen above the constraints of their time; however, they were unable to bring about a lasting change for all women, mainly because when one or two women try to break free of tradition, the power structure is easily able to isolate and ostracise them— sometimes by deification, more often by vilification. But if whole groups of women begin to demand change, this is much more constructive. Obviously, when challenging an entire system or ideology, the power of a group is always greater than the power of an individual.

- *Empowerment processes must begin by creating a separate 'time and space' for women, in which to collectively and critically examine their lives, develop a new consciousness, and organise and act for change.* This space and time—away from men and household pressures—enables women to look at old problems in new ways, analyse their environment and situation, recognise their strengths, alter their self-image, access new kinds of information and knowledge, acquire new skills, and initiate actions that challenge the dominant ideology, transform institutions and structures, and enable them to gain greater control over resources of various kinds.

- *Empowerment is a spiral—not a cycle—which leads to greater and greater changes.* Consciousness, problem identification, action for change, and analysis of that action and its outcome lead to higher levels of consciousness and better-honed and executed strategies.

- *The empowerment spiral transforms every person involved: the individual (including the change agent), the collective and the environment*—although not necessarily at the same pace or depth. By this definition, therefore, *empowerment cannot be a top-down or one-way process.*

- *Empowerment is not merely a change in consciousness, but a visible manifestation of that change which the world around is forced to acknowledge,* respond to, and accommodate as best it can. Armed with their growing collective strength, women begin to assert their right to control material, human and intellectual resources, and participate equally in decisions within the family, community and village. Their choice of issue, their priorities, may often surprise or baffle the outsider, but inevitably indicate a sound understanding of strategy and tactics.

- *Empowerment therefore means making informed choices within an expanding framework of information, knowledge and analysis of available options.* After all, choices can only be made within the menu of known or experienced possibilities (for example, pay dowry and marry off your daughter, don't pay and let her remain a spinster and a stigma on your family; contract yourself as a migrant worker in a foreign country or let the family suffer in poverty). So empowerment is a process that must enable women to discover new possibilities, new options—a growing repertoire of choices.

- *The struggle to gain access to and control over resources is integral to the empowerment process.* As poor women begin to identify and act on the problems and issues that they have chosen (through a process of collective analysis), they struggle for land, employment, better wages, access to fuel, water, fodder, forests, housing, credit, healthcare, childcare, legal redress, and a myriad other resources. This is often the stage at which the external agency supporting the empowerment process has to make its own set of choices and strategic decisions. This is when they must repeatedly ask themselves the question: 'How do we support this struggle in a way that will further empower women (not us) the most?'

- *Clearly, an empowerment process is one that tackles both the condition and the position of women*; a process in which questions about the structures of power and, within these, gender subordination, are continually raised and explored. Due to the acute poverty and overwhelming work burden of poor women in our countries, there is a genuine dilemma facing most empowerment activists: should they respond to women's immediate problems ('condition'), or take the longer route of raising their consciousness about the underlying structural inequalities that have created these problems ('position')?

- *Women's empowerment must become a political force if it is to transform society at large.* In the ultimate analysis, this is possible only through an organised mass movement that challenges and transforms existing power structures. Thus, if the struggles of village or neighbourhood-level collectives have to make a larger impact, they must begin to coalesce into larger networks and become a mass movement of poor women (and men). The reason for this is again obvious: just as individual challenges can be easily crushed, so can the struggles of small local collectives of women at a larger social-political level.

- This is probably the most important turn of the empowerment spiral: *only mass movements and organisations of poor women (and men) can bring about the fulfillment of women's 'practical' and 'strategic' needs, and change both the 'condition' and the 'position' of women.*

- *The process of empowerment should also generate new notions of power itself,* and the purpose for which it is wielded. Present-day notions of power—evolved in a hierarchical, male-dominated society—are based on divisive, destructive and oppressive values that encourage aggression, competition and corruption, regardless of whether it is men or women wielding power.

- *The need is for a new understanding of power itself*—not one of control and exploitation for personal gain, but the power of together constructing a new society in which the potential of every human being can be realised, without regard to gender, race, class, caste, ethnicity or region. As one group put it,

> We would not like women's empowerment to result in women taking over men's powers within the same exploitative and corrupt society. Women's empowerment should lead to ... a situation where each one can become a whole being, regardless of gender, and use their fullest potential to construct a more humane society for all ....[5]

Similarly, women gaining control over resources should not result in their using them in the same selfish and ecologically destructive manner that male-dominated capitalist societies have done.

- *Women's empowerment should thus lead to a world where women—and the 'new men'—ensure that resources are utilised not just equitably, but sanely and safely; where war and violence will be eliminated, and our earth restored to a clean, green place for the coming generations.*

---

[5] Farida Akhtar, UBINIG, December 1992, personal communication.

The impact of women's empowerment on men

It is obvious that poor men are almost as powerless as poor women in terms of access to and control over resources. This is exactly why most poor men support women's empowerment processes when they enable women to bring much-needed resources into their families and communities, and/or challenge power structures which have oppressed and exploited poor men as well as women. The resistance, however, comes when the same women begin to question the power, attitudes or behaviour of men in the family.

The question then arises: *can women be empowered without disempowering men?* There can be no denying the fact that if the women of any class, caste, or region are to gain greater control over resources, and hence decision-making power, then those who traditionally enjoyed such power will have to give up at least some of it. Does this mean that any process of women's empowerment is inevitably directed against men, as many activists fear?

We must be clear that *women's empowerment, if it is a real success, does mean the loss of men's traditional power and control over women both within and outside the family*: control of her body and her physical mobility; the right to abdicate from all responsibility for housework and care of the children; the right to physically abuse or violate her; the right to spend family income on personal pleasures (and vices); the right to abandon her or take other wives; the right to take unilateral decisions which affect the whole family; and the countless other ways in which the patriarchal system has given men of every class unjust control over women. However, it is important to emphasise that *women's empowerment is not against men, but against the system of patriarchy and all its manifestations* (Bhasin 1991: 6).

The point that is often missed, however, is that *the process of women's empowerment will also liberate men*: they will be freed from the roles of oppressor and exploiter which distorts and limits their humanity and potential. They will also be relieved of gender stereotyping, which forces them to deny many innate traits (like sensitivity, the need to care for others), interests and latent abilities in order to conform to socially-determined notions of 'manliness' and 'masculinity', just as it forces women to adhere to codes of behaviour that are 'womanly' and 'feminine'. Yes, men will have to share in housework and childcare and stop all forms of violence against women—but they will also find themselves with women who are ready to share traditional male burdens in exchange.

The impact of women's empowerment on women

While fears of men's disempowerment are rampant, there is hardly any recognition of the losses women sustain in the process of empowerment. It is assumed that for women, empowerment is a win-win situation. But the reality is far more complex for most women: empowerment in its full sense is a frightening, disconcerting process, as women lose the comfort and security of the sheltered, protected lives they have led; there are no safe, clear-cut roles and stereotypes to fall back on; they must emerge from the sanctity of the veil or the courtyard into a bewilderingly complex world, which they have to cope with without having had either exposure or preparation; they must deal with people, situations and issues they had never before encountered; they must learn all kinds of new and disturbing ideas. Most of all, in the churning up of traditional social relations, women stand to lose a large number of the props and securities which supported them in the old order.

For many women, it is tempting to turn and run. It is only the strength and support of collectives that averts this, as well as the growing realisation that change is never a neat, tidy process, but an extremely chaotic and messy business. Above all, women press ahead only when they are sure that however uncomfortable and confusing the new order may be, the gains for them will be greater than the losses.

Essential features of the empowerment process

- The capacity to question traditional beliefs and practices, and develop a critical approach to one's environment;

- Developing a positive self-image and recognising one's strength, including valuing one's existing knowledge and skills;
- Exploding myths, misconceptions and stereotypes about women in society;
- Critically analysing structures of oppression and exploitation;
- Becoming aware of one's rights as an equal citizen and a woman;
- Defining and sharing one's strengths and weaknesses with other women;
- Building strong collectives through which individual and collective problems are identified and addressed;
- Learning to organise and build collectives, and function in and as collectives, including collective decision-making, action, critical reflection, accountability;
- Learning to confront oppressive practices within and outside the home and family, and changing one's attitudes and practices with one's own children, including giving daughters opportunities for learning;
- Seeking access to new kinds of information and knowledge relevant to the critical issues of one's life, as well as for understanding the world beyond our horizons;
- Learning about and critically analysing the dominant ideology, including social and gender relations, development policies, national and local politics;
- Evolving alternative agendas and collectively working for change by developing new strategies and methods, including forming strategic alliances with other groups of exploited and oppressed peoples;
- Studying the available resources—physical, human, financial—including government/non-government services and schemes;
- Learning to access resources and public schemes/services independently, demanding accountability, and working for changes in schemes and programmes that are inaccessible/inappropriate;
- Learning to access information independently, including by becoming literate and numerate;
- Learning to negotiate with public institutions and systems (local

councils, elected representatives, banks, government departments, etc.) independently;

- Learning to set up and collectively manage one's own services and programmes whenever needed;
- Understanding political structures and systems of governance, and how to participate in these and demand accountability;
- Organising and building networks at local, regional, national and global levels, through which poor women can become a social, economic and political force; and
- Learning other empowering skills, for example vocational, managerial, literacy, basic data collection skills for conducting their own surveys, etc., which enable poor women to become a force to reckon with in society.

Enabling and disabling conditions for empowerment

The process of empowerment of women (or indeed any group of poor and powerless people), including empowering education, is facilitated by certain enabling socio-political conditions. The absence of these enabling conditions, or the presence of disabling ones, make empowerment difficult—or perhaps even impossible—to achieve. What are the conditions that enable and disable women's empowerment?

Box 3.3
Enabling and Disabling Conditions

Enabling conditions for empowerment:
- Peace
- Democracy
- Constitutional/legal guarantee of equal rights to women

Disabling conditions for empowerment:
- Suspension or curtailment of democratic rights for economic reasons
- **Denial of rights on the basis of citizenship**
- **Suspension or curtailment of democratic rights for political reasons**

Enabling empowerment

Peace

The poor in general, and women in particular, cannot be organised to challenge their subordination or lack of control over resources when they are living in situations of conflict. *By peace is meant not only an absence of war, but of other conditions of systematic, organised violence and civil strife*—caste conflicts, terrorism, civil and military wars, communal/ethnic clashes, and so on. All of these disrupt normal civil life, threaten basic survival, cause displacement and migration of people from their homes and livelihoods, and produce emotional and physical trauma.

When the 'politics of violence' prevails, communities and families tend to close ranks and draw inwards. Conservative traditions and values tend to get strengthened, as people struggle to survive under external threats. These forces affect women even more deeply. First, women are invariable targets of violence in conflict situations, since they are seen both as part of the enemy's property to be conquered and enjoyed, and as symbols of their honour and self-respect. The rape of women has always been considered one of the 'spoils' of war. So the protection of womenfolk becomes paramount in conflict situations, resulting in strong re-assertions of patriarchal gender relations: women's physical mobility and exposure to external influences are severely curtailed.

It is precisely this argument that has been used for centuries to push women into the home, into re-accepting conditions of subordination which they may have overthrown. In fact, even so-called 'progressive' movements and political struggles argued that women must defer their demands for equality until 'after the revolution'. In many conflict situations, women are also expected to docilely provide sexual services to the heroes fighting the battle, as their contribution to the 'cause'.

In other cases, women themselves retreat into family, kinship and community codes and support systems, as they are well aware of the danger they are in. Even when they are forced by circumstances to fend for themselves (because their menfolk have been killed, abducted, or are missing), they are in no position to question the prevailing order—or disorder—as they struggle for simple physical survival.

Some situations of struggle—such as the independence movements in British India, Algeria, Palestine and Vietnam, for instance—actually mobilised women in large numbers to fight for the cause alongside men. In many ways, these mass movements, which created war-like situations, resulted in empowering women and bringing them into the mainstream of the change process. This is possible, however, only when the liberation of women and gender equality is part of the overall agenda of a struggle. But in most strife-torn parts of the world today, that is hardly the case. Even if women are involved in actual fighting, they are often used as cannon fodder and shock troops, and in suicide missions (witness the LTTE member Dhanu, who carried the belt-bomb which killed Rajiv Gandhi).

There is little historical evidence, therefore, that women can be empowered where conflict prevails; sustainable and effective women's empowerment processes are thus most successfully initiated in conditions of peace and normal civil life. In their absence, those concerned with women's empowerment must join forces with other movements involved in the struggle for peace, and against militarism and violence. The restoration of peace, in these contexts, is the first task in empowering women.

Democracy

The process of empowerment is also nearly impossible outside a democratic political system—*only democracy allows space for mobilisation, struggle and dissent, all of which are integral to empowerment.*

Since empowerment is dependent on consciousness-raising, organising and challenging existing orders, it can only be initiated and sustained where there is space for mobilisation, struggle and dissent—where the rights of citizens to organise and assert their rights are recognised, respected and protected by law. Certain political regimes, especially those whose economic policies are dependent on suppressing dissent and upholding unequal power relations, will not allow genuine processes of empowerment to occur; they are also, more often than not, patriarchal in nature, subscribing to the 'natural' justice of male superiority.

Adult franchise is the engine that drives democracy, which means that mass movements can find political expression through the ballot box, and subsequent popular pressure on the elected representatives, to achieve their goals.

While most democratic countries are far from ideal democracies, the fact remains that they allow the relatively free flow of ideas, and it is from ideas that popular movements can arise. Although in many cases there has been violent repression, there is also much evidence of movements surviving and forcing changes in the dominant power structure.

The process of women's empowerment, as we have seen, must also become a popular mass movement in order to change the basic structures of subordination. Only in a democratic environment—where the principle of basic civil and political rights are accepted, and which provides a constitutional basis and space for the struggle for gender equality—can such a women's movement survive and succeed. In political systems where women's equality is not accepted and constitutionally guaranteed, the struggle for empowerment must begin at this basic level, and will be a longer, more perilous process.

Constitutional/legal guarantee of equal rights to women

Democracy itself is usually based on the principle of equal rights for all citizens, providing a constitutional basis and space for the struggle for gender equality, even where it does not exist in practice. There are usually constitutional guarantees of certain individual 'fundamental rights' and freedoms—as, for instance, the right to free speech, movement, association, religion, etc. Most modern democracies guarantee freedom from discrimination on the grounds of sex, race, caste, creed, ethnicity, etc. In such a context, therefore, women's empowerment processes are only acting to realise for women the rights that have already been formally conferred.

This is impossible in regimes based on entrenched ideologies of gender discrimination—where gender equality is not only *not* accepted constitutionally, but support for the subordination of women is drawn from religion. Here again, empowerment struggles must first ally themselves with those progressive democratic movements which have a gender perspective.

Disabling empowerment

All the above enabling conditions, however, become irrelevant when certain other factors impinge on the capacity of people to organise themselves for empowerment.

Suspension/curtailment of democratic rights for economic reasons

Unfortunately, in the Asia-South Pacific region today, many nations have curtailed the democratic rights of their people in order to promote economic growth. The rights of workers, for instance, or those attempting to organise them, have been restricted or removed altogether to ensure that so-called 'labour unrest' does not imperil the rate of growth of these economies. These economies are utilising relatively cheap, unorganised labour—who live and work in appalling conditions—to maintain their global competitiveness and export earnings; there is a fear that this will be adversely affected if workers organise and demand higher wages and better working conditions. Such countries, therefore, are democracies on paper, but civil and political rights within them have been sacrificed to economic growth.

Denial of rights on the basis of citizenship

The empowerment process seeks to organise the poorest and most oppressed and exploited sections of people, and assumes that, being full-fledged citizens of the nation in which they are subordinated, they have the right to demand socio-economic and political changes from the leadership. We assume, therefore, that the group one seeks to empower is eligible for all the civil rights—even if limited—of that nation.

In today's globalising economies and labour markets, however, we are increasingly witnessing the problem of migrant labour who are residents, but not citizens, in another country. Their rights to organise and negotiate their interests are by no means recognised by the political regimes of the host countries; attempting to do so could at best lead to instant deportation, and at worst to imprisonment. Migrant workers' contracts often contain clauses prohibiting them from organising in any manner. The situation is aggravated when the labour-exporting countries are themselves subordinate, in economic and political terms, to the importing ones, and so do not have much clout at the inter-governmental level.

Suspension/curtailment of democratic rights for political reasons

A significant proportion of vulnerable groups—especially women—are denied their basic rights to organise for change, even when they enjoy full citizenship, for reasons of 'internal security', 'defense reasons', or because they live in 'sensitive areas', etc. We have, in the region, situations in which the legal rights of citizens in their own countries have been suspended for various reasons—their race, ethnicity, location; due to military objectives; or other factors. These are often areas in which serious political unrest and/or separatist movements have taken root. In this scenario, the affected people's right to organise, challenge state policies, or even make themselves visible is non-existent.

What is the meaning of empowerment in such a context? How can women be empowered in an eco-political environment that is fundamentally disempowering? Obviously, neither organising women for empowerment nor empowering education is possible in an environment where one can be instantly criminalised for engaging in such activities.

In such a context, women's empowerment activists have little scope for grassroots organising, and must attempt other strategies, such as international lobbying and advocacy, with the support of global networks working for human rights, democracy and women's empowerment. They must also ally themselves with those groups within the country who are working for a restoration of basic democratic rights.

References

Bhasin, Kamla. 1991. 'Education for Women's Empowerment: Some Reflections'. Lecture delivered at the First General Assembly of the Asia Pacific Bureau of Adult Education (ASPBAE), Tagaytay City, Philippines, December.

KRITI. 1993. *Patriarchy*, I (3): 12–13.

Molyneux, Maxine. 1985. 'Mobilization without Emancipation? Women's Interests, the State, and Revolution in Nicaragua', *Feminist Studies*, 11 (2): 227–54.

Olsen, M. E. and M. N. Marger (eds). 1993. *Power in Modern Societies* (Boulder: Westview Press).

Walters, Shirley. 1991. 'Her Words on His Lips: Gender and Popular Education in South Africa', *ASPBAE Courier*, 52.

Young, Kate. 1988. *Gender and Development—A Relational Approach* (Oxford: Oxford University Press).

4. Challenging Ritual Caste Oppression: The Tegampura Story*

TEGAMPURA is a small village in the backward district of Bidar in Karnataka state in southern India. Even in the early 1990s, the social structure of this region was highly feudal, with a rigid caste hierarchy. A few 'upper'-caste families owned most of the land, and working as agricultural labourers in their fields was the only source of livelihood for the Dalits.[1] This region also carried an antiquated custom which symbolised the social subordination and economic dependence of the labouring class/castes on the landowners: At the end of the day's work in the fields, the Dalit labourers had to stand outside the back verandah of the landlord's house and ritually beg for food, their hands raised, palms out. Only after the landlord's wife had thrown the previous day's stale bread into their hands would they be paid their day's wages of grain and a little cash. And only after the act of ritual begging were they permitted to cook their evening meal.

Even four decades after Indian independence, after untouchability was abolished and its practice made punishable by law, no one thought to question this shameful custom. Until 1991, when the activist-educators of a government-initiated women's empowerment programme called Mahila Samakhya entered Tegampura and its surrounding villages and began organising Dalit women. Mahila Samakhya literally means 'Women Valued as Equals', and is the name given to a programme of Education for Women's Empowerment launched by the Ministry of Education, Government of India, in 1988. It was one of several initiatives taken after the

---

* This essay was written in April 2006, but based on events that occurred in 1993.
[1] 'Dalit' means the oppressed, and the term was coined in the late 1960s by progressive leaders of what the Indian Constitution called the 'Scheduled Castes'—a list of former 'untouchable' castes.

New Education Policy of 1986, which included the stated objective of making education an instrument for women's empowerment and gender equality. The programme was launched in several states of the country, including Karnataka, through specially formed autonomous organisations headed and staffed, for the most part, by feminist activists.

The Mahila Samakhya strategy was that of feminist popular education, with a strong emphasis on building collectives of the poorest women at the village level (called 'Sanghas' or 'Samoohs'). Its women activists were trained to create a space and time for poor women to talk about their problems, critically analyse them, and begin challenging the dominant ideology and practice of inequality in gender and social power relations in thought and action.

Mahila Samakhya activists began working in Tegampura in late 1991. Early in 1992, a small but cohesive collective of about twenty-five Dalit women had been formed. They began to discuss the custom of ritual begging, and poured out long-suppressed feelings of rage and humiliation. At one of their weekly meetings, their outrage culminated in a decision to refuse to perform the begging ritual, which they decided was meant purely to reinforce their subjugation as Dalits, and to demand their wages as a right. The Mahila Samakhya activist was not even present at the meeting where this revolutionary decision was taken.

When the women went home and communicated their resolve to their families, their men and elders were terrified. They begged and pleaded with them not to go through with their decision. 'There will be a caste war!' they said; 'They will burn our huts, rape our daughters and slaughter us'; 'We are too weak to win against the landlords.' But the women were adamant. 'What is the use of our living without dignity or respect? How can we allow our children and grandchildren to continue to be humiliated like this—and their children after them? If they kill us, all the better! The government will have to take notice and stop it. The begging must end.'

The women had decided that they and their men would refuse to work the fields until the landlords agreed to pay their wages without the begging. But they were too smart to rush into implementing their decision. Anticipating the landlords' reaction, they spent the next few weeks going to surrounding villages and asking their fellow labourers not to come in as substitute workers if the landlords tried to hire them. They also planned their act of rebellion for a time when the crops were ripe for harvesting, and even a few days' delay would mean a huge loss.

When all was in readiness, the women led the way. One fine day, after completing the day's work in the fields, they stood outside the landlords' houses and boldly demanded their wages. Incensed at their audacity at refusing to perform the ritual of begging for food, the landlords refused to pay their wages, and threatened them with dire consequences. They declared a sort of lock-out, refusing to let the Dalits work in their fields. But thanks to the women's wily preparations, the landlords' attempt to bring in labour from nearby villages failed, and the crops stood wilting in the fields. The Dalit families of Tegampura were supported with meagre supplies from neighbouring areas, or simply gave up eating twice a day, and struggled to survive the boycott. They were hungry, but their spirits were high— they knew the landlords were nervous about resorting to violence, knowing the women had outside support and contacts because of the Mahila Samakhya programme.

Desperate, the landowners even employed a local 'witch doctor' to cast a spell on the movement's ringleaders, using a local belief in possession by spirits called 'banamati', and ensuring that the women knew they had done this (the spell doesn't work unless you know it's been cast). The belief in the power of possession was so strong in their culture that some women actually surrendered to it, becoming lethargic and morose. Others, though, saw it for the tactic it was and refused to submit. Rather, they turned the tables by waylaying a marriage broker on his way to negotiate an alliance for one of the big landlord's sons, and telling him that any girl given to these families would be subjected to witchcraft! The broker promptly reported this to his clients who withdrew the marriage offer for the young man, much to the landlord's chagrin.

In less than two weeks, as their crops lay withering, the landlords caved in. They asked the Tegampura women and their families to return to the fields, and agreed to pay their wages without the begging ritual.

The women had won a great victory. Economically, of course, nothing much had changed. They still earned paltry wages, well below the legal minimum, and depended on the landowners for work. Yet, everything had changed—the power structure had been shaken up by a small band of courageous women. They had sent out a signal to their oppressors, they had eradicated a centuries-old custom, they had changed the power equation between themselves and their men, and between the Dalit community and the dominant one.

All this happened because someone came along and helped the women look at their reality with new eyes. Someone helped them voice and analyse their sense of injustice, bring to the surface their revolutionary anger, and believe in their power to change things themselves. This is how the women of Tegampura experienced and demonstrated the meaning of empowerment.

5. The Transformation of Political Culture: The Mahila Samakhya (Karnataka) Experience*

Women and political power—the central issues

It is abundantly clear that a sustainable and long-term reversal of the subordination of women can happen essentially through a political process, and can be successfully completed only when women storm the bastions of political power that have thus far been controlled by men from the dominant social groups. However, becoming representatives in corrupt and unaccountable political bodies is not the crux of the matter—the very nature of politics and the very way political power is exercised have to be transformed. Obviously, there is no reason why only women should be concerned with this—this is a social project in which both men and women have a stake. But women have a special opportunity to take a lead in this process by virtue of the fact that there is, in our country, a women's movement which is itself built on the re-examination of and challenge to existing power relations, and is engaged in the quest for an alternative ethical framework for the practice of power.

Experience shows that generally, whenever and wherever women have entered politics and political institutions, one of two things have happened: They have either been co-opted and/or corrupted by the dominant political culture (which also often means distancing themselves from the needs and issues of the mass of women); or, if they are unwilling to play by the rules of the game, they are rendered

---

* Paper presented in the sub-theme on 'Women, Political Participation, and Politics of Organising', Seventh National Conference of the India Association of Women's Studies, Jaipur, 27–30 December 1995.

ineffective and marginalised. Either way, the cause of women is not advanced, and neither is the nature of politics itself challenged or altered in any meaningful way. There are three main reasons for this, in my view.

1. Lack of a critical mass of women in political institutions

The number of women entering formal political institutions like the state and national legislatures, or even the old (pre-Constitutional Amendments) Panchayati Raj bodies, has been woefully inadequate. Figures for the Lok Sabha, for instance, show several revealing trends: The increase in the percentage of women MPs to total MPs between 1952 and 1991 is only 2.2 percentage points—that is, from 4.4 per cent in 1952 to 6.6 per cent in 1991 (Kaushik 1992: 40).[1] At the state level, the picture is little better: In Karnataka, for instance, the percentage of women MLAs in the State Assembly has *decreased* from 5 per cent in 1952 to 3 per cent in 1994. Until the 1985 Karnataka Panchayati Raj Act, which mandated a 25 per cent reservation for women, the nation-wide custom of nominating one or two women members ensured that their presence in these bodies was virtually irrelevant. Even in West Bengal—whose Panchayat system is considered a model, and whose revised Panchayat Act of the early 1980s broke the power of the traditional rural elite in the Panchayats—we find that women's representation prior to the seventy-third Constitutional Amendment was dismal: less than 5 per cent (Development Dialogue 1995).[2]

Obviously, there *must be a critical mass of women—and that too, women with a radical, feminist consciousness—to materially affect the culture and functioning of political institutions*, and to usher in policies,

---

[1] Mahila Samakhya is a programme launched by the Department of Education, Ministry of HRD, Government of India, in late 1988, with the stated objective of 'Education for Women's Empowerment'. The programme is implemented through autonomous registered societies at the state level, and is currently operational in five states, viz., Andhra Pradesh, Bihar, Gujarat, Karnataka and Uttar Pradesh.

[2] Bidar, Bijapur and Mysore; the programme was expanded into the districts of Gulbarga and Raichur in 1991, and currently covers over 700 villages in the five districts.

laws and programmes for gender justice. Conceptually, this is where reservation politics must be placed: They create an enabling condition for a critical mass of women to enter the political arena. However, reservation is only a beginning, for it cannot ensure that the women entering politics through it will function any differently from their male counterparts.

2. Lack of linkage between the women's movement and women in politics

Women entering the formal political system in India have not necessarily come from, been accountable to, or been supported by a mass-based and progressive women's movement in the country, especially a movement that has become a political force in its own right, and is thus capable of influencing the political system while simultaneously maintaining a supra-political stance. Indeed, this could be said to be the case with the majority of our politicians, barring some exceptions who have emerged from mass-based peasant organisations or trade unions. This means that most women in politics owe their allegiance to the political party that fielded them, and to the interest group, region and constituency from which they hail, in that order. All of them have had an unimpressive track record on women's issues; in fact, some political parties have abjured any specific agenda about women on the grounds that this is divisive and reformist, while others remain obscurantist in their position on women.

How can women in political institutions, coming from such diverse backgrounds and ideologies, play a positive role for the advancement of all women? Clearly, this will be possible only if they have emerged from a strong-progressive movement, which not only continues to support them in both ideological and practical ways, but to which they are also accountable.

3. Women's experience of power in the private and public spheres

Finally, women's experience of power in the public sphere—or the lack of it—is a critical factor affecting their performance and effectiveness in the formal political system. Since women have been denied power in the public domain for millennia, their only experience in the exercise of power is, by and large, in the familial or private sphere. Even here, they have generally had to exercise power indirectly, through their influence on the key men of the household, or in very limited areas of decision-making, such as arranging marriages or policing other women. Thus women have been conditioned, from earliest childhood, to uphold male power, and to seek power through men. *They have little experience of joining together with men—much less with other women—in the pursuit of wider social projects,* or of using power for a different end.

Conversely, women's only model for the exercise of power in the public sphere is that created by the patriarchal dominant class and caste. The culture of power that they have witnessed has been that of *power over, not power on behalf of, or for a larger social good.* The model of political power surrounding women in our society has increasingly come to mean bribes, corruption, patronage networks, and the promotion of narrow interests. Corruption and criminalisation of the electoral process has resulted in facile justifications of post-electoral corruption and malpractices. Women entering the political system for the first time thus have no alternative models of political culture to emulate or promote, but are under constant pressure to fall in line and conform to the existing norms.

All these factors imply that the Indian women's movement must have a clear political agenda, and a strategy for entering and transforming political structures—including political parties, trade unions and peasant associations, and institutions of governance. The time has come for such an agenda to be formulated with maturity and far-sightedness—which means a radical change in postures. For instance, the movement has often demanded accountability from women in politics, asking them what they have done for the cause of women. Perhaps now, in addition, we must ask ourselves: *What is our responsibility, as a movement, to support and enable women in politics to work for the cause of gender and social equality, and also to alter the nature of politics itself?*

With one-third reservation for women in Panchayati Raj institutions—and serious lobbying for similar reservation in State Assemblies and the Lok Sabha—we must now formulate a strategy for accessing political power while simultaneously maintaining a supra-political stance. It is in this context that a small experiment undertaken by the Mahila Samakhya[1] programme in Karnataka can provide several insights about such a strategy.

Lessons from the Karnataka experience

The Karnataka Panchayati Raj Act of 1985, hailed as the most radical in the country, was the first to implement reservation of 25 per cent of all seats for women, cutting across other reservation categories such as SC, ST, OBC, etc. Thus, when the Mahila Samakhya (hereafter MS) programme was launched in three districts of Karnataka[2] early in 1989, there was already a large number of grassroots women representatives in the Mandal and Zilla Panchayats. It soon became evident that a majority of these women had been forced to stand for election, and there were multiple barriers to their effective participation, which have been well-documented elsewhere. The most common were—illiteracy; lack of awareness of their rights and responsibilities; manipulation by male caste members or men of their own strata; lack of knowledge of the Panchayat Act and the rights and duties of the Panchayats and their members; and most importantly, the triple burden which rendered the opportunity cost of participation very high.

The Mahila Samakhya strategy was to organise poor rural women into collectives; the Karnataka programme did not follow the 'Saathin' or 'Sakhi' model, but focused on the building of *mahila sanghas* by the programme activists, known as Sahayoginis, each working in about ten villages/hamlets. It happened quite naturally, therefore, that many women PRI members became active members of the *mahila sanghas* as well. As part of its consciousness-raising and political education strategy, MS district teams helped the village *mahila sangha* to strategise on how best to lobby the Mandal Panchayats[3] which, under the 1985 Act, has the power to allocate

---

[3] The Karnataka Panchayati Raj Act of 1985 has created a two-tier system of self-government within the district: Mandal Panchayats covering an approximate population of 15,000, and Zilla Parishads at the district level. This was then revised,

over 90 per cent of the district's development resources. Women members of the Panchayat became the natural targets of such lobbying, which raised the issue of their core capacity to function in, much less influence, Panchayat decisions. This led, inevitably, to recognising the need for special training and support interventions for women members of the PRIs, and very soon, for all SC/ST and Backward Caste members, women and men.

A series of special workshops were then organised for local Mandal Panchayat SC/ST members (men and women), and later, for all women and members, regardless of caste. The latter were very useful exercises in learning the extent to which women, as a gender, could transcend the social divisions amongst them and formulate some common agendas, regardless of caste and class. These workshops were sometimes quite explosive, but very good sensitisers, since upper-caste women had to stay and eat together with Dalit women if they wanted to attend the training opportunities being provided by MS. This forced both groups to introspect on the limits and potentials of gender solidarity, on where their caste and class interests converged and diverged. For example, upper-caste women representatives of one Mandal supported the Dalit members' demand for a separate cremation ground, but were not willing to back the Dalit's alternative demand to cremate their dead in the upper-caste *ghat*.

In the process, it became clear that the *sanghas* should strategise much more purposively to contest the next round of Panchayat elections: identifying and preparing potential women; training themselves before, rather than after, entering the local bodies; and on how to break out of the confines of reservation policy by contesting and campaigning to win open category seats—this naturally brought up several critical questions about the relationship of such women with the *sanghas* during the election process, and after they entered the Panchayat bodies. These questions are in essence the same as the questions we would have to ask about the relationship between women entering politics from the women's movement, and the women's movement as a whole, viz.:

---

in 1993, to a three-tier system of Gram Panchayats, Taluk Panchayats and Zilla Panchayats.

1. Would women candidates for the *mahila sanghas* be allowed to contest in the name of the *sangha*, or use their membership of the *sangha* as a campaigning strategy?
2. If elected, would the women members continue to be members of the *sangha* and participate in the decision-making process?
3. What would be the accountability of successful women candidates to the *sangha* after election, in their capacity as members of the Panchayat body?
4. How would the *sangha*, in turn, relate to the women Panchayat members elected from amongst them, and to the Panchayat bodies as a whole?
5. How would the *sangha* handle changes in the attitudes/behaviour/values/goals of its members after they became Panchayat representatives?

The women's *sanghas* in MS districts and villages prepared for over three years in various ways to contest the 1994 Gram Panchayat elections. Countless workshops and training programmes were held to build critical analysis and awareness of the prevailing political culture and structures; the nature, powers and functioning of political institutions like the PRIs, the state Assembly and the national legislature; the problems faced by women and SC/ST members; becoming functionally literate and numerate; and learning about the brass tacks of Panchayat functioning—including meeting notice, sitting fees, framing resolutions, keeping minutes, procedures, gram sabhas, etc. Over 300 *sangha* women in five MS districts contested elections, including about fifty who contested open category seats not reserved for women.

Most importantly, the *sanghas* hammered out answers to the above questions—and I believe that the answers some of them found have a great deal to teach us about the role of the women's movement in enabling women's access to political power, while simultaneously struggling to alter the dominant political culture.

• First, most *sanghas* decided that while selected women from amongst their membership would stand for elections in their own names, they could actively use their membership and political record in the *sanghas* in their campaigning. That is, they did want the *sangha* to become tantamount to a political party and be subverted by the unsavoury party politics surrounding them; however, since their members would not woo voters with the usual means (distributing liquor, making untenable promises about distribution of benefits, etc.), they would use, instead, the considerable respect earned by the *sangha* and its members for integrity and activism on behalf of poor women. What is more, the *sangha* members themselves campaigned for their candidates, capitalising on the *sangha's* record of struggles for equitable distribution of public resources, its militancy in protecting and promoting women's rights, and the greater awareness and preparedness of its candidates for effective participation in the Panchayats.

- Successful candidates—about 200 in all five districts, including several women who won general category seats—are allowed to continue to be members of the *sangha*. Most *sanghas* view this as vital, both as an ongoing support to the women and in order to demand accountability from them. However, formal leadership positions or responsibilities within the *sanghas* must be relinquished.

- *Sangha* members who became Panchayat representatives have several responsibilities vis-a-vis the *sangha*: They must advocate the *sangha's* agenda for women's rights and development in the Panchayat's decision-making process (for example, the selection of women beneficiaries for various schemes, correct application of poverty norms in beneficiary selection for schemes like the IRDP, Jawahar Rozgar Yojana, etc.); they must provide information about the Panchayat's decision and allocation of resources to the *sangha*; and they must inform the *sangha* of any decisions that are likely to be prejudicial to the interests of the large constituency of poor women and their families.

- In turn, several forms of practical, intellectual and moral support are extended by the *sangha* to elected women representatives (in most cases, whether they are *sangha* members or not); for example, they can appeal for the *sangha's* support in situations where their rights as women, or as Panchayat members, are being infringed, or their ability to function is being adversely affected (such as sexual or caste-based harassment or discrimination; non-payment of sitting fees; resolutions passed in their absence or without the requisite quorum; husbands/sons forcing them to stay at home and attending meetings in their stead; helping out with childcare, fuel gathering, cooking, or other tasks to enable her to attend meetings, etc.). They can also continue to access the various learning awareness and skill-building opportunities provided to the *sanghas* by MS or other NGOs.

- In cases where women's attitudes, values, behaviour, or solidarity with the *sangha* (and with the interests of the poor women that it represents) begins changing, or signs of corruption or co-option by other interests become evident, the *sanghas* have used several accountability weapons. There are several examples of women *sangha* members changing colour after becoming Panchayat members. *Sanghas* have dealt with these situations in a variety of ways: First, there are open discussions in the *sangha* meeting, in the presence of the errant member, about the changes and what they represent. The individual is advised, warned, cajoled, persuaded. If there is no change even after this, *sanghas* have been known to terminate their membership; withdraw their support in material and psychological terms; organise protests, publicise and campaign against the errant individual and/or the lobby she has become a part of; pose a public challenge at the Gram Sabha; and, most importantly, deny access to the learning and skill-building opportunities provided to the *sanghas* by organisations like the MS. These are powerful weapons, which act as deterrents more often than they are actually used. The *sanghas* have acted not only as watchdogs, but also as guides and supporters. This dual role is critical to whatever little success they have achieved in the 200-odd villages where their members have become part of the Gram Panchayats.

This is where the role and importance of the relationships and links between women in politics, and a larger, vibrant, politically conscious and ethical women's movement comes in. In the MS programme, a strong effort was made to build a different culture and model of power within the *sanghas* themselves. Through experiments with collective leadership, rotating leadership, strong mechanisms of collective planning, action, analysis and accountability, an effort is being made to build a new culture of power, and a different value system. Simultaneously, the MS programme teams have maintained their inputs for consciousness-raising and critical analysis, and a continuous upgrading of information, knowledge, skills and collective strategies. Together, the *sanghas* and MS have strengthened the search for alternative values and new ways of exercising power, so that they do not reproduce the inequitable power relations of a patriarchal and socially stratified society.

This has not been an easy task. The external social and political environment is enormously powerful and resilient, and continually saps the process in multiple ways—quite often through women's own internalised attitudes. From within, women are struggling with their own conditioning in a feudal and patriarchal society, which has been training them to accept their place in the social and gender hierarchy, to embrace dependence and eschew autonomy. From without, it is all too easy for the politics of narrow, divisive identity, personal aggrandisement and affluence, patronage and patriarchy to take over. After all, these women are swimming against the social tide, and it is inevitable that they will often fail.

For instance, experiments in changing the dominant, patriarchal single-leader model have brought a host of problems in their wake: rotating the joint leadership of the *sanghas*[4] leads to situations where the 'best and the brightest' are unhappy when their turn is over—which is often when they are really feeling ready to 'take charge'—and are not always willing to share their abilities when the situation demands. Collective leadership alienates and frustrates highly motivated and articulate individuals who feel they are criticised for domination if they take the initiative in a given context, and are damned, in hindsight, for not doing so. Finding gender unity across caste, community and ethnicity was difficult and extremely rare. Indeed, there were deep divisions between equally marginalised

---

[4] Such as the nomination of three or four members to act as sangha 'Sahayakis' for a fixed period of time (for example, one year), after which a fresh group takes on this role.

women: for example, Dalit women belonging to Hindu, Muslim and Christian faiths demanded separate *sanghas*, or were far more suspicious of each other than they were of the upper castes!

It would be foolhardy indeed for Mahila Samakhya in Karnataka or anywhere else to claim to have successfully changed such deeply ingrained social divisions, values and attitudes—but certainly, there are growing beacons of hope. The experiences of MS Karnataka activists, filmmakers preparing modules for training Panchayati Raj members,[5] and at least one independent study (ISST 1995) confirms that women GP members from the *mahila sanghas* are a force to reckon with in their Panchayats, and are bringing changes—no matter how seemingly insignificant—in their functioning. *Sangha* women who have become Gram Panchayat members have not only been found to be consistently more articulate, aware, assertive and effective as GP members, but they also appear to be creating some meaningful changes in the conduct and culture of the GP as a whole—for example, ensuring that no drinking and carousing takes place in the Panchayat office, calling to order meetings where proper procedures are not being followed, forcing disciplinary actions against errant GP secretaries, and ensuring that *gram sabhas* are regularly held and the GP budgets correctly prepared and presented.

These are no mean achievements, and bear testimony to a more important lesson the *sanghas* are teaching us: that they are actively analysing and transforming the culture of the institutions of political power from both *inside and outside*. They are struggling to create viable mechanisms for changing the dominant model of power and politics in the public domain. This is a messy and laborious process, with many reversals and failures. But what is far more important is that it has been undertaken with great seriousness and a spirit of hope. These women are bringing change by believing in change. The women's movement at large can do no less.

---

[5] Personal communication with Deepa Dhanraj, film coordinator for the GRAMSAT experiment in televised two-way training launched by the Department of Women and Child, Government of Karnataka, 1995.

References

Development Dialogue. 1995. *Women in Panchayati Raj—A Study in West Bengal* (Uma Resource Centre: Institute of Social Studies Trust).

——. 1995. *Women in Panchayati Raj—Perspectives from Different States* (Bangalore: Institute. of Social Studies Trust).

Institute of Social Studies Trust (ISST). 1995. *Challenge and Opportunity: A Study of Women Panchayat Representatives in Karnataka* (Bangalore: Uma Resource Centre, ISST).

Kaushik, Susheela. 1992. 'Women and Political Participation', in *Women in Politics: Forms and Processes* (New Delhi).

6. Taking the Power out of Empowerment*

Of all the buzzwords that have entered the development lexicon in the past thirty years, empowerment is probably the most widely used and abused. Like many other important terms that were coined to represent a clearly *political* concept, it has been 'mainstreamed' in a manner that has virtually robbed it of its original meaning and strategic value. It is one of the best examples of what I have elsewhere described as the

> ... distortion of good ideas and innovative practices as they are lifted out of the political and historical context in which they evolved and rendered into formulas that are 'mainstreamed'. This usually involves divesting the idea of its cultural specificity, its political content, and generalizing it into a series of rituals and steps that simulate its original elements, but lacking the transformative power of the real thing. Thus good ideas—evolved to address specific development challenges—are altered into universally applicable panaceas. Transferring the correct rhetoric—buzzwords and catch phrases emptied of their original meaning—is a vital part of this legerdemain (Batliwala 2007: 89–94).

A brief history[1]

Both the word and the concept of empowerment have a fascinating history. According to some recent research into the origins and meanings of the term (Gaventa 2002), 'empowerment' can be traced back as early as the Protestant Reformation in Europe, and reverberates through the centuries in Europe and North America

---

* First published in *Development in Practice*, 17 (4 & 5), August 2007: 557–65.
[1] I am deeply indebted to Jonathan Gaventa for his masterly overview of the origins, meanings and usages of empowerment; 'Empowerment: A Briefing Note', unpublished monograph prepared at IDS Sussex, July–September 2002.

through Quakerism, Jeffersonian democracy, early capitalism, and the Black power movement. In other linguistic equivalents the concept of empowerment was embedded in many other historic struggles for social justice—in my own state of Karnataka in southern India, for instance, the twelfth and thirteenth-century Veerashaiva movement against caste and gender oppression called for the redistribution of power and access to spiritual knowledge through the destruction of these forms of social stratification. However, the term was revitalised and acquired a strongly political meaning in the latter half of the twentieth century, when it was adopted by liberation theology, popular education, Black power, feminist, and other movements engaged in struggles for more equitable, participatory and democratic forms of social change and development.

From these historically, politically and geographically diverse locations, empowerment was hijacked in the 1990s into increasingly bizarre locations, converted from a collective to an individualistic process, and skillfully co-opted by conservative and even reactionary political ideologies in pursuit of their agenda of divesting the 'big government' (for which, read the welfare state) of its purported power and control by 'empowering' communities to look after their own affairs. Management gurus discovered the term and infused it into the human resource development and motivational practices of the corporate world, turning it to the service of profit-making and competitiveness in the marketplace. Thus, the 1990s witnessed a massive co-option of the term by corporate management, neo-con political movements, and consumer rights advocates.

What's in a word?

Should we be troubled by what many may consider the inevitable subversion of an attractive term that can successfully traverse such diverse and even ideologically opposed terrains? I believe we should, because this represents not some innocent linguistic fad, but a more serious and subterranean process of challenging and subverting the politics that the term was created to symbolise. This political project is most clearly evident in the domain of women's empowerment, and I shall use the subversion and de-politicisation of the term within this context, particularly in my country—India—to demonstrate why it is a matter of concern.

The concept of women's empowerment emerged from several important critiques and debates generated by the women's movement throughout the world during the 1980s, when feminists, particularly in the Third World, were growing discontented with the largely apolitical and economistic 'WID' (Women in Development), 'WAD' (Women and Development) and 'GAD' (Gender and Development) models in prevailing development interventions. There was growing interaction between feminism and the concept and practice of popular education, based on the 'conscientisation' approach developed by Paulo Freire in Latin America in the 1970s as part of his 'liberation theology'. The latter, though a powerful new framework that contested the more top-down, paternalistic 'community development' approach prevalent till then, nevertheless ignored gender and the subordination of women as a critical element of liberation. The re-discovery of Gramsci's 'subalterns' and the hegemonic role of dominant ideologies, and the emergence of social construction theory and post-colonial theory were also important influences on activists and nascent social movements at this time.

The interplay of these powerful new discourses led, by the mid-1980s, to the spread of 'women's empowerment' as a more political and transformatory idea for struggles that challenged not only patriarchy, but the mediating structures of class, race, ethnicity—and, in India, caste and religion—which determined the nature of women's position and condition in developing societies. By introducing a hitherto absent gender dimension to theories of conscientisation and popular education, by recognising women as part of Gramsci's subaltern classes, feminists incorporated gender subordination and the social construction of gender as a fundamental category of analysis in the practice of social change and development. Feminist movements in the Third World, and particularly in Latin America and South Asia, evolved their own distinct approach, pushing mere consciousness-raising into the realm of radical organising and movement-building for gender equality. The influence of these discourses had led to the widespread adoption of the empowerment concept in many other development and social justice arenas as well (such as education, healthcare, rural development, workers' rights, etc.). By the beginning of the 1990s, empowerment held pride of place in development jargon. And although it was applied in a broad range of social change processes, there is little doubt that the term was most widely used with reference to women and gender equality.

It is not surprising, therefore, that the term—if not the concepts that informed it—soon became a trendy and widely-used buzz word. The sharp political perspective from which it arose became diffused and diluted. Development assistance agencies (multilateral, bilateral and private), eternally in search of sexier catch phrases and magic bullets that could somehow fast-track the process of social transformation, took hold of the term and began to use it to replace their earlier terminology of 'people's participation' and 'women's development'. The Fourth World Conference on Women in Beijing played a critical role in introducing the 'e' word to state actors, and governments anxious to demonstrate a progressive approach to gender quickly adopted the catch phrase of women's empowerment. For instance, signatories to the Beijing Declaration stated that they would dedicate themselves to 'enhancing further the advancement and empowerment of women all over the world …' (United Nations 1995: 7).

The most important point, though, is that all efforts to more clearly conceptualise the term stressed that empowerment was a *socio-political process*, and that the critical operating concept within empowerment was *power*, and that empowerment was about shifts in political, social and economic power between and across *both* individuals *and* social groups.

How power left empowerment—the Indian experience

Let us now use the Indian case to demonstrate how the once powerful idea and practice of women's empowerment degenerated into a set of largely apolitical, technocratic and narrow interventions that create nothing close to the radical transformation envisioned by early women's movement leaders—and how it was brought to serve neo-liberal economic ends.

Borrowing from the usage of the term by feminist popular educators in other parts of the world, empowerment entered the women's movement lexicon in India by the mid-1980s. Almost at the same time, it replaced the earlier terminology of 'women's welfare', 'women's development' and 'women's upliftment' used by the government and major donor agencies supporting work with marginalised women. In 1986, for instance, I co-designed and authored a critical new programme template for the Department of Education, Ministry of Human Resource Development, entitled 'Education for Women's Equality', in which the *empowerment* approach (roughly similar to feminist popular education methods) was strongly advocated. Thus, empowerment as a term entered the gender equality arena in India through distinctly different political routes—that of feminists challenging patriarchal gender relations, of progressive government policy, and of aid agencies anxious to do something new. By the beginning of the 1990s, therefore, everybody concerned with women's issues and gender equality—state actors, aid agencies, development professionals, and feminist activists and advocates—were using the term 'empowerment'. But, like a latter-day development Babel, there was no clarity about what exactly this meant to its various proponents, since the meanings they attached to the term were seldom articulated in any clear or specific way. It was common, in those days, to come across the annual reports of NGOs or donor agencies talking about how their objective was empowerment, but it was impossible to find a comprehensive definition of what the term signified to them.

In an attempt to clear the conceptual and strategic cloud, I was invited, in 1992, to undertake an exercise to examine how empowerment was understood and operationalised across South Asia by grassroots women's and development organisations with a stated objective of women's empowerment. Through a wide process of consultation and discussion with over twenty-five organisations across South Asia and a number of leading feminist activists, a (then) new conceptual and strategic framework was collectively and painstakingly developed over the course of a year: 'Women's Empowerment in South Asia: Concepts and Practices' (Batliwala 1993). At the time, this document provided one of the first detailed conceptualisations of empowerment, constructed from the perception and practice of those consciously engaged in the empowerment of women and in advancing gender equality. This coincided with Naila Kabeer's own research and her influential book *Reversed Realities* (1994), which echoed and greatly enhanced the framework in the South Asia document.

The South Asia document defined empowerment as a process, and the results of a process, of transforming the relations of power between individuals and social groups. Since feminist activists were among the first to use this word widely, it also had a specific gendered meaning—the transformation of the relations of power between men and women, within and across social categories of various kinds. The document defined empowerment as a process that shifts social power in three critical ways: by challenging the ideologies that justify social inequality (such as gender or caste); by changing the prevailing patterns of access to and control over economic, natural and intellectual resources; and by transforming the institutions and structures that reinforce and sustain existing power structures (the family, state, market, education, media, etc.). The document emphasised that transformatory empowerment could *not* be achieved by tackling any one of these elements of social power—even at that early stage, its architects were clear that there was no 'one-shot' magic bullet route to women's empowerment, such as providing women with access to credit, enhanced incomes, or land titles. The framework stressed that the ideological and institutional change dimensions were critical to sustaining empowerment and real social transformation.

Through the 1980s and early 1990s, initiatives around the subcontinent, and particularly in India, were engaged in a diverse range of experiments that attempted to enact the process of empowerment on the ground with various marginalised communities, most often focused on poor rural and urban women.[2] These approaches tried to depart from past interventions that treated women as beneficiaries of services, or as producers or workers, and adopted

---

[2] The Women's Development Programme in Rajasthan and the Mahila Samakhya Programme in several states of the country are the earliest examples of this.

feminist popular education strategies that created new spaces for women to collectivise around shared experiences of poverty, exclusion and discrimination, critically analyse the structures and ideologies that sustained and reinforced their oppression, and raise their consciousness of their own sense of subordination. These spaces and the activists working within them facilitated women to recognise their own agency and power for change—their power to organise themselves to confront and transform the social and economic arrangements and cultural systems that subjugated them. The main inputs in these processes were new ideas and information, not hand-outs or services; an opportunity for women to locate and articulate the changes they wanted to make, and evolve strategies to do so. Grassroots women in different corners of the country, in cities, towns and villages, were mobilised into 'sanghs' or 'samoohs'[3] through which they developed a political and personal agenda for change, and the collective strength and creative power to move their agendas forward.

These basic strategies found expression in a range of activities across the country. Women's groups and grassroots women's collectives began to address their unequal access to economic and natural resources, to education, health services, to reproductive health and rights, and change the gender division of labour and access to training, technical skills and employment. Micro-credit programmes successfully shifted productive resources into poor women's hands, and they in turn demonstrated how their enhanced incomes were applied to raise household nutrition levels, and improve the health and educational status of their children. There were struggles to make visible and redress the pervasive and diverse forms of violence against women—dowry-related violence and murders, rape, female infanticide and foeticide, domestic violence, caste and communal violence that targeted women, and state-sanctioned violence. Large public campaigns were launched for legislative reform and enforcement—for special cells for women in police stations, for

---

[3] Several sections of this paper also borrow heavily from my chapter, 'Women's Empowerment in 21st Century India—Changing meanings, contexts and strategies', in Shiva Kumar and Rajani Ved (eds), *The Wellbeing of India's Population*, forthcoming.

greater representation of women in Panchayat Raj[4] Institutions, for changes in the rape law that would shift the burden of proof from the victim to the perpetrator, for banning or regulating sex determination and sex-selection technologies, and for more stringent punishment for dowry harassment and domestic violence.

Interestingly, during this entire phase, women's movements saw the state as a critical enabler of the empowerment process, even if their stance was adversarial. In turn, several arms of the Indian state—and especially some committed senior bureaucrats—took the lead in supporting and launching programmes that were built upon a transformative notion of empowerment, providing space for the mobilisation and organisation of some of the country's poorest and most oppressed women to challenge and change their social, political and economic conditions, even when this meant confronting other sections of the state and its policies and programmes.[5] This support was not entirely altruistic, of course, but often sprang from an astute understanding that these women's empowerment processes might better enable the administration to deliver its schemes and services, outperform other states and provinces in development indicators, and lower the poverty line.

Donor agencies quickly followed suit, and abandoned their earlier 'WID', 'WAD' and 'GAD' approaches to embrace the empowerment framework as both an objective and a methodology. While donors did not play a critical role in India in defining or advancing the empowerment approach, they quickly promoted it amongst their development partners, and many NGOs and women's development organisations were compelled to switch their language, if not their strategies, to fit the new empowerment mantra. This was a huge factor, along with the government adoption of the term, in spreading the use of the empowerment terminology, and eventually rendering it into a meaningless buzzword.

In retrospect, it is the early successes of the empowerment

---

[4] 'Sanghs' / 'Samoohs' are local terms for collectives or informal organisations.

[5] The structures of local self-government at the village and provincial levels, based on pre-colonial Indian units of local government that existed in some parts of the country.

approach—despite contemporary angst about how difficult it was to measure, or how it took too long to have an impact, and other anxieties—that contributed inadvertently to its subsequent instrumentalisation, and its conversion into a magic bullet for poverty alleviation and rapid economic development, rather than a multi-faceted process of social transformation, especially in the arena of gender equality. By the mid-1990s, India had enthusiastically embraced neo-liberal economic policies, but it was also an electoral democracy where the poor—particularly the rural poor—formed the largest vote banks, and who routinely threw out regimes who failed their interests and needs. Opening up rural markets and raising the incomes of the poor were thus critical to political survival. In India's populist politics, empowerment was a natural target for co-option by varying political agendas, most of whom were anxious to limit its transformatory potential.

Consequently, political parties of various hues and ruling regimes rapidly adopted and simultaneously constricted the concept and practice of women's empowerment into two relatively narrow and politically manageable arenas: the so-called 'self-help' women's groups (SHGs), which were meant to simulate the empowering nature of the sanghs and samoohs mentioned earlier, but in reality engage in little else but savings and lending; and reservations for women within local self-government bodies, which is deemed to lead to political empowerment. Both of these are described as 'women's empowerment' approaches, although there is little evidence that either results in sustained changes in women's position or condition within their families, communities, or society at large. Indeed, there is a growing body of analysis showing that the empowering effects of these interventions are complex, and that they can consolidate existing power hierarchies as well as create new problems, including manipulation and co-option by dominant political interests, growing indebtedness, doubling and tripling of women's workloads, and new forms of gendered violence (Burra et al. 2005; Cornwall and Goetz 2005: 783–800; Fernando 2006).

Although virtually every government policy claims to support women's empowerment, a deeper scrutiny of both policy and implementation strategies (available on the websites of every ministry concerned with poverty eradication, marginalised social groups, women and girls) reveals that the broad-based, multi-faceted and radical consciousness-raising approaches fostered in programmes like the Mahila Samakhya in the 1980s and early 1990s have more or less disappeared. Every department's narrow-bandwidth intervention, in an era of increasing divestment and privatisation, is packaged in the language of empowerment. India's rural development policy describes its objectives as poverty alleviation and empowerment, and states that these will be achieved through the strategies of self-help groups and strengthening local governments, the twin sites of 'women's empowerment'. The Education Department's Women's Empowerment Project offers an even better example of this 'downsized' empowerment strategy:

> Since the overall empowerment of women is crucially dependent on economic empowerment ... the main purpose of the Women Empowerment Project (WEP) is to organize women into effective Self Help Groups ....

In the larger political arena, we have witnessed an equally disturbing trend where the idea of women's empowerment has been distorted and co-opted into the ideological frameworks of the religious fundamentalism that has become deeply entrenched in Indian politics—the status of women in certain minority groups, and their need for 'empowerment' (in its vernacular equivalents), was a key component of the Hindu nationalist's ideological and political project, as was the construction of the Hindu woman as the educated, equal, empowered opposite—all while they remain deeply hostile to the questioning of the disempowerment and subjugation of millions of women with the spread of particular regional and upper-caste Hindu practices such as dowry and female foeticide through sex-selective abortions (Hassan 1998; Sarkar 1998).

A requiem

In the new millennium, the once-ubiquitous term 'empowerment' has virtually disappeared from the Indian development discourse, including in the context of gender equality, except in a few niches of government policy. I attribute this to several tendencies that began emerging in the late 1990s: the overwhelming sway of the micro-credit model and SHGs as substitutes for the more comprehensive empowerment processes of early feminist activism; the displacement of empowerment by the emergence of the 'rights-based approach' within critiques and counters to neo-liberal reductionist and instrumentalist strategies for economic development and social justice; and the management-influenced 'results-based' approach that has been adopted by a large number of development assistance programmes and donors, including those who had remained steadfastly opposed to fast-track strategies.

With donors increasingly abandoning empowerment as a no-longer fashionable—indeed, *practical*—methodology, and enthusiastically championing (with a few exceptions) large-scale micro-finance programmes as the quickest route to women's empowerment (*and* overall economic development!), the old feminist empowerment concept and practice has been interred without ceremony. Grassroots practitioners and movements find they can no longer fund-raise with the language and strategies of empowerment, or must disguise these within more *au courant* frameworks / rhetoric (rights, micro-finance, transparency, accountability, and so forth). Some donors have moved resources out of broader-based empowerment approaches because they don't apparently show 'countable' results, and/or because they do not work fast enough.

Since the process—and its effects and impacts—was so shaped by the interests and contexts of those engaged in it, and hence was less predictable in its outcomes, the empowerment approach is not considered sufficiently 'results-oriented', an important priority in current development funding. In such agencies, the 'rights-based' approach (as though empowerment is about anything but rights!) finds greater favour because rights-based interventions—greater access to redress, achievements of the Millennium Development Goals, new legislation—are more readily quantified. But these approaches often shift agency into the hands of professional intermediaries (lawyers, NGO activists, policy specialists), and *away* from marginalised women and communities. They also focus more on formal structures and equality, rather than the informal institutions and cultural systems that older empowerment processes attempted to transform (although not always successfully).

Meanwhile, in keeping with the insidious dominance of the neo-liberal ideology and its consumerist core, we see the transition of empowerment out of the realm of societal and systemic change and into the individual—from a noun signifying shifts in social power, to a verb signalling individual power, achievement, status. 'Empower yourself', screamed a billboard ad for jobs in yet another IT company in Bangalore, my home town, last year. Ironically, the permeation of the concept into corporate management practices reflected some of the principles that infused it in the world of social change: reducing hierarchy, decentralisation, greater decision-making power, and autonomy for managers on the ground—all essential to efficiency and competitiveness in the era of global corporations (Cook and Macaulay 1996; Willcocks and Morris 1995). But this journey out of social struggles and into management practice is deeply disturbing: Can the empowerment of the local manager of a multinational corporation achieve the same social good as the struggles of impoverished Dalit women I have worked with for the right to burn their dead in the upper-caste cremation ground or have their children seated in the classroom with caste-Hindu classmates; or of indigenous women to regain their traditional rights to forest produce; or of pavement dwellers to secure housing in India's burgeoning metros? Would these women equate their experiences to that of the manager who is advised to hold an exercise on Friday afternoon where they are asked to 'Present an award for the best bit of empowerment, the most empowered person of the day?' (Willcocks and Morris 1995: 77).

Postscript

I called this an experiential account because I did not want this paper to pretend to be an exhaustive, thoroughly-researched analysis of the buzzword 'empowerment'—and also because I was an unapologetic champion of the powerful and transformatory concepts and practices that it represented at the height of feminist grassroots organising in another India. But today, I ask myself a simple question:

If this word, and the idea it represented, has been seized and redefined by populist politics, fundamentalist and neo-con ideologies, and corporate management, if it has been downsized by micro-finance and political quota evangelists, and otherwise generally divested of all vestiges of power and politics, is it worth reclaiming? These very processes signal the vagueness and lack of political accuracy that its critics always highlighted. They also warn us that the subversion of powerful political techniques that organise the marginalised will always first occur through the co-option and distortion of its language.

Clearly, we need to build a new language in which to frame our vision and strategies for social transformation at the local, national or global level. I, for one, intend to do so not by re-reading Foucault or Gramsci or other great political philosophers, but by listening to poor women and their movements, listening to their values, principles, articulations and actions, and by trying to hear how they frame their search for justice. From this, I suspect, will emerge not only a new discourse, but also new concepts and strategies that have not yet entered our political or philosophical imaginations.

References

Asia South Pacific Bureau of Adult Education (ASPBAE/FAO). 1993. *Women's Empowerment in South Asia: Concepts and Practices* (New Delhi: ASPBAE).

Batliwala, Srilatha. 1993. 'Women's Empowerment in South Asia: Concepts and Practices' (New Delhi: ASPBAE [Asia South Pacific Bureau of Adult Education]).

———. 2007. 'When Rights Go Wrong', *Seminar*, 569: 89–94.

Burra, Neera, Joy Deshmukh-Ranadive and Ranjani K. Murthy (eds). 2005. *Micro-Credit, Poverty and Empowerment: Linking the Triad* (New Delhi: Sage Publications).

Cook, Sarah and Steve Macaulay. 1996. *Perfect Empowerment: All you need to get it right first time* (London: Arrow).

Cornwall, Andrea and Anne Marie Goetz. 2005. 'Democratizing Democracy: Feminist Perspectives', *Democratization*, 12 (5): 783–800.

Fernando, Jude L. 2006. *Microfinance: Perils and Prospects* (London: Routledge).

Gaventa, Jonathan. 2002. 'Empowerment: A Briefing Note', unpublished monograph, IDS, Sussex.

Government of India, Ministry of Human Resource Development, Department of Education. 2006. http://india.gov.in/outerwin.htm?id=http://education.nic.in/ (accessed February 2006).

Hassan, Zoya. 1998. 'Gender Politics, Legal Reform, and the Muslim Community in India', in Patricia Jeffery and Amrita Basu (eds), *Appropriating Gender: Women's Agency, the State, and Politicized Religion in South Asia* (London: Routledge), pp. 71–88.

Isserles, Robin G. 2003. 'Microcredit—the Rhetoric of Empowerment, the Reality of "Development as Usual"', *Women and Development: Women's Studies Quarterly*, 31 (3&4): 38–57.

Kabeer, Naila. 1994. *Reversed Realities—Gender* .... (London: Routledge).

Morris, Steve and Graham Willcocks. 1995. *Successful Empowerment in a Week* (London: Hodder and Stoughton for the Institute of Management).

Sarkar, Tanika. 1998. 'Woman, Community and Nation—A Historical Trajectory for Hindu Identity Politics', in Patricia Jeffery and Amrita Basu (eds), *Appropriating Gender: Women's Agency, the State, and Politicized Religion in South Asia* (London: Routledge), pp. 89–106.

Shiva Kumar, K. and Rajani Ved (eds). 2010. *Handbook of Population and Development* (New Delhi: Oxford University Press).

United Nations. 1995. Beijing Platform for Action, p. 4, point 7, http://www.un.org/esa/gopher-data/conf/fwcw/off/a—20.en.

II. Beyond Empowerment

Introduction

IN this section, I have included slightly abridged versions of some very lengthy documents that I wrote in the past decade, at least two of which are similar in scope to my 1993 'women's empowerment' paper. Both 'Changing Their World—Concepts and Practices of Women's Movements' and 'Feminist Leadership for Social Transformation' were attempts to pin down complex and abstract concepts and make them accessible, in ways very similar to what I first attempted with the women's empowerment paper. What is more, these papers tried to make these complex concepts accessible and practicable for those engaged in actual gender equality work, whether at the grassroots or at the global level, whether in policy arenas or in communities.

I call this section 'Beyond Empowerment' because the chapters in it reflect my shift of focus from empowerment to other processes equally critical to gender equality, particularly processes whose meanings have been lost or distorted by neo-liberal politics and donor discourse. They are a reflection of how I came to realise that ultimately, empowerment is not an end in itself, but is in fact a methodology, a building block. Empowerment is not a goal, but a foundational process that enables marginalised women to construct their own political agendas and form movements and struggles for achieving fundamental and lasting transformation in gender and social power structures.

The first chapter in this section—'Changing Their World: Concepts and Practices of Women's Movements'—was my first major work for the Association of Women's Rights in Development (AWID), and was prepared as a base document for AWID's eleventh International Forum held in Cape Town, South Africa, in November 2008. It is in some ways a recent application of the approach I first honed while writing the 'Women's Empowerment in South Asia' paper more than fifteen years earlier. It is a 'pracademic' piece—a conceptual framework developed by a 'practitioner-academic', based on both experiences from the ground as well as a studied review of theory.

The scholarly component for this paper came out of my research as a Civil Society Research Fellow at the Hauser Center for Nonprofit Organizations in Harvard University (2001–09), on the literature on social movements. I undertook this research on movement theory with my research assistant Sarah Titus, and we ploughed through an impressive mountain of tomes theorising social movements, from MacAdam and David Snow and Charles Tilly and Sidney Tarrow, to the 'New' Latin American Social Movement theorists like Arturo Escobar, Evelina Dagnino, and Sonia Alvarez. The grounded part came from the case studies of ten women's movements from around the world that AWID had commissioned in the previous year, to feed into the document. The conceptual framework was thus as unique, in its own way, as the Women's Empowerment framework developed in 1993, but informed by a far more rigorous study of practice, since ten different researchers wrote the case studies for the movement document, while I alone did both research and theorisation for the empowerment document.

Thanks to the power and accessibility of the Internet, 'Changing Their World' has exceeded 'Women's Empowerment in South Asia' in popularity—it has been downloaded more than 5,000 times since it was first put online in early 2009, not to mention that all 1,200 hard copies printed in English, Spanish and French before the 2008 Forum have been distributed. The version I share in this volume, however, is an abridged version of the second edition's introductory and concluding chapters, written in 2011. The process of extensive feedback and change that these sections went through deserves some explanation.

Unlike 'Women's Empowerment in South Asia', 'Changing Their World' received almost immediate and extensive feedback from users—partly because of the Internet, but more importantly, because I began to use the conceptual framework and key insights into women's movements in regular teaching and training contexts. These

were mainly—but not limited to—the 'Institutes' for young feminist
activists organised by Creating Resources for Empowerment in
Action—CREA[1]—and AWID's Young Feminist Activism Program's
online training, among others. These interactions with activists
interested in doing movement-building work helped me hone the
framework in multiple ways, and correct some of the shortcomings
of the conceptualisation that went into the first edition of 'Changing
Their World'.

For instance, I found that people needed much more clarity about
the distinction between organisations and movements, and about
the nature of organisations. My work with the CREA team[2] also
made me feel a strong need to supplement the case studies of women's
movements to include the movements of women uniquely
marginalised by virtue of their sexual orientation, ability/disability,
occupation in sex work, and location in a conflict zone. Lydia Alpizar,
AWID Executive Director, and Programme Director Cindy Clark
felt much the same, and strongly endorsed the need for these
additional case studies. The second edition therefore has *fourteen*
women's movement stories from *thirteen* different countries/regions
of the world. The case studies now include the struggles of women as
diverse as Indigenous women in Mexico, Dalit women in India,
domestic workers in the United States, young mothers in the Czech
Republic, sex workers in India, poor lesbians in the Philippines,
disabled women across the world, women in conflict-ridden Sudan,
women factory workers in Argentina, women survivors of violence
in South Africa, grassroots rural women in Kenya, and Roma (gypsy)
women in East Europe, among others. The conceptual framework
and analysis of lessons learnt also gained in strength and clarity. I
feel fortunate to be able to share this considerably stronger and clearer

---

[1] One of the very dynamic feminist organisations that I work with regularly in a
teaching capacity because of their strong focus on building young women's leadership
to sustain movements for gender equality, and sexual and reproductive health and
rights. See www.creaworld.org for more information about CREA's 'institutes', which
are in high demand.

[2] And especially with CREA's Count Me In project, which documented violence
against women marginalised for being lesbian, disabled, or sex workers; see http://
www.countmeinconference.org/ for more information.

version with the readers of this volume, because I know I am offering you my best and sharpest thinking on the concepts and practices of women's movements.

Feminist leadership

The next major chapter in this section follows in the tradition of both 'Women's Empowerment in South Asia' and 'Changing Their World: 'Feminist Leadership for Social Transformation—Clearing the Conceptual Cloud'. Like its predecessors, it takes on another amorphous yet critical concept that we struggle to practice: feminist leadership. The feminist leadership paper was commissioned by CREA in early 2008—yes, 2008 was a very challenging and productive year, one that saw me writing up two major think pieces! —and proved far more difficult, however, than 'Changing Their World'.

I decided to apply the framework I had developed at the Hauser Center for my working paper on civil society to develop the conceptual framework on feminist leadership, viz., answering the five key questions: 'What is it?' (definitions); 'Where is it?' (sites and locations); 'What does it look like?' (features, characteristics); 'What/ Who is in it?' (social, conceptual and other boundaries); and 'How does it work?' (power dynamics, key actors). But when I began the research, I was alarmed by the thousands of definitions of leadership, mostly from management literature. I was far more shocked at the scarcity of clear definitions of feminist leadership, which I had never anticipated. So I had to enlist the support of a researcher who could get at non-virtual resources in the library of the Center for Women's Global Leadership at Rutgers University in the United States—this helped yield quite a few additional feminist definitions. But the leadership paper was challenging for more reasons than this, and the chapter itself will give readers a sense of why that was so. Leadership is such a complex and multi-faceted concept that one has to mine many different disciplines and conceptual frameworks to unpack it— theories about power, about organisations, theories about identity and the self, to name just a few. And then putting it all together again in a coherent, usable framework is another challenge altogether.

It is not surprising, therefore, that this paper took a long time to consolidate, and went through many drafts and gained strength and clarity from the suggestions and comments of many, many readers from around the world. I would single out for special thanks all the participants of the meeting, 'Building Feminist Leadership—Looking Back, Looking Forward', organised by CREA in Cape Town, South Africa, in November 2008, and especially Charlotte Bunch, Ireen Dubel, Bisi Adeleye-Fayemi, Michel Friedman, Rakhee Goyal, Joanna Kerr, Helen Kim, Frances Kunreuther and the CREA team, among others. Vinita S., Michel Friedman and Pramada Menon continued to read different versions and provide intensive and useful feedback. Caroline Earle of CREA's New York office researched and provided invaluable inputs to the second draft of the document, and the incredible Charlotte Bunch and Peggy Antrobus shared generously the oral history of the earliest searches for meaning in the idea of feminist leadership. And most of all, I'm grateful to Geetanjali Misra, founder and director of CREA, for pushing and supporting me to make this paper happen, and for her vision and foresight in knowing how much a piece like this was needed! I know from my experience of teaching this framework at the CREA and AWID courses for young activists that it was a huge missing piece of the feminist puzzle for many young people. And a huge source of angst was the lack of good role models of feminist leadership—most had experienced senior feminist leaders as domineering, insecure, authoritarian, and unwilling to surrender power or open space to younger women.

The paper thus provides some guidelines to help them get it right as they emerge in leadership roles, or to help each other see where they might stumble and fall, just as their seniors did. In fact, for this very reason, OXFAM NOVIB has supported CREA in the creation of a toolkit based on the leadership concept paper, which can help groups and individuals struggling for clarity about the nature and practice of feminist leadership.

I hope readers will enjoy delving deep into the rich and complex ideas and frameworks offered in the lengthy chapters in this section, which incorporate a lot of what I learnt through my study and practice of women's empowerment, but go much beyond that.

7. The Power of Movements: Clarifying our Concepts

If you do not change direction, you may end up where you are heading.

Lao-Tzu

THIS saying of the great Chinese philosopher Lao Tzu seems particularly apt for those of us concerned with the state of feminist movements worldwide at the present time. At some levels, our movements seem to have lost much of the momentum, coherence and impact that they had even a decade ago, while at others, women seem to be building their collective power in vibrant new ways. Where movement building has weakened, we see a far greater focus on implementing short-term projects and providing services. While these are certainly useful, they are often palliative, without a clear political agenda aimed at transforming gender and other social power relations in the longer term. So although we continue to speak of a 'global women's movement', it is unclear whether this exists more in our nostalgic memory than in reality. There are many factors that have contributed to this loss of focus on movement building.

Externally, donors have moved away from support for movement-building strategies, towards 'gender mainstreaming' and 'gender components' in larger development projects. Governments have co-opted and de-politicised strategies developed by feminist-thinking groups to transform gender power; take, for example, the case of micro-credit or political participation. Finally, social movements that were once quite gender-sensitive, or at least felt pressured to focus on women's concerns and leadership within their movements (for example, the environment, human rights, or economic justice movements), are now far less so, or tend to instrumentalise women's concerns without genuinely gendering their perspectives, agendas, or strategies.

Internally, feminist activism has lost some of its earlier movement-building focus and momentum. The struggle for organisational or personal survival, for retaining autonomy while also having to compromise with changing funding priorities, and the backlash against feminist agendas and women's human rights defenders in many locations have all taken a toll. Conflicts and schisms within and between groups have led to fragmentation and increased competition for limited resources, without necessarily widening the impact of feminist organising.

Perhaps most critically, however, there has been growing confusion, internally, about what constitutes a movement. At a number of international women's meetings, it has been striking to witness the word 'movement' used quite sweepingly, without much clarity. All kinds of aggregations of women's organisations, all varieties of campaigns and activities related to women's issues are now described as movements: for example, groups of organisations working in a particular region (the 'African Women's Movement'), or country (the Indian women's movement), or sector/issue (the women's health movement, the reproductive rights movement, the gay/lesbian movement) are described as 'movements', whether or not they bear the characteristics of one.

Today, there is a vast body of literature on social movements, organisational development, and related subjects. But most of this material has not been developed within a feminist perspective, and so does not really illuminate the concept and practice of building feminist movements. Even today, some of the 1980s writings on engendering the analysis of development and social change processes,[1] and 1980s and 1990s writing on women's empowerment processes[2] are still the closest approximations or guides to a movement-building praxis for feminists.

At the Association for Women's Rights in Development (AWID), we believe that these conditions mean that the time is ripe

---

[1] Such as Maxine Molyneux and Kate Young's work on women's practical needs and strategic interests, and on women's condition and position in societies.
[2] Such as DAWN, Naila Kabeer, Srilatha Batliwala and Diane Elson's conceptualisations.

for a re-examination and clarification of our understanding of movements, movement-building and, most important of all, feminist movements. The strategic initiative of AWID, 'Building Feminist Movements and Organisations', was launched to help contribute to this clarity. But this is not intended as an academic exercise; its purpose is to help ourselves and other groups to re-cast our strategies and catalyse a new wave of movement building that can bring feminist agendas back into global and local politics with renewed clarity, energy and impact.

The basic questions

It seems obvious that we cannot locate new strategies to strengthen our movement-building work until we find the answers to some basic questions:

- What is a movement?
- What is a feminist movement?
- Why do movements matter?
- What are the challenges facing women's/feminist movements?
- What is the relationship of organisations and individuals to movements?
- What are the elements of a movement-building approach?

We know that there cannot be a single, final, authoritative answer to any of these questions. But this paper is an attempt to at least begin to answer them by laying out some tentative concepts, definitions and characteristics of movements, and an initial analysis of some of the current challenges that must be confronted and overcome in order to move forward. We hope that this will help us achieve greater clarity about building movements, and particularly feminist movements and movement-building, and the relationship between organisations, individuals and movements. AWID would like to see the paper stimulate debate and discussion, a contextualisation of the concepts and analysis, thereby leading to both refinement and greater precision in our collective understanding and strategies. Finally, we try to provide some basic tools to help us examine our own work—no matter where we are located geographically, thematically, or strategically—so that together, we can begin a new journey of reclaiming feminism, revisiting our current strategies, and revitalising our movements. We also aim to revive a sense of hope, of the power of resistance and rebellion—as the recent popular uprisings in the Middle East have so magnificently demonstrated—in sum, to reinstate the idea that movements can and will make other worlds possible, especially for women. To make the paper more accessible, we have avoided footnotes and references in the text, but provide a list of readings and source materials at the end for those who would like to probe these issues in greater depth.

What is a movement?

While there are many scholarly definitions of social movements, sifting through these shows that movements can be simply defined as *an organised set of constituents pursuing a common political agenda of change through collective action*. Thus, movements are distinguished by these characteristics:

1. *A constituency base or membership that is mobilised and collectivised;*
2. *Members collectivised in either formal or informal organisations;*
3. Some *continuity over time* (that is, a spontaneous uprising or campaign may not be a movement in itself, although it may lead to one);
4. *A clear political agenda*—that is, the constituency has a shared analysis of the social / structural conditions that have disempowered them, and the changes they seek to make in these structures;
5. *Collective actions and activities* in pursuit of the movement's political goals;
6. *Use a variety of actions and strategies*—from confrontational, militant actions (including violent protests), to peaceful protest / non-cooperation (a la Gandhi), to public opinion-building or advocacy strategies; and
7. *Clear internal or external targets* they will engage in the change process, such as:
   • Their own membership or communities (such as in

movements against discriminatory customs and social practices like female genital mutilation [FGM], violence against women, machismo, etc.).

- Society at large (to change negative attitudes, biases or perceptions of themselves—for example, racial, gender-based, caste-based, ethnic or religious discrimination, or exclusion by virtue of sexual orientation, ability, or occupation).
- Other social groups who violate their rights or exclude them (such as discrimination and violence by majority groups against racial, religious, ethnic or sexual minorities, or claiming land rights or fair wages from landowners or employers).
- The state or regimes in power (in demanding, for instance, greater democracy, transparency, accountability, legal reforms, or policy changes).
- Extra-state actors (such as drug cartels or criminal networks who terrorise and use direct and indirect violence against women as a means of control).
- Warring factions in civil or military conflicts, who disrupt the conditions for daily survival and use violence against women as a weapon of war.
- Private-sector actors (corporations and employers who violate women's labour rights, cause environmental damage, or restrict women's access to natural resources, etc.).
- International institutions (such as the World Bank, UN, IMF or WTO), whose policies and prescriptions have impacted women's lives directly and indirectly.
- A combination of some or all of the above.

To answer the second question (What is a feminist movement?), we may first have to re-formulate what feminism itself means in the world today, in the light of recent history and present reality.

What is feminism today?

- The past three decades of activism, advocacy, research and theorisation, as well as the changing global geo-political context, have generated powerful insights into and experience about our gains, setbacks and the challenges of the future. These have also enabled us to re-frame our philosophy and approach, and create a broader vision for ourselves and the world we want to create. Through this process, feminism has evolved as an *ideology, an analytical framework, and a strategic framework.*

- As an *ideology*, feminism today stands not only for gender equality, but also for the transformation of all social relations of power that oppress, exploit, or marginalise any set of people, on the basis of their gender, age, sexual orientation, ability, race, religion, nationality, location, class, caste, or ethnicity. We do not seek simplistic parity between the sexes that will give us the damaging privileges and power that men have enjoyed, and end up losing many of the so-called 'feminine' strengths and capacities that women have been socialised to embody. But we do seek a transformation that will create gender equality within an entirely new social order—one in which both men and women can individually and collectively live as human beings in societies that are in harmony with the natural world, based on social and economic equality and the full body of human rights, liberated from violence, conflict and militarisation.

- As an *analytical framework*, feminism developed / transformed the concepts of *patriarchy* (the social order of male rights and privilege) and *gender* (the socially constructed relations of power between men and women), and created a range of analytical tools and methods for unpacking the hidden and normalised power imbalances between men and women in various social institutions and structures—for instance, the gendered division of labour in the household and in production, control of women's sexuality and reproductive life, etc. Feminist scholars have also developed radically new frameworks for analysing the way in which multiple forms of discrimination and exclusion operate together, rather than incrementally, in people's lives (for example, concepts like intersectionality [Crenshaw 1989] and social exclusion). Feminism is also embracing new notions of gender and gender identities that go beyond the social construction of just two genders, thanks to the work of queer scholars and activists, and LGBT studies (for instance, Butler 1990, 2004; Vance 1989).

- *As a social change strategy*, feminism prioritises the empowerment of women, the transformation of gender power relations, and the advancement of gender equality within all change interventions. Feminism believes that change that does not advance the status and rights of women is not real change at all: for instance, economic interventions that increase household incomes without giving women the greater share of that income or altering the gender division of labour in the production of that income, or improvements in healthcare that do not address the specific barriers that may prevent women from accessing such care, are *not* feminist strategies. Thus, feminism views all change interventions through a 'gender lens'—viz., examining how the change is impacting women—so whether the change strategy is focused on an issue (health, education, the environment, human rights, economic rights, etc.), or a location (a set of villages, a province, a country, a region), or population (indigenous people, workers, the urban poor, etc.), feminism will examine whether gender equality and women's rights are being consciously addressed and advanced by that change process.

- In the current global crisis of rising food prices, exorbitant energy costs, and the nightmare of climate change, feminism **stands for economic policies based upon food security, clean renewable energy and ecological soundness, in order to ensure a sustainable future for the planet, all its species and its natural resources.**

- Given the gendered and inequitable impacts of neo-liberalism and globalisation, we also stand **for economic transformation that creates greater social equity and human development**, rather than mere economic growth. Feminism challenges all economic models that ignore the gender dimension of production, access to productive resources, income, trade and financial structures, even if they are otherwise considered 'progressive' or 'alternative'. For example, there are many economic justice movements that have sought wealth distribution to poor and marginalised people, without considering how patriarchal familial structures may continue to keep women out of the ownership of assets or decision-making over newly acquired assets and resources.

- We stand **for political transformation that guarantees full citizenship rights, the full body of human rights, and for secular, plural, democratic regimes that are transparent, accountable and responsive to all their citizens, both women and men.**

- Escalating levels of war and civil conflict, the conflict-related displacement and subjugation of both women and men, and the increasing use of sexual violence against women as a political tool, have led feminists to **oppose violence** of any kind, and to **stand against wars and conflicts that displace, violate, subjugate and impoverish both women and men.** Conversely, **we stand for peace and non-violence**—and for the peaceful resolution of disputes achieved through inclusive and participatory processes. Given the worldwide increase in attacks on women's human rights, the rolling back of hard-fought gains, and violence against women's human rights defenders, feminism stands for the right of women to organise and build movements and organisations for social justice without let or hindrance, and asserts the responsibility of states to protect such movements and activists from violence and intimidation.

- We stand for **responsible co-dependence rather than individualism,** but believe in the **freedom of choice of individuals** with respect to their private lives. We oppose the rampant promotion of consumerism that continues to objectify both men and women, and which promotes the wasteful use of the planet's natural resources and devastates the environment.

- **Feminism stands for the power to, for and with, and not power over**—we struggle to **change the practice of power,** both within our own structures and movements, and in the social, economic and political institutions we engage with. This has created a set of 'feminist ethics' which, while varying in different parts of the world, contain some common principles at the core: such as creating less vertical and more horizontal, participatory and democratic structures; greater transparency and openness about internal and external processes and finances; ensuring a voice and role for all key stakeholders, internal and external; and building a sense of solidarity / sorority / inclusion, a strong sense of accountability to our constituents and to the larger movements we are linked to; creating flexible, gender-sensitive internal policies and practices based on respect for different capacities; and generally, pursuing non-violent strategies of action. These ethics underlie the struggle, in most feminist movements and organisations, to create distinctly *feminist* ways of working.

- Consequently, we support the **renewal of our own organisations and movements** through empowering new generations of actors and leaders, and **creating respectful spaces and roles** for the beginners, the experienced and the wise, regardless of age, class, caste, race, ethnicity, ability or sexual orientation.

- Finally, **we stand against all ideologies and all forms of fundamentalisms that advocate against women's equal rights, or against the human rights of any people,** be it on the basis of economic, social, racial, ethnic, religious, political or sexual identity.

What is a feminist movement?

Given our definition of movements, and of feminism in the present global context, feminist movements would contain all the features of movements mentioned earlier, but in addition, would have certain particularly *feminist* characteristics:

- Their agenda is built from *a gendered analysis* of the problem or situation they are confronting or seeking to change.
- *Women form a critical mass* of the movement's membership or constituency—women are the subjects, not objects or 'targets', of the movement.
- Open espousal of *feminist values and ideology* (gender equality, social and economic equality, the full body of human rights, tolerance, inclusion, peace, non-violence, respectful spaces and roles for all, etc.), even if they do not call themselves 'feminist' or articulate these values in more culturally specific ways.
- They have systematically centred *women's leadership* in the

movement, at all levels—that is, they do not treat women instrumentally (as good for increasing numbers and resistance, but without real decision-making or strategic power in the movement).

- The movement's *political goals are gendered* (they seek not only a change in the problem, but a change that privileges women's interests and seeks to transform both gender and social power relations).

- They use *gendered strategies and methods*—strategies that build on women's own mobilising / negotiating capacities, and involve women at every stage of the process.

- They create more *feminist organisations*—that is, organisations that create more transparent systems and structures, consciously address the distribution of power and responsibility across roles, build a feminist practice of leadership (see, for instance, Batliwala 2011), strong internal and external accountability and learning systems, and actively experiment with change within their own structures and movements.

This is not to claim that all existing feminist movements—or ones that would claim to be feminist—necessarily manifest all these qualities. Rather, this is an attempt to frame an ideal prototype—or as ideal as we can presently conceive—that feminist movements should aspire to emulate. This is a critical point since many mainstream movements, with very radical agendas, often reproduce the very politics and power hierarchies that they seek to challenge and change elsewhere—the structures of privilege, agenda-setting, and decision-making power and exclusion. Unfortunately, many feminist organisations and movements are guilty of the same; so it is all the more important for us to create a framework that enables us to consciously tackle these negative dynamics within our own processes and structures.

Why do movements matter?

It is possible to argue that women can be empowered without necessarily building movements, through grassroots work and policy advocacy. Some would assert that macro changes—such as the CEDAW convention or the reproductive and sexual rights guaranteed in the Cairo Plan of Action—were achieved through the research, documentation, activism and advocacy efforts of individuals and organisations, without the sort of movement characteristics that were detailed earlier. While this is true, a consideration of the major changes in favour of women and gender equality that have occurred over the past several decades makes evident that none of these could have been achieved without building some kind of *collective power*— whether of individuals, organisations, or a combination of both. Thus, various UN policies and norm structures—such as CEDAW, the Beijing Platform of Action, or the recognition of women's rights as human rights, or policy changes at the national level recognising women's equal right to education, healthcare, employment, access to credit, etc.—were all the result of organised lobbying by women's organisations / feminist activists and advocates, through their collective action, without the affected constituencies being directly mobilised or involved in acting for these changes.

However, *the reason movements matter is their capacity to create sustained change at levels that policy change alone cannot reach.* As one veteran African women's rights worker puts it,

> We are now in a world in which so called 'advocacy' [read that as lobbying and taking members of parliament to a nice workshop!] is the strategy of choice. Getting more women at the table is the other. But unless these women and these lobbying activities are backed up by the power of numbers, by the power of women who speak for themselves and have strong movements, then change is never going to be sustainable, and in some cases, it won't even come! Worst case, it will be rejected by the very women it might claim to benefit, for example, policy change, or new legislation. We have seen this happen in this part of the world [South Africa].

This, however, is not just one individual's viewpoint—extensive empirical research over the past two decades have highlighted why 'change from above' (that is, policies, laws, etc.) cannot make gender equality a lasting reality: because they do not address all the elements that contribute to the subordination of women. Several feminist strategic frameworks have also been developed on the basis of this research. One of the earliest feminist frameworks postulated that lasting change in gender relations cannot be achieved by addressing women's *practical needs* alone (healthcare, water, income, childcare), without addressing their strategic interests (dismantling patriarchal norms and practices, giving women access to and control over resources, changing the gender division of labour, etc.).[3]

Another framework developed from practice (Batliwala 1992) asserts that social transformation that creates both gender and social equality involves challenging and changing at least three core elements of the existing power structures:

1. The ideologies that justify and sustain inequality (that is, the beliefs, attitudes and practices designed to uphold social hierarchies);
2. The way resources—material, financial, human and intellectual—are distributed and controlled; and
3. The institutions and systems that reproduce unequal power relations—the family, community, state, market, education, health, law, etc.

Another approach (Rao and Kelleher 2002) is to shift power by challenging and changing:

1. Who gets what—the distribution and control of resources;
2. Who does what—the division of labour;
3. Who decides what—decision-making power; and
4. Who sets the agenda—the power to determine whose issues / priorities come to the table for discussion.

Evidence from around the world suggests that movements can bring about change in some of these dimensions far more effectively, deeply, and in a more lasting manner than other interventions. Figure 7.1 places the different dimensions of change needed for a sustained, lasting transformation in women's *position and condition*, in *their*

---

[3] See the works of Maxine Molyneux, Kate Young and Caroline Moser, written in the 1980s and early 1990s.

practical needs and strategic interests, in a diagrammatic form. Here, the various domains of change emerge through two intersecting continuums or axes. The 'y' axis runs from the individual to the community level, and further down to the level of larger systems, and the 'x' axis cuts across, representing a continuum from the informal to formal social, cultural, economic and political arrangements. These two axes thus create four quadrants or domains of change that must be tackled to bring about sustainable transformations in gender and social power.

Figure 7.1
The Dynamic of Change

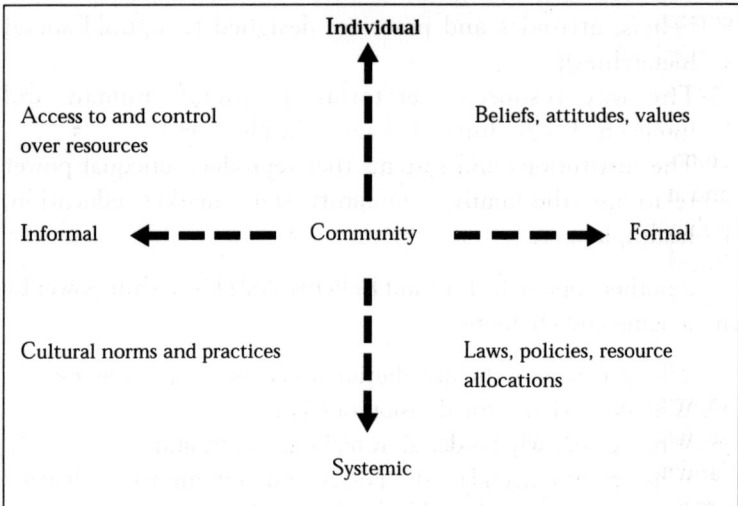

	Individual	
Access to and control over resources	↑	Beliefs, attitudes, values
Informal ← ─ ─ ─	Community	─ ─ ─ → Formal
Cultural norms and practices	↓	Laws, policies, resource allocations
	Systemic	

Source: Adapted from Rao and Kelleher 2005: 60.

On the right, we see the *formal* mechanisms that influence individual and collective status: individual resource ownership (land, house, a job, educational level, access to healthcare, etc.) and the laws, policies and resource allocations at the systemic level that determine the affluence, poverty, or status of different groups (equality guaranteed in the law and constitutions, affirmative action policies, or special budgets for women's social or economic development programmes; or laws criminalising same-sex relationships or sex work). These are the domains that can be challenged and transformed through research, advocacy, campaigns, and other interventions, without necessarily building movements of marginalised or discriminated groups. The campaigns for the inclusion of women's unpaid subsistence work in national accounting systems, advocacy for gender budgeting or quotas for women in education, employment, training and political bodies, and advocacy for changing discriminatory laws, are all examples of interventions that have brought about changes in the *formal* individual, community, or systemic domains.

On the left of the diagram are the *informal* cultural and social systems that are internalised by individuals and operate within communities, and which usually determine women's access to the opportunities, rights and entitlements provided through changes in the *formal* domains. These informal dimensions include the traditions, beliefs, values, attitudes, norms and practices that are deeply embedded in culture, and which operate at systemic, community and individual levels. Culture is far slower to change than formal policy or law, and law and policy do not automatically create changes in culture. Thus, the culture of discrimination, marginalisation and exclusion is the most challenging domain, where formal changes often do not penetrate.

Women must cross many hurdles in order to access their rights, most of which lie in the informal domain of cultural norms and socialisation. Let us take the example of rape—while the laws of the land may have been reformed to give women access to justice, there are many cultural barriers she must cross to reach it. First, the victim's own belief systems must be transformed to recognise that this is a crime of violence, and not something to be hidden for fear of being shamed or shunned by her family or community. Then, her family must support, rather than hinder or prevent, her in filing a complaint with the police and making the matter more public. The attitudes of the police must be changed to avoid further harassment or shaming of the victim, or to prevent their aligning themselves with the rapist, if he hails from a more powerful group, and refusing to take up the case. She and her family need the support of the larger community, whose traditional taboos against making such matters public need to be altered. Then, she must have the resources—in terms of time, money, etc.—to seek legal assistance. And finally, legal services or courts must not only be available, but must also provide appropriate services to the victim—such as closed hearings and sensitive judges. This clearly shows that the existence of formal laws and rights is no guarantee that women can actually reach them to obtain justice. We can cite similar examples from many other areas—lesbian women seeking partnership rights, sex workers fighting for healthcare, married women seeking contraception, or girl children wanting the same educational opportunities as their brothers.

This is where the special power of movements, and especially grassroots movements, comes in. While individual feminists (such as lawyers, doctors, feminist researchers) and women's organisations have successfully campaigned for equality under law, for millions of women, especially in the South, formal law is too remote, expensive and difficult to access. Their rights are determined not by formal courts but by customary laws and practices, administered by traditional clan, caste, or community mechanisms, where gender equality is considered contrary to custom and culture, and where patriarchal and other hierarchical belief systems are deeply embedded. So while feminist advocacy may have resulted in pro-women policies, laws and resource allocations, unless women themselves, and their families and communities, are able to break the hold of tradition and taboo, these positive gains have little meaning. Constituency-based movements, using consciousness-raising, political awareness, and other strategies that challenge the power and practice of patriarchy, are far better able to tackle and bring down the barriers to women's equality in the sites where they are most deeply embedded.

The other reason why movements matter is that their impact is usually on a scale that single organisations, no matter how radical, effective and successful, are able to achieve. We have all seen evidence of how dedicated organisations working with a feminist agenda have tackled forms of oppression and exploitation, and created significant shifts in cultural attitudes and practices at the local level. But for these transformations to occur on a larger scale, building feminist movements becomes critical.

Building feminist movements and feminist movement-building

Movement-building is a process of mobilising the constituency that implicitly benefits from a particular social, economic or political change; organising the constituency in some way and building a clear political agenda (or change agenda); and preparing the constituency to choose its targets, strategies and actions to bring about the change they seek. In this context, it is important to distinguish between the ideas of *building feminist movements* and *feminist movement building*.

Building feminist movements is a process that mobilises women (and their allies or supporters) for struggles whose goals are specific to gender equality outcomes—for instance, to eradicate practices like female genital mutilation, bride-burning and female foeticide, or violence against women; or for expanding equality of access to citizenship (for example, franchise), land or inheritance rights, education, employment, health, or reproductive and sexual rights. In this sense, the struggles to change customary inheritance rights in Kenya and Tanzania, the anti-FGM movements in several countries of Africa, movements against the repeal of gender-equal legal rights in several parts of the Middle East, the sex workers' movements in several parts of Asia Pacific, Europe and North America, the Afro-Brazilian women's movement in Brazil, the reproductive rights movements across Latin America, the anti-dowry and anti-sex determination movements of India, the current struggles against honour killings in Pakistan, against the trafficking of women in the Philippines and Indonesia, or for the rights of migrant women in China—all these are examples of the *building of feminist movements*.

Feminist movement building, on the other hand, could be defined as the attempt to bring feminist analysis and gender-equality perspectives into other movements—classic examples are the efforts of many feminists to engender the analyses, goals and strategies of the environment, peace, human rights, and peasant and labour movements around the world. Code Pink, created to engender the peace movement that arose in the US against the invasion of Iraq and the war in Afghanistan, is a good example of feminist movement building. Greenbelt Kenya, led by the late Nobel laureate Wanghari

Mathai, is an environment movement with a strongly gendered analysis, but mobilises poor women and men in a larger struggle for protecting and preserving the natural resource base of their homelands. Shack Dwellers International and its national chapters struggle for the rights of tenure and safe habitat of slum dwellers, but with a strong feminist analysis and women's leadership. Feminist Sandinistas played a strong role in attempting to bring gender equality issues to the centre of the political struggle in Nicaragua. Indigenous women across Central and South America work for the recognition of their rights and concerns as part of broader indigenous people's struggles. South African feminists have played a similar role in the anti-apartheid movement, and now in the movements around HIV-AIDS. These are all examples of how feminists change and influence the building of movements with other agendas, to ensure that gender-equality outcomes are not marginalised or forgotten.

Where are feminist movements today?

Several factors have weakened and fragmented feminist movements, particularly over the past ten or fifteen years, and they act in complex and inter-linked ways. Some of the most damaging are:

- The co-option and / or distortion of feminist ideology, discourse and agendas by mainstream institutions and social forces, such as governments and multilateral institutions, fundamentalist projects, donors, business interests and the media. The term 'empowerment', for instance, which was claimed by feminists to signify the challenging task of shifting gender and social power relations in favour of women, especially poor women, has been taken over and virtually divested of meaning and political content. Not only is empowerment now conflated with uni-dimensional interventions like micro-credit, but it has also been claimed by management gurus in the human resources field as an individualised motivational tool. At another level, the media has played a mainly negative role, simultaneously demonising feminists and appropriating their language to appear progressive and 'modern'. Private interests have also co-opted and distorted feminist ideas of equality for questionable commercial ends:

promoting images of 'empowered' and 'liberated' women to sell products or lifestyles that have nothing to do with feminism.

- **The resurgence of fundamentalisms of various kinds**—economic, religious, ethnic, and others—have posed possibly the greatest threat and setback to feminist agendas and activism. Economic fundamentalism has imposed an economic order on the world that has resulted in the decreased sovereignty of nation-states, and intensified the tyranny of structural adjustment programmes and market dominance that we have been ill-prepared to confront. The resulting impacts on women and gender relations have been complex—the burgeoning demand for women's labour in some sectors ('feminising' of the labour force), and pockets of acute and escalating poverty where poor women bear the burden of household survival with the least support or resources to do so. Religious and ethnic fundamentalisms worldwide have created similarly complex challenges. On the one hand, there is the rabid and overt attack on feminist agendas in all regions where they have had a visible impact on policies, laws and social norms, ensuring inheritance, equal pay, labour protection, reproductive and sexual rights for women, or raising public awareness of gendered violence and discrimination. Here, the fundamentalist project has been to discredit feminists as man-haters, baby killers, family breakers and sexual deviants. On the other hand, there has been a cunning co-option and distortion of feminist projects—such as the demand for equality under law or a greater role in civil and political life—to spread fear and hatred, vilify and demonise other communities, or instrumentalise women into becoming armed militants in ethnic conflicts. In still other groups, there is a straightforward attack on and attempts to rescind women's social and political gains of the past decades, and the re-assertion of medieval forms of patriarchal gender relations. In most cases, feminists and women's groups have been ill-equipped to face these serious, complex and multiple challenges. This has led to retreat, or piecemeal responses, or a kind of underground activism that has further weakened and fragmented our movements.
- There has been a gradual but accelerating **flow of major donor**

resources *away* from movement-building approaches *towards* projects and interventions that supposedly show more 'visible' and 'measurable' returns. While this has been a long-standing perception amongst many of us, AWID's 'Where is the Money for Women's Rights Research' (2006) has now established this fact with rigorous data. This de-funding is in turn a product of more serious and subterranean political trends in many developed countries: a backlash against feminist ideology, politics and power; a growing tide of political and social conservatism; pandering to the sexist and conservative elites in developing countries; and above all, a growing suspicion of approaches that do not somehow return benefit to the investing countries—for example, opening up markets for their exports, increasing purchasing power, creating better trained but low-cost labour for overseas production, lowering trade barriers and investment controls, and so on. And of course, movement-building approaches are above all suspect because they are considered too political, and therefore threatening to the interests of the developed countries or their elite allies in the South.

• **The magic bullet syndrome** is a result of this larger politics, but is another factor that has had a very negative impact on building feminist movements. This has produced one of the great ironies of our times: even as there is an apparent increase in the global commitment to poverty eradication and social justice—as witnessed by the great fanfare surrounding the MDGs (Millennium Development Goals) and their centrality to the new aid architecture—there is a growing delusion that there are magic bullets and quick fixes which can override the need for more fundamental but painful and longer-term transformative processes. Feminist activists have always understood that positive and lasting change in the status of women can only result from processes that tackle the basic structures of power and privilege, and truly transform our societies in favour of women and all marginalised and excluded people. Today, though, our organisations are unlikely to be resourced for such work; but the money will come streaming in if we offer to implement some of the magic bullets that are currently popular shortcuts to women's empowerment and gender equality, viz., gender mainstreaming, women-focused micro-finance projects, and quotas for women in politics. Many of these are rooted in feminist ideas and advocacy, but have been divested of the complex transformative strategies within which they were originally embedded, and reduced to formulas, rituals and mantras.

• **The 'NGOisation' of feminist movements** is another critical factor that has weakened our movement-building capacity and focus. The search for resources and sustainability led feminist activists and movement builders to found organisations within the NGO paradigm. National legal and regulatory requirements impose certain kinds of structural norms on these, and donor requirements and priorities impose another set of norms. Such organisations, often born out of movements or to support movement-building work, are gradually pushed into running projects and services, some of which may actually contravene their politics, ideology, or even their own experience of what really works. Many feminist scholars believe that this has also gradually shifted power away from the constituency that movements organised and into the hands of organisations and an organisational leadership that is increasingly less connected and accountable to the constituencies they claim to serve.

• The complexity and breadth of issues that feminists have tackled over the past three decades, and the emergence of new issues, voices and interest groups have also led to a level of **specialisation and diversification** that is considered by some to have fragmented and splintered feminist movements. Today, we have an overwhelming spectrum of distinct struggles and formations of and by women: economic empowerment and labour rights groups; indigenous women, peasant and landless women's groups; women's health, reproductive and sexual rights movements; land and inheritance rights struggles; housing and slum dwellers movements; lesbian and transsexual groups; struggles of women displaced by economic development projects or wars and conflicts; sex workers' movements; anti-trafficking and violence against women campaigns; women's legal rights campaigns—not to mention struggles against specific forms of discrimination (such

as FGM, dowry, caste), struggles of women of particular
ethnicities and religious groupings (such as Muslim women,
Roma women, Chiapas women) or occupations (fish workers,
street vendors, small women farmers, piqueteras), women living
with or caring for people affected by AIDS—this list could go
on and on. Each of these has its own agenda, goals and strategies,
presenting a bewildering array of priorities and movements that
testify to the vibrancy, but also the segmentation, of women's
movements. While there is nothing inherently problematic about
this, it presents some challenges in terms of creating an
overarching and shared political agenda to which all these
components would subscribe—the problem of speaking on at
least some set of issues with a unified voice. This fragmentation,
without some mechanism for cohesion, also enables outside forces
to 'divide and rule' more easily.

• Feminist movements have also lost some of their early clarity in
terms of their **theory of change**. In the 1970s and 1980s, for
instance, feminists who were mobilising around the world to
enhance women's role and representation in politics and political
structures were operating with a theory of change that looked
something like this:

  – That the transformation of both the *position* and *condition* of
    women at the societal or macro level could be lastingly
    achieved only through political change (enabling policies,
    legislation, enforcement and protection of rights);

  – That women in politics would advance the cause of gender
    equality and women's rights;

  – That unless women themselves were represented in local,
    national and global political bodies, the momentum for such
    change could not be sustained;

  – That a critical mass of women in political institutions would
    also initiate change in broader policies of development and
    international relations—by fostering and promoting policies
    of peace and non-violent conflict resolution, sustainable and
    socially just development, access to and protection of the full
    body of human rights, and placing people above profits; and

  – That a critical mass of women in political institutions would transform the very nature of power and the practice of politics through values of cooperation and collaboration, holding power in trusteeship ('power on behalf of, not over'), greater transparency and public accountability, etc. In other words, that women would *play politics* differently and *practice power* accountably.

Work on women's empowerment in the 1980s and 1990s was similarly based on a notion that the long-term transformation of gender relations would occur only when feminist movements were able to challenge and transform (*a*) the ideologies that justified gender discrimination; (*b*) the access to and distribution of both public and private resources that privileged men in every social strata; and (*c*) the institutions (family, market, state, community) and structures (economic, political, social, cultural—such as policies, religious practices, political barriers, and other exclusionary structures such as race, class, caste, religion, etc.) through which patriarchal and elitist norms of privilege and power were perpetuated. This analysis provided a kind of clarity—no matter how illusory—that informed and framed strategies of women's empowerment, and helped ensure that they did not focus on only one of these dimensions at the cost of the others.

Today, the tough lessons of experience have humbled us—we know that structures of power are incredibly resilient. We have seen that they find ways of both overtly accommodating us (such as signing the Beijing or Cairo Platforms of Action, creating national women's commissions, or even reforming biased laws), and covertly marginalising or subverting our agendas in unforeseen ways (through the travesty, for instance, that gender mainstreaming has become, or by making micro-credit programmes stand in for women's empowerment). Globalisation and its attendant impacts on women and their communities—social, economic and political—are something we have yet to fully absorb or understand, much less be capable to tackle. We have not yet synthesised or built upon these lessons to create a new theory of change—and indeed, there are precious few spaces in which to do this important 'thought work', given the end of the global conference era and the de-funding of 'talk shops'.

So it is difficult to find any clear theory or analysis of how to achieve a broader gendered social transformation informing feminist activism. The theory of change underlying many of our actions and strategies is often too narrow or limited, or too short-term and pragmatic, forgetting the longer-term social transformations that would lead to sustainable shifts in gender and social power relations. This is all the more critical since the forces of globalisation, fundamentalism, violence and conflict, and the intensifying backlashes against feminist agendas mentioned above, require responses that arise from a comprehensive, powerful analysis of how these forces are acting on both gender and social power. We need, therefore, to re-articulate a theory of change for our times—this would then become the basis for building the common agenda that is either missing or too weak in our current politics and vision.

Movements and organisations—a Relational view

The relationship between movement and organisations is a complex and sometimes contradictory one. To begin unravelling this intricate relationship, it is helpful to start by focusing on the central concept within the term 'movement', viz., that movement means something dynamic, something moving towards some goal. It cannot be used to signify something that is either static or in a constant state of reproducing goods, services, or relations. Organisations related to movements must therefore possess the same qualities—they must be in a state of motion, moving towards some particular set of goals or changes that they were set up to promote. We are in search here of a better understanding of what makes for feminist 'movement-building' organisations—and hence, organisations that can be said to be part of feminist movements.

To enlighten us, it may be helpful to develop a typology of organisations to clarify how different types of organisations stand in relation to movements and movement-building work. One distinction made in the literature on non-profit organisations is between 'member-serving' and 'other-serving' organisations. Within women's and feminist movements, we have both types.

Member-serving organisations are those set up by movement constituents/ members to structure and govern themselves more democratically and effectively, to gain greater visibility and voice, make coherent and strategic decisions, and/or coordinate their collective power and action: unions or workers' federations (such as that of self-employed women, home-based workers, street vendors, sex workers, etc.), ascriptive associations or organisations of particular identity groups (indigenous women, Dalit women, lesbian and transsexual groups, etc.), and associations of women and communities that transcend traditional sociological categories and are based on new identities emerging from their social or political experience, leading to shared agendas (piqueteras, slum and barrio women, migrant, displaced, and conflict-affected women). Such organisations, since they arise from the movement's constituency base, stand at the centre of movements, and have little problems with establishing their credibility or legitimate right to represent the interests of their members to the external world. They can, however—including feminist member-serving organisations—become static, hierarchical, less democratic, or be dominated by authoritarian styles of leadership, and these trends have to be examined and corrected, regardless of the legitimacy they enjoy in the eyes of others.

Other-serving organisations, under which the majority of feminist groups and NGOs fall, stand in a far more complex and contested relationship to movements. Debates have arisen as to whether these organisations are or are not part of particular or generic feminist movements. This is itself the result of the co-option, specialisation and hierarchisation that we discussed earlier under the challenges facing feminist movements. In many regions of the world, as regimes became friendlier to gender equality goals, both governments and donors played a role in converting groups that were once operating autonomously or even confrontationally into their technical assistance arms, or in-house 'gender experts'. Can such groups be considered a part of the feminist movement?

Similarly, many feminist and women's organisations that were formed to support and strengthen movement-building and movements have diverted their energies to executing donor- or government-driven projects and sub-contracts, simply in order to survive and sustain themselves. Here, some difficult questions must be answered about the rationale that guides these compromises, and whether the altered focus genuinely serves the final social and political purpose for which these organisations were originally established.

There are also many other-serving women's organisations—including some with relatively sound feminist thinking—that exclusively provide some set of services to women: shelters, or childcare, or credit, or legal aid. They too are important, and may have a conscious relationship to movements, but this would mean they have to do something more than service provision to become what we might term 'movement organisations'. They too must have internal monitoring and accountability mechanisms to check how their services and activities are contributing to a movement or its political agenda. We must acknowledge that sometimes, movements need these services in order to enable their constituents to engage in organising and action towards their agenda, or to protect their members and leaders from legal or political attacks. We need to put such organisations in a separate and valued category, which we might term **'movement serving'** rather than movement-building.

It is important to emphasise that **we should not place our organisations in a hierarchy**, where only those claiming to be movement-building organisations are valued, valorised, or glamorised, and those providing critical services—shelters and safe houses, childcare, community kitchens, crisis loans, legal assistance—to women or their communities, or those helping women to survive in politically or economically hostile environments, are placed at the bottom of the pile. Figure 7.3 illustrates one model of the relationship that can exist between member-serving, other-serving and service-providing organisations and a hypothetical grassroots women's movement, to help us understand where we can all stand within a movement if we have a shared agenda.

Another divide that has opened up in many regions is that between **autonomous feminist groups and feminist NGOs**. In the 1970s and 1980s, autonomous groups prided themselves on their independence from government, donors and business interests—particularly from funding from any of these sources—and their voluntarism. Most members of autonomous groups supported

Figure 7.3
Movements and Organisations—A Relational View

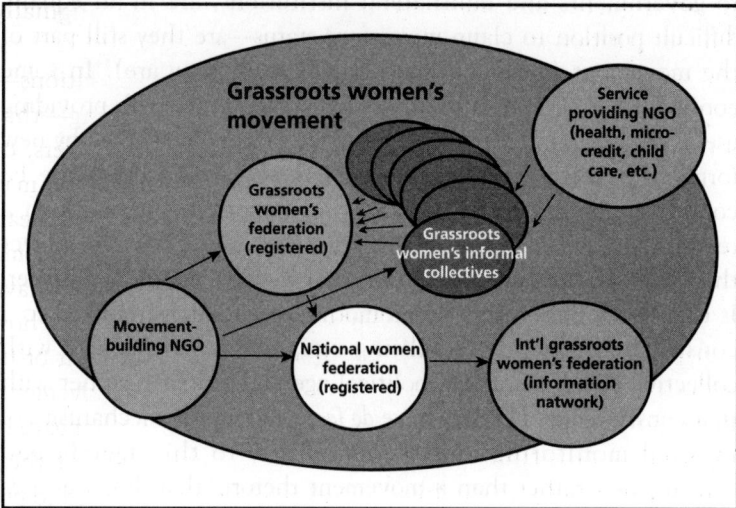

themselves through jobs in the academy, the media, or independent consulting, and were thus able to contribute their time to feminist activism without financial survival concerns. However, the changes in the political environment and the institutionalisation that occurred in the 1990s, significantly in Latin America and Asia, led many of these groups to mutate into NGOs. Many academic feminists also became 'femocrats' in governments or donor agencies, or elected representatives.

Many autonomous feminist groups have been the fiercest critics of the NGO-isation of the women's movement, and challenge the right of the latter to be considered feminist or even within the movement at all. However, these same groups have often become isolated pockets of individuals with a strong sense of ideological superiority, unengaged in any kind of mobilisation or larger movement-building work, or unconnected to constituency-based movements in their regions. Other feminist activists are often critical of these groups for these very reasons, and question their right to speak for the movement.

Feminist NGOs, on the other hand, who have become mainly involved in donor-driven project implementation, or sub-contracting to governments and multilateral institutions, are in an equally difficult position to claim movement status—are they still part of the movement (although many would insist they are)? In some contexts, it is such organisations that have, or are still, providing useful resources and some voice or space to women affected by new forms of poverty or violence—women who would otherwise be completely marginalised, isolated and forgotten. But to claim a relationship with feminist movements, they would have to subject themselves to the same litmus tests that we have mentioned earlier: Is their work either directly promoting or consciously linked to a constituency base, or mobilising one, and moving ahead with collective power towards a political agenda created together with that constituency? Do they have *de facto* and visible mechanisms of internal monitoring and accountability to this agenda and constituency, rather than a movement rhetoric that disguises a *de facto* accountability to their funders? This is a difficult tightrope to walk for most.

Movements and Individuals

Our definition and analysis of movements, and our focus on the relationship between organisations and movements, should not result in diminishing the important and often critical role that individuals play. Feminist movements, in particular, have been strengthened and sometimes even propelled by the role of individual feminists, many of whom did not belong to feminist, women's or progressive organisations of any kind. In some parts of the world, in fact, individual feminists, working in mainstream professions and institutions, became critical intellectual and strategic leaders of feminist movement-building. They were scholars and scientists in the academy, doctors and healthcare professionals in hospitals, health centres, or government health departments or ministries; they were demographers and population experts, economists, teachers and educators; they were journalists and media professionals, and lawyers and legal scholars; they were feminists in donor agencies, or in multilateral, bilateral and international financial institutions. These were a multitude of feminist women deeply committed to the feminist agenda and to marginalised and excluded women and men.

This trend continues to be a reality, and these women can legitimately claim membership of movements. These are individuals who are not necessarily part of the affected group or constituency organising for change—they need not ally themselves with movements, they have professional careers and job security—and yet they choose, for ideological reasons, to commit themselves to advancing women's rights and social transformation both within their own institutional settings and by supporting feminist and women's movements on the ground. Throughout the world, these individuals have played critical roles at some historic moments, in even the survival of feminist movements and activists.

In Latin America, for instance, during the era of authoritarian regimes that clamped down on social movements and arrested their key leaders and activists, feminist women in the academy provided spaces to convene and sustain each other until better times; some even provided financial support and legal aid to activists under threat. In South Asia, individual feminists in various professional locations have provided vital support to grassroots struggles and movements of marginalised people (such as LGBT groups or sex workers unions) in the form of legal aid, convening spaces, policy analysis, research for advocacy, etc. In many parts of the world, individuals have acted as whistle-blowers when movements and/or their leaders have been attacked or suppressed, providing critical exposure in the media, with international or national human rights commissions, and creating vital public awareness and debate locally, and even internationally.

Individuals stand in a range of relationships to movements— some enter and exit on an *ad hoc* or need basis, some associate themselves with specific time-bound projects, programmes, or research studies, and others form long-term relationships of solidarity and accompaniment. All these roles are important to strengthening movements, and greatly expand the intellectual resources and expertise they can access in their struggles. They also provide a set of alliances that, in certain circumstances, lend movements greater credibility, legitimacy and power.

Movement building—some key elements of a feminist process

Strong and sustainable feminist movements will arise from processes that contain most of these elements—one can almost argue that it is these elements that make a process both feminist and a movement.

- **Consciousness raising / awareness-building:** Feminists more or less invented consciousness-raising, since early feminist analysis understood that women's participation in, co-option by, or reproduction of their own oppression, exclusion and subordination were results of the false consciousness in which they existed. This false consciousness is created through the processes of both socialisation (conditioning into particular values, beliefs, worldviews and roles), and structural barriers and threats (intimidation or violence against women who strayed from their allotted position). Raising their consciousness of their oppression and exploitation thus became a critical first step in building feminist movements. A plethora of innovative and powerful consciousness-raising tools were created by feminist popular educators around the world—tools and methods that have sadly fallen into disuse in current times, as the consciousness-raising process has itself often been abandoned in favour of other first steps such as forming savings and credit groups. Latin American feminist popular educators also gave their sisters the powerful idea of putting Freirian liberation pedagogy to feminist use, and thus enabled women's consciousness-raising processes to lead to a gendered analysis of the larger social, economic and political structures of oppression in which women lived.

- **Building a mass base:** The mobilisation of aware, conscious women into varied forms of collectives or groups, named and framed using culturally and locally appropriate and familiar forms—the 'sanghas' and 'samoohs' of Indian women's empowerment programmes, for instance, or the 'marais' of New Zealand, or the 'mothers centres' of Germany and the Netherlands, or the market women's groups of East and West

Africa, the 'mehfils' of the Magreb, etc. These collectives formed the foundation of early feminist organising and movement building, since it helped to organise the movement's constituency or mass base into visible and accessible units that could then link up and amplify their voice, vision and struggle. This constituency base and its organisational and leadership structures were distinct and autonomous from the NGOs that might have mobilised them. In other words, it was they who were at the vanguard of the movement, not the NGO, although the NGO continued to provide strategic analysis and support, new ideas and, occasionally, protection from backlash. Building this foundation was painstaking business, but irreplaceable—it gave feminist movements their teeth, their legitimacy and their power. The diversion of energy into other activities has cost us a great deal, including our political power.

- The question, though, is: **Do numbers really count?** Lesbian or transsexual movements, or feminist disability groups, might argue that it is not numbers but tactics, and that their smaller numbers do not make them less of a movement. The answer probably lies somewhere between these poles: numbers do count, but not in some absolute quantitative sense. They matter because to qualify as a movement, we have to demonstrate an organised constituency base that has engaged in some collective action—so whether it's 100 or 100,000, it is the level of organisation, cohesion, a shared political agenda, and the exercise of collective power and action in pursuit of that agenda that matters. Fifty people or organisations, meeting at a conference or workshop on some issue of shared concern, do not constitute a movement, although a movement could easily be born in such a space.

- Feminist movements will have **clearly crafted political agendas** that are informed and framed by a theory of change that incorporates both gender and social transformation. These agendas will be generated through bottom-up processes that use the process of agenda building itself as a consciousness-raising tool. In other words, they would not have 'ideologues' who create the agenda and vision, and 'followers' who are converted to and mobilised around this. Feminist agendas will arise through debate and democratic discussion, in which constituents have a large and even defining role.

- A **spiral** of mobilisation, organisation, building a theory of change, common political agenda, action strategies, and critical reflection and re-grouping should characterise feminist movements. That is, they should be **dynamic, learning movements,** not static ones reproducing the same analysis and strategies without spaces for critical reflection and re-grouping for greater impact. They will also attempt to expand their constituency base with each round of the spiral, in order to increase their collective power and political clout.

- Given the importance of learning and change, **building a new kind of knowledge, and a new politics of knowledge building,** would be a key feature of feminist movements. Feminist movements would challenge the monopoly of knowledge professionals (academics, researchers, development and gender 'experts') by democratising the processes of learning and knowledge generation within and by their movements. They should create space, respect and concrete mechanisms for their members to participate in theorising, analysing, monitoring and evaluating their experiences. They make it possible for knowledge to be created in multiple forms that do not privilege the written word and patronise other forms of expression—oral traditions, street plays, art, or music. They may use the most modern technologies of documentation and communication, but will make these a part of the knowledge 'democracy' rather than the 'knowledge economy' by challenging concepts like patents and copyrights. They would also resist the exploitation and expropriation of their knowledge (of plants and seeds, or organic farming methods, for instance) by external forces such as multinational corporations.

- Most importantly, feminist movements would be concerned **not just with changes at the formal institutional level, but also at the informal level** or within the actual contexts and communities in which their constituents transact their lives and live their realities (that is, not just changes in legislation or policy, but in the attitudes and practices of families and communities). There will be a strong emphasis, therefore, on substantive rights and not just on formal structures that often do not reach women in their life contexts (a legal reform, for instance, without the organising and consciousness raising at the community level that enables women to access and assert these rights).

- Finally, feminist movements should **focus on transforming their own practice of power,** and build new models of power and leadership within their own structures and processes. This has been a distinct feature of many feminist movements worldwide—the attempts to break away from patriarchal models of power and create more shared models of leadership, authority and decision-making. While these have not always been successful—the insidious and hidden power structures that have emerged, for instance, in overtly 'flat' feminist organisations like autonomous women's groups, for instance— they are worthy examples of the search for new ways of governing ourselves, making decisions, and sharing both power and responsibility.

The Lifecycle of Movements

Movements, like people and organisations, also have lifecycles. They arise, grow, thrive, achieve impact and even fame, and then, sometimes, go into phases of dormancy, retreat, or decline. Chronologically 'old' movements are not necessarily the most vibrant or successful ones. Movements do not have to live forever—indeed, if they are successful, they probably should fade away as their political agendas have been achieved and their constituents are reaping the fruits of change. Some movements give birth to others—witness the number of other movements that early feminist movements have themselves mothered. But if their agenda has not been achieved, or their collective power has diminished, it is vital for movements to renew and re-build themselves.

Interesting work on the lifecycle of non-profit organisations has highlighted five stages in their lifecycle, and we have adapted these to approximate the lifecycle of movements as well.

Box 7.1
Lifecycle of Movements

Stage One: **Imagine and Inspire**
We know what we want to change, and who needs to be involved in the change
Stage Two: **Found and Frame**
Building our theory of change and deciding how we will begin the process of change
Stage Three: **Ground and Grow**
Mobilising and building the organisations of our constituents
Stage Four: **Struggle and Learn**
Engage the targets of change and experiment with different strategies to see what works
Stage Five: **Review and Renew**
What have we learnt so far, and how do we re-configure our structure, agenda, strategies and tactics for the next stage of action?

We are clearly in a historic moment when feminists must review and renew their movements, and locate the strategies that can best achieve this in the current global and local political and economic context. In the essay 'Great Transitions: The Promise and Lure of the Times Ahead', Raskin et al. say:

> In the past, new historical eras emerged organically and gradually out of the crises and opportunities presented by the dying epoch. In the [current] planetary transition, reacting to historical circumstance is insufficient. With the knowledge that our actions can endanger the wellbeing of future generations, humanity faces an unprecedented challenge—to anticipate the unfolding crises, envision alternative futures and make appropriate choices. The question of the future, once a matter for dreamers and philosophers, has moved to the center of the development ... agendas (2002: 24).

What women's movements teach US

In 2007 and then 2010, AWID supported the study of fourteen diverse and vibrant women's movements from different parts of the world, and these were published under the title 'Changing Their World: Concepts and Practices of Women's Movements'.[4] These case studies were commissioned to help us build a theory of women's movements and movement-building processes from practice, rather than the other way around. Table 7.1 provides a list of the movements studied and their location, if any.

The case studies comprise a huge diversity in terms of their political and social contexts, the issues, interests and exclusions that triggered their formation, the methods used to mobilise and build the movements, the strategies used to advance their cause, the multiplicity of targets they engaged, the challenges and setbacks they faced, and the extraordinary range of their achievements. They generated a wealth of information, insights and lessons. The following

Table 7.1
The AWID Women's Movements Case Studies

Movement	Region/Country	Movement	Region/Country
Czech Mothers Centers	East Europe	Iranian Women's Movement	Middle East/ Iran
Disabled Women's Movement	Global	Palestinian Women's Movement	Middle East/ Palestine
Dalit Mahila Sanghathan— Dalit Women's Movement	South Asia/ India	Piqueteras	Latin America/ Argentina
Domestic Workers Alliance	North America/ United States	One in Nine Campaign	Southern Africa/ South Africa
GALANG—Poor Lesbian Movement	Southeast Asia/ Philippines	Roma Women	East & Central Europe
GROOTS Kenya— rural/urban grass- roots women's movement	Africa/Kenya	Suwep Sudan Women's Peace Movement	Northeast Africa/ Sudan
Indigenous Women's Movement	Central America/ Mexico	VAMP/ SANGRAM	India/South Asia

[4] This document, as well as the full case studies of which it contains summaries, can be downloaded at http://www.awid.org/AWID-s-Publications/Movement-Building.

analysis is an attempt to distil the key messages these movements are sending us with respect to building movements.

Historical and political contexts

The greatest diversity among the case studies lies in the range of socio-political and historical contexts in which they have arisen. The various movements and their political contexts can be categorised as follows:

- Post-colonial states with neo-liberal democracies (India, Kenya, South Africa, the Philippines)
- Post-communist states with neo-liberal democracies (Czech Republic, East and Central Europe)
- Neo-liberal democracies (USA, Mexico)
- Neo-liberal democracies with secessionist struggles (Mexico)
- Post-dictatorship states with neo-liberal democracies (Argentina)
- Post-revolutionary theocratic states (Iran)
- Occupied states with struggles for political autonomy (Palestine)
- States in conflict or civil war (Sudan)

In some cases, such as the disabled women's movement, they have emerged in the global space, with roots in multiple national political and social contexts, but with the similarity of exclusion contributing to their need to organise themselves, both locally and globally. And similarly, the sex workers and lesbian movement case studies may have arisen in a particular political context, but have strong influences on, or links with, the regional or global movements of these constituencies.

The fact that these women's movements have arisen in such widely differing contexts suggests that our theories about 'enabling' and 'disabling' conditions for movement building need to be reconsidered. For instance, the movements in Palestine, Iran, Argentina, Sudan and Mexico were built amidst the most disabling conditions imaginable: the occupation by Israel and daily violence and conflict; repression by the theocratic Iranian regime, which is profoundly suspicious of and hostile to even the most basic of women's rights; the chaos following the economic meltdown in Argentina;

the decades-long civil war, gendered violence and disruption of life in the Sudan; and an armed secessionist struggle violently and militarily suppressed by successive Mexican governments blind to the cultural hegemony and racism of its policies towards indigenous people. So clearly, strong women's movements are not only possible, but could even be a response to hostile conditions that affect not only women themselves, but also their families and communities.

Another widely-held belief challenged by these movement stories is the necessity of liberal democracy, or rather, a 'democratic space', for popular organising to occur. Indeed, the Czech, Sudan and Iranian cases show that women have found ingenious and subversive ways of mobilising even when that space is limited or absent. For instance, since the 1979 Islamic revolution, Iranian women have not had a legitimate, legally ensured democratic space to organise or protest against the inexorable rolling back of their rights. Therefore, they formed a highly decentralised, 'headless' movement that works both under and above ground. Women meet in private homes or under the guise of 'religious meetings'; the cells of organised women are widely dispersed in both rural and urban areas across the country; and the movement is not led by one particular set of high-profile leaders whose detention can weaken it. All of this makes it virtually impossible for the regime to successfully repress or destroy this resilient struggle.

Several of the cases also highlight the particular nature of exclusion faced by certain women by virtue of their sexual orientation, their occupation in sex work, or their level of ability. These stories highlight how mainstream women's or other progressive social movements themselves have been either consciously or unconsciously exclusionary towards these constituencies. These case studies tell the story of women organising—or being organised— because they cannot find space or voice even within their own male-dominated movements (disabled women), or within women's movements, sometimes because of insensitivity or tokenism (disabled women), sometimes because of genuine political ambivalence on their issues (sex workers), and sometimes because they fall outside the class norm of the mainstream movement (poor lesbians).

Strategic insights

The case studies generated some highly significant insights into the power and character of women's movements, and the strategies used to build their movements.

- **Women build movements around particular identities and interests.** These movements were launched by women not essentially around their identity as women, but as women of *particular identities, categories and circumstances*—for example, women of particular ethnicities / social groups (Roma women, Dalit women, indigenous women); women facing particular forms of exclusion or voicelessness (sex workers, disabled women, lesbian women, mothers of young children, poor grassroots women); in particular occupations or economic situations (domestic workers, Piqueteras, sex work); or in particular political circumstances (Iranian women, Sudanese women, Palestinian women). In the words of Esther, a Zapatista woman,

    'I'm indigenous and I'm a woman, and that's all that matters right now.'

- They demonstrate that the power of movements—and particularly of women's movements—lies in the fact that their constituents/members have become *primary agents of change*. I want to contrast this with the notion of **'agency'**, which is popular in both feminist and development rhetoric, because while even an effective feminist NGO will enable women to use their agency, they may not, consciously or unconsciously, actively move women of the constituency into primary leadership. The leadership that is built at the base is often secondary to the leadership of the NGO or support organisation. But many of the case studies—the domestic workers, sex workers, disabled women, Piqueteras, indigenous women, women peace-builders in Sudan and violence survivors in South Africa, the grassroots women of Kenya, and the Czech mothers—are replete with examples of **primary agency**, symbolised best, perhaps, by these words from a Piqueteras leader:

    In other times I would never have dreamed of being so far from home and fighting for demands that I believe are just ... Trying to tell people about the struggle of my factory and my people, well ... these things ... I'd never have seen myself doing this. I'm sure I always had the ability hidden away and that it was part of me, but I had never developed it.[5]

- **Some movements are more 'explicitly' feminist than others**, and this is something worth unpacking. Why do some movements openly adopt the ideology and label of feminism, while others hesitate to do so, even when they are mobilising isolated, marginalised or excluded women to gain visibility, voice, power, influence? GROOTS Kenya, Domestic Workers and Czech mothers are either hesitant to call themselves feminist or have possibly felt distanced from feminist movements because of specific encounters or experiences.[6] This forces us to question how feminism has become positioned in a way (and not always by feminists themselves) that is exclusionary to women with an implicitly feminist agenda, or needs to engage them to advance—and possibly radicalise—their agenda. The Czech Mothers, for instance, do not appear to have as yet challenged the gendered nature of childcare responsibilities, but may do so without disclaiming or surrendering their role and rights as mothers. They have, so far, considered the needs of heteronormative families in their 'family friendly' cities campaigns, but might move, gradually, to include other types of families. So they might be willing to adapt their agenda in several ways if they do not start out feeling that feminists would somehow reject them, making them defensive about their focus on the very gendered work of women, one for which feminism in an earlier phase demanded recognition, respect and economic value.

---

[5] Quote from Celia Martinez, cited in the Piqueteras case study by D'Atri and Escati, p. 4.
[6] The late Monika Jaekel, one of the founders of the German Mothers Centers, told me in an interview conducted in 2003 that despite repeated efforts, they failed to find a legitimate space and recognition for the participation of the Mothers Centers movement within the German Feminist movement.

- In several ways, **the movements are reclaiming and reframing feminism**—sometimes from urban middle-class feminist issues, sometimes from the Western model of individual liberation, and sometimes from the instrumentalist approaches of men's movements. The indigenous women have created, for instance, an analysis that asserts their unique culture and the power of their relationships with land and natural resources, while simultaneously challenging not only their culturally-rooted oppression, but also the dominance of mainstream culture and government policies. Roma women are struggling to do the same. Domestic workers are creating new links between their status as immigrants and a critical but exploited workforce, with their status as marginalised women in need of accessible health and reproductive services and childcare responsibilities. The One in Nine campaign is seeking to establish a new conceptual frame that locates sexuality at the core of women's struggles for justice and freedom from violence.

- In other ways, **some of the movements are actually exploding and advancing the traditional political and conceptual boundaries of feminism in radical new ways.** While much of early feminist theorisation was based on challenging the patriarchal notion of anatomy as destiny, disability theorists and the disabled women's movement have interrogated ideas of 'bodily integrity' that lay unquestioned at the heart of feminist theory and practice for decades. They have shown us how feminism itself assumed certain norms of 'embodiedness', about what constitutes ability and bodily 'integrity', and about the very transient and problematic nature of our understanding of physical or mental 'wholeness' and ability. The queer movement has forced us to interrogate the traditional male-female gender binary that was so central to feminist analysis, challenged the notion of the social construction of gender into two simple categories, and demonstrated that gender identity lies along an infinite and complex continuum, with huge variation. Sex workers' movements have also forced us to question our own internalisation of ideas about the sanctity of certain parts of the female body, which arise from patriarchal controls over female sexuality. They have also confronted the notion that trading sex for money is somehow worse than performing any other kind of service for a fee, and compelled us to address their demand for recognition of sex work as work, and their rights as workers, moving the debate away from moral positions and into the realm of rights.

- What is emerging, therefore, is **a far more complex feminist analysis and theory** that shows the intersecting nature of women's practical needs and strategic interests, and the ability to act on this understanding in powerful new ways. The refusal of the indigenous women, for instance, to step outside the larger movement for indigenous rights, while consistently challenging patriarchal reconstructions by male leaders of supposedly 'traditional' gender relations, is a good example of this. So is the way the Sudanese women's movement demonstrated that peace and a culture of peace were essential both for meeting their practical needs and advancing their gender interests; and the way domestic workers reached out to a range of unlikely but similarly marginalised groups in their local mobilisations, in order to build a wider base of support and greater political clout for their advocacy.

- Some movements are therefore very **strategic about how and when to claim an autonomous identity**—for example, the indigenous women, the Dalit women, the Piqueteras, disabled women—and when to ally with, or embed their agendas within, other movements. This is a particular kind of political strategy, which recognises that the political agenda of the larger movement is critical to their own rights, and which seeks to avoid splintering movements in a way that could be exploited by the regimes and power structures they are challenging—we could easily imagine, for instance, how the Mexican government could seek to concede the demands of the indigenous women's movement, but not of the indigenous movement at large. So, as the Indigenous Women's National Coordinating Committee recognises,

> We women say that autonomy for indigenous peoples is the path

towards initiating a new relationship among ourselves, to the Mexican government, to other Mexican people, and between men and women ... (Carlsen 1999).[7]

- On the other hand, **retaining multiple identities**—as women, and as part of an excluded and marginalised group—**has proved challenging for some.** Disabled women's particular and unique concerns, for instance, have fallen between two stools, with the disabled people's movement assuming that their particular needs and interests as women will be dealt with by women's movements, and women's movements assuming that their needs and interests as people with disabilities will be handled by the disability movement. This, however, has resulted in neither movement addressing these women's specific issues; as Umoh E., Founder Director of the Nigerian NGO Family Centered Initiative for Challenged Persons, puts it:

> The issue of women with disabilities is excluded in two areas; there is a great oversight of disabled women's issues within the women's movement, they think it is a matter for disability movement, while the disability movement think it is a matter for the women's movement. So, we are at a crossroad and sometimes I am almost tempted to think that we are beginning to lose our gender because of a disability.

- **Some movements have used mainstream development interventions and services**—such as self-help groups, home-based care, or managing subsidies—**as the base for movement building,** and appear to be going successfully beyond the usual limits of these activities to create political consciousness and a longer-term political agenda. The self-help member groups of GROOTS Kenya, for instance, have emerged as key challengers to local power structures, claiming inheritance rights for widows and orphans from customary tribunals, running for local

---

[7] Quote from the document presented by the EZLN in the second phase of the dialogue and the Indigenous Rights and Culture table in the sub-group on women; the document was not accepted by the government, cited by Marusia Lopez in her case study of the Indigenous Women's movement.

elections, and ensuring that the local governance is responsive to their priorities and agenda. The Czech Mothers have earned a similar place of authority vis-à-vis town planning and urban development processes.

- There is a very **strong emphasis**, in several of the movements, **on building leadership, and especially on new (not necessarily 'young') leadership.** The domestic workers have taken this to the most sophisticated level by building leadership training into their governance model, and ensuring the development of 'new' leaders. However, leadership building to strengthen and sustain their movements is a key concern and practice in several others—indigenous and Dalit women, Piqueteras, grassroots women, members of the OINC, etc.

- **The role of struggle as the best school for leadership and political consciousness** is firmly attested by several of the movements—an achievement that cannot be claimed by the training programmes offered by even the best feminist NGOs. The clarity, courage and strategic insight of the indigenous women, of the Piqueteras, of the domestic workers, of the sex workers in VAMP, or of the Dalit women would be hard to equal!

- The case studies also teach us that **we must define the 'radical' nature of political agendas and activism within the socio-political context in which movements have evolved,** and not against some absolute ideological standards. The framing of issues by the Czech Mothers, for instance, could appear rather conventional (viz., centred around the isolating process of nuclear-family motherhood and child-rearing) if we fail to recognise that their organising began in the Soviet era. This was a time when public gatherings and civic action were dangerous, and the women who founded the movement were forced to meet on street corners to discuss their concerns—they were thus acting very radically. Their mobilisation of other women and the resources to start mothers centres in a region where neither men nor women had the privilege of acting independently in their own interest was not only radical, but also a shrewd use of the space that the 'Velvet Revolution' opened up. Similarly, the initial demands of the sex workers' movement—not to be ignored by HIV/AIDS prevention programmes as though they were completely dispensable—could be viewed as a narrow attempt to gain access to health services. But this was in fact a profoundly radical challenge to the dominant discourse and positioning of sex workers as disease vectors, and led to the formation of a movement that has transformed the attitudes and practices of a wide range of actors, including feminists and feminist movements.

• The framing of political agendas by these movements is also a fascinating process. In some movements, the evolution is from one or two gendered interests/issues (home-based care for the ill, collective spaces for mothers, recognition of domestic work as labour, removal of caste-based discrimination, access to health services, or inclusion in peace negotiations) to a more complex and intersectional analysis. As Klara Rulikova, a leader of the Czech Mothers Centers, puts it, '…With the mothers center, we did not think about how we were trying to change society, it was simply about being together with others like myself.'

In other cases, the agenda quickly assumes complexity and sophisticated analysis (OINC, IW), even if collective action is focused on particular struggles. The Roma case, however, demonstrates the contestation between older and younger activists, and different Roma women's formations (IRWN and JRWI) over the framing of the agenda, and intense but respectful negotiations between the two to create a more feminist agenda. Overall, the movements also demonstrate, much more so than male-dominated movements, a concern for building broader, more inclusive agendas that often integrate the interests of a wider range of communities.

Stages of movement growth and maturity

The case studies also show that movements have a distinct evolutionary path, and can be placed along a continuum of growth and maturity, which includes decay and decline. Some of the movements are in the making, some are emerging into full-blown movement form, and some are mature movements. And at least one, the Piqueteras, has declined and decayed. Sometimes, movements grow in dramatic leaps, in both scope and scale. As the Czech Mothers case study says, for example,

> In the last fifteen years, these women have gone from creating one mother center in Prague; to organizing and managing over 250 mother centers … to federating a country-wide network of women who work collectively on a broader set of values and goals that demonstrate why and how Czech society must become 'family friendly'.

The stages of movement growth are discernible in the number of movement characteristics they exhibit at different levels of evolution. Specifically,

- Some movements are more 'mature' than others (Czech mothers, Sudanese women's peace movement, indigenous women, domestic workers, the sex workers)—that is, they have a more conscious and well-articulated ideology and/or political agenda, an organised mass base, organisational and decision-making structures, processes for building and renewing leadership, and have clearly delineated relationships (in terms of strategic and other decision-making) with allies and support NGOs that work with them. They have developed sophisticated strategies, alliances and relationships, and there is growing recognition from governments, other movements and the public.
- Some are emerging movements (Iranian women, disabled women)—they have achieved a higher level of mobilisation and collective power, an increasingly clear political agenda, and autonomous leadership structures, but are yet to achieve sustainability, political or policy impact, or changes in public perceptions of their issues or in the larger discourse.
- Others are at a more nascent stage of movement formation (poor lesbians, Roma women), and need continued support to sharpen their politics, agenda and strategies.

These movement 'stages' suggest a 'maturity' continuum that is presented in Figure 7.4. The use of this term is not to suggest that earlier stages of movement formation constitute 'immaturity'. Rather, this is intended to provide movement-building organisations and movements with a useful trajectory along which to place themselves,

Figure 7.4

Continuum of Movement Development and Maturity

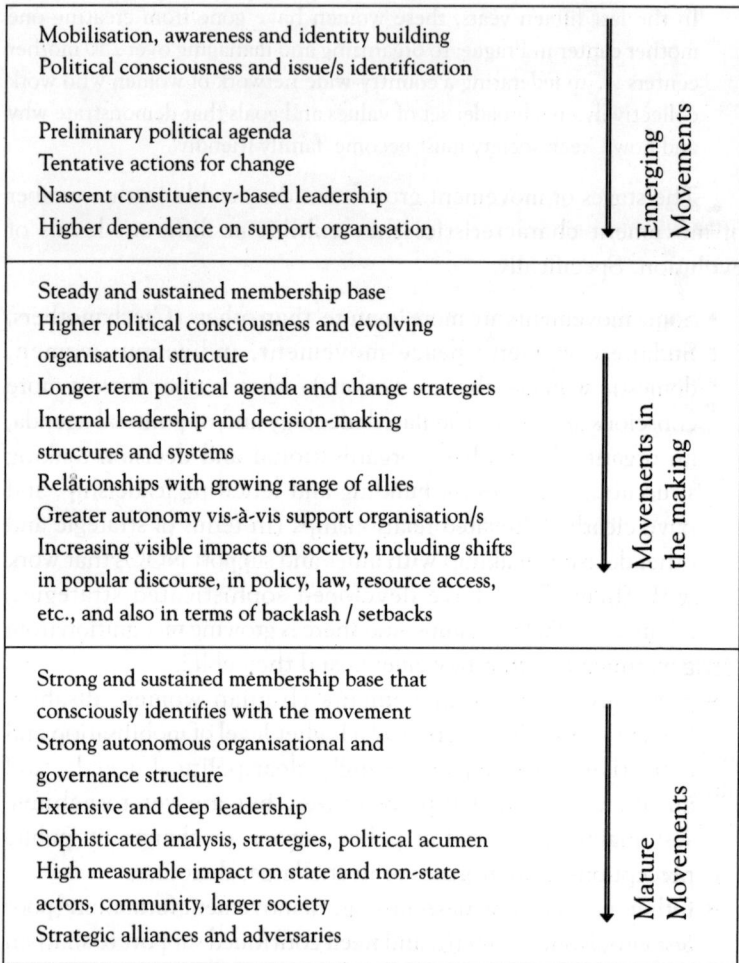

Mobilisation, awareness and identity building Political consciousness and issue/s identification Preliminary political agenda Tentative actions for change Nascent constituency-based leadership Higher dependence on support organisation	Emerging Movements
Steady and sustained membership base Higher political consciousness and evolving organisational structure Longer-term political agenda and change strategies Internal leadership and decision-making structures and systems Relationships with growing range of allies Greater autonomy vis-à-vis support organisation/s Increasing visible impacts on society, including shifts in popular discourse, in policy, law, resource access, etc., and also in terms of backlash / setbacks	Movements in the making
Strong and sustained membership base that consciously identifies with the movement Strong autonomous organisational and governance structure Extensive and deep leadership Sophisticated analysis, strategies, political acumen High measurable impact on state and non-state actors, community, larger society Strategic alliances and adversaries	Mature Movements

and to help them assess how to take their movements to the next stage of development so that they can achieve greater political impact.

At the risk of oversimplification, it may also be useful to reflect on what our case studies tell us about the basic steps involved in movement building—how they got from their point of catalysis to where they are now (Figure 7.5).

Figure 7.5
Steps in Movement Building

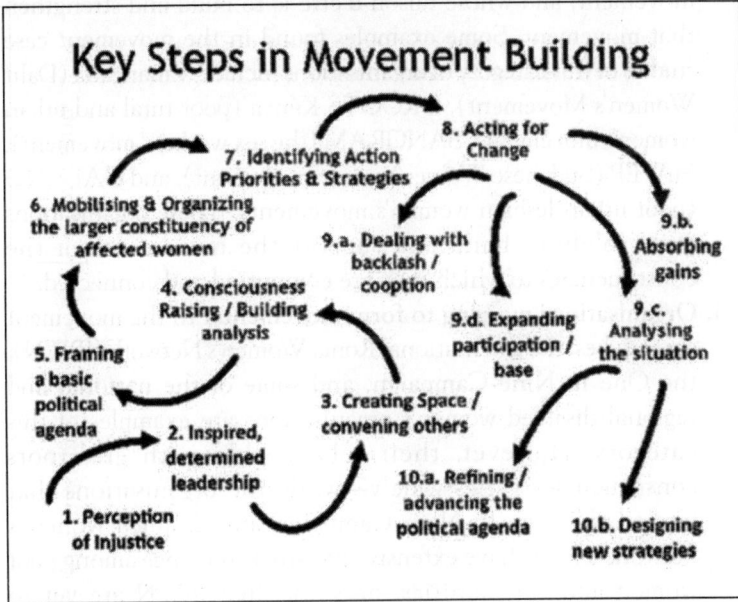

Key Steps in Movement Building

8. Acting for Change

7. Identifying Action Priorities & Strategies

6. Mobilising & Organizing the larger constituency of affected women

9.a. Dealing with backlash / cooption

9.b. Absorbing gains

4. Consciousness Raising / Building analysis

9.c. Analysing the situation

5. Framing a basic political agenda

9.d. Expanding participation / base

3. Creating Space / convening others

2. Inspired, determined leadership

1. Perception of Injustice

10.a. Refining / advancing the political agenda

10.b. Designing new strategies

Organisation-movement relationships

Earlier in the chapter, we discussed the range of organisation-movement relationships. The movement case studies beautifully illustrate the complex and variegated range of organisations that exist in relationship to movements, viz.:

1. **Movement created organizations** (MCOs): That is, formal and informal organisations set up *by movements* to govern themselves and strengthen accountability to their constituency/members, promote visibility, democratise representation, voice and decision-making, manage services, and negotiate movement members' interests and priorities with other actors; examples of MCOs can be found in the case studies of the Piqueteras, indigenous women, domestic workers, Dalit women, sex workers, disabled women, Sudan women's peace movement and the Mothers Centers.

2. **Movement-building or supporting organisations** (MBOs): These are organisations that stand in relationship to a specific movement, and whose raison d'etre is to build and strengthen that movement. Some examples found in the movement case studies of this category of organisations include Vanangana (Dalit Women's Movement), GROOTS Kenya (poor rural and urban women's movement), SANGRAM (the sex workers' movement), SuWEP (Sudanese Women's peace movement), and GALANG (poor urban lesbian women's movement). These organisations exist solely to build and support the movements of the constituencies to which they are committed and connected.

3. **Organisations merging to form movements:** In the movement case studies, the International Roma Women's Network (IRWN), the One in Nine Campaign, and some of the national and regional disabled women's organisations are examples of this category. However, their relationship with grassroots constituencies varies widely—while the organisations that formed the One In Nine Campaign and disabled women's networks clearly have extensive grassroots presence among poor women and communities, networks like IRWN are yet to successfully mobilise and organise the mass of poor Roma women, whose rights and interests they seek to advance.

4. **Organisational allies of movements:** A range of these were found in the movement case studies, from trade unions to political parties, feminist academics, women's studies centres and research groups. While some of these relationships resulted in co-option and derailment of the movements they allied with, others have provided capacity building, critical linkages, access to resources and new political spaces, and other forms of support. UN agencies, as well as some bilateral donors, have also proved critical allies in several cases.

The relationship dynamics in each of these configurations can be unpacked and explored to deepen our understanding of how organisations and movements work together. In the fourteen case studies, several patterns or directionalities were discernible.

- **Equilateral/circular.** Not surprisingly, the movement-created organisations in the case studies exhibit the 'flattest' and most equilateral relationships of all. Having been created by the movement, these organisations—such as the Mexican indigenous women's groups, the domestic workers' local organisations, the Dalit women, OINC, or the Mothers Centers—exist to serve and structure the constituency's organising and strategic goals. Several of the movements, however, have exhibited remarkable foresight and understanding of how formal positions, even within MCOs, can lead to unhealthy power dynamics. So most of these movements have planned or actually put in place a number of mechanisms to neutralise this tendency, ensuring leadership training opportunities for ALL their members, or systems of rotating leadership or term limits in formal roles. In this, they are holding up a very critical mirror to mainstream women's organisations, where lack of leadership change and concentration of power have become major challenges.

- **Symbiotic.** In this dynamic, neither the movement-building organisation nor the movement has greater overall control or power, but exist in a synergistic and symbiotic relationship with each other—the relationship of Vanangana to DMS in the Dalit women's case, or SANGRAM to VAMP in the sex workers case, for example. It is also noteworthy that some of the movement-building organisations (MBOs) in the case studies have changed their role over time, ceding many of their initial roles to the movement-created organisations they helped catalyse. This is an important lesson for MBOs to reflect on—if your role hasn't changed over time, it is possible that you are not allowing the movement's internal organisations and leadership to mature and take over.

- **Paternalistic / instrumentalist / clientelist.** Here, the allies, supporters or movement-building organisations are in command, with the movement leadership and its organisations (if any) being in a dependent or instrumental relationship with the former. The IRWN or JRWI in the Roma case, the political parties and trade unions in the Piqueteras case, or the Palestinian Authority, donors and professionalised women's NGOs in Palestine, and male-dominated disabled people's federations like Disabled

People International, are all good examples of this. The negative impact of this kind of relationship on movements is also clearly illustrated in these cases—viz., the subversion of powerful movements (for example, the Piqueteras); loss of credibility, relevance and mass support (Palestinian women's movement); the inability to mobilise the larger mass of the constituency (the Roma); or losing the ability and legitimacy to represent the larger mass of the constituency (indigenous women, disabled women).

The movements described in the case studies also contain the full continuum of formal to informal organisations discussed in the Introduction to this volume. At the formal end are the well-defined governing structures of the Czech Mothers Centers, the National Coordinating Committee of Indigenous Women in Mexico, and the two unions that formed the Domestic Workers Alliance. At the most informal end are loose relationships built on common understanding or shared agendas, but with few governance, financial or other controls, most beautifully illustrated by the Iranian women's movement.

Another visible factor is the strength of the 'glue' that binds the organisation-movement relationships. The Domestic Workers Alliance, for instance, is a looser coalition than the National Coordinating Committee of Indigenous Women or the Czech Mothers' National Council. The Piqueteras, at the height of their movement, and the Iranian women, are at the other end of the spectrum: very loosely federated networks of neighbourhood groups, bound more tightly by ideology and cause than by any organisational structure. The absence of the glue—or its gradual dilution—was a major problem with the women's NGOs in the Palestinian and in the Roma women's context, while SuWEP, Vanangana, GROOTS Kenya, GALANG and SANGRAM would barely have a reason to exist without the movements they are building, supporting and resourcing. Clearly, the 'glue' factor overrides the organisational structures visible in these movements.

One of the cases also highlighted the issue of *competition* in the organisation-movement relationship, and how competing for resources, or a narrow focus on practical needs at the cost of strategic interests, can impede movement building. In the disabled women's case study, an African disability activist is quoted as saying:

> Without solidarity, without an understanding that the fight that we lead is not done in the interest of a sole disabled people's organization, but in the interest of all, we will never achieve any results. Each disabled people's organization to understand that the fight that we lead outweighs the competition and that we have to go forward together to succeed in getting long lasting results.

Governance and decision-making structures

The case studies showed that women have used, adapted and transformed structural forms that have evolved in the civil society and social movement terrain over centuries—mass assemblies, unions, federations, networks and coalitions. Registered legal entities—non-profits or NGOs—are also a part of the spectrum, both those created by movements as governance or representational structures, and those that exist precisely to build, support and serve movements. The case studies depict three broad categories of structural forms assumed by these movements:

- **Coalitions/Networks/Federations:** These are women's organisations or collectives connected with varying degrees of cohesion and closeness around a particular political agenda, and acting together on that agenda. The case studies abound with these forms: coalitions like the One in Nine Campaign; disabled women's networks like the South Asia Network of Disabled Women, the National Network of Sex Workers in India, or the networks that constitute SuWEP in North and South Sudan; and federations like the Indigenous Women, the Czech Mothers Centers, or the Domestic Workers unions.
- **NGO-federation partnerships:** Such as the Dalit women and Vanangana, the sex workers of VAMP and SANGRAM, or GROOTS Kenya and its women's groups in Nairobi and other provinces.
- **Underground networks:** This is the unique form of the Iranian women's movement, which has to use word-of-mouth and other

informal means of communication to make strategic and other decisions.

Depending on the age, stage and geographic spread of the movement, the structures evolved for planning, strategising and governance have an equivalent number of layers. The **older and more mature movements have often developed more complex structures** than the younger and emerging movements. What is clear, though, is how all are struggling to create highly accountable, democratic and bottom-up decision-making systems that give their constituents a real sense of voice without sacrificing their agility. The Piqueteras used the informal but very powerful format of popular assemblies and '*fogados*' reminiscent of the French Revolution. The One in Nine Campaign functioned by convening as many member organisation representatives as possible for taking decisions on the run, while the Dalit Women use 'cluster committees'. And a major constituent union of the Domestic Workers (viz., the MUA) uses the '*Comite Corazon*'—the campaign coordinating 'heart' committee—to make rapid decisions. The challenges of creating appropriate decision-making systems are summarised by Dawn Cavanagh, one of the leaders of the One in Nine Campaign:

> We were running on pure energy, and it was very untidy, it was messy at first; those who were willing and able to do the work, they were the ones doing it, and decisions got made by whoever was able to just be there, and everyone accepted that, it wasn't until later that we got to sit down and design proper terms of reference and map out a more longterm strategy, we weren't responding to a pre-planned anything, with a budget, and so on, we were just building as powerfully as we could, it was a totally new way of organizing for us ....[8]

The systems of governance created by these movements—and particularly the older ones—suggest a **need for us to interrogate notions of 'formal' and 'informal' structures** in movement-building. Clearly, even the most informal-seeming structures—the Piqueteras assemblies, GROOTS Kenya's annual retreats, and OINCs day-to-day consultations—were highly organised and participatory. But then,

---

[8] Quoted by Jane Bennett in the case study 'Challenges Were Many', p. 9.

so also are the more formal structures of the Indigenous Women's National Coordinating Committee, the VAMP sex workers' collective, SuWEP's coordinating committees and the Czech Mothers council. Some, such as OINC, have seen a need to move from more informal styles of decision-making in its early stages to a more systematic and democratic approach in order to ensure that it adheres to the feminist values and principles they have consciously adopted for their struggle.

Regardless of the form the structures take, though, a remarkable feature of the movements is that they have all struggled—and largely succeeded—in creating deeply **democratic, representative, and layered governance and decision-making structures**. The structures reflect the operation of certain core principles that are clearly feminist, whether the movement calls itself feminist or not, viz.:

- **Ensuring voice and representation** for all their members/ constituents, especially at the grassroots.
- **Nominating or electing leaders/representatives from each level of their constituents** who form the base, or foundation, of the movement.
- **Forming accessible, participatory units or layers of decision-making** as the movement spreads geographically or grows numerically—'cluster committees', local unions, county- or province-level units, local mother's centre board.
- Many of **the structures have ensured accountability to the movement's base or membership**, displaying a concern for ensuring that the 'apex' decision-making body or NGO is not too powerful, unaccountable, arbitrary, or disconnected from the base. In other words, the process of agenda-setting and decision-making is itself bottom-up rather than top-down. As the GROOTS Kenya case study puts it,

> The regional groups consistently inform the strategic direction of the organization, and their involvement is multi-faceted. For instance, at the annual retreat, the representatives of the various regions determine the annual fund raising plan of the secretariat. In addition, through the regional focal point leaders, mentorship and direction is provided to the sub groups, so that there is regular

consultation and inflow of information from focal point leaders, to
the secretariat and back to the various groups in the region. Even at
donor meetings, the regional representatives at times negotiate grants
on behalf of their regions, while at other times fundraising is done
for Groots Kenya.

Another fascinating question is: **How autonomous are the
various constituent units of these movements**, and over what types
of issues or actions do they exercise that autonomy? This is worth
debating not only in relation to the NGO-movement relationships
in the case studies, but even in the movement-created organisations
and governance structures. Many of the constituent units of the
movements obviously run their own programmes and services at the
grassroots level—such as livelihood programmes, credit schemes,
schools and childcare services—relatively independent of the larger
federation or umbrella organisation of which they are a part (for
example, see the indigenous women, Palestinian women and
GROOTS Kenya case studies). The network and coalition-type
structures—such as those used by the domestic workers or disabled
women—also follow this approach, with local unions developing
their own strategies and tactics. But while there is a high degree of
autonomy in designing activities at the local level, most of the
movements demonstrate that there is coherence and unity in acting
on the collective political agenda. For instance, no section of the
Indigenous Women's movement will go off to negotiate their own
agreements with the Mexican government—this will only be done
through their National Coordinating Committee, after reaching
consensus throughout their layers.

The leadership structures are also largely drawn from the mass
membership or grassroots constituents of the movement. Even
campaigns like OINC, formed by a coalition of NGOs, have ensured
that leadership is in the hands of the women who have directly
experienced the forms of violence the campaign is addressing, rather
than women from the privileged or dominant groups. Where multiple
layers of leadership exist, several movements have developed very
democratic processes of selection/election and representation (see
the Dalit Mahila Samiti, VAMP, Domestic Workers and Czech
Mothers case studies, for example). The systems of accountability of

the leadership to the constituents are very strong in some and less clear in other cases. In contrast, a very nascent movement-building process like GALANG is experiencing the severe challenges of creating local leadership and ownership.

Overall, the data present in the case studies indicates that these women's movements **'model' both the principles and practice of feminist decision-making and governance structures.**

Forces and Actors engaged

In pursuit of their diverse political agendas, these women's movements have resisted, challenged and/or engaged an incredibly wide and varied range of actors, institutions and processes, including:

- **Formal institutional actors** at local, national and international levels. Despite the domination of the neo-liberal paradigm and the alleged shrinking role of the state, our case studies suggest that the state and its various arms and layers (national and provincial governments, urban municipal councils, etc.) are key institutions engaged by women's movements everywhere. Clearly, women are not ready to abandon—or allow governments to abandon—the primary responsibility and accountability of the state to citizens, and politicians and political parties holding state power are also frequently targeted in the process. International institutions like the UN and its various units and commissions (UNIFEM, CSW, CSD, etc.), and other international bodies have also been sites of engagement for advocacy or alliance building.
- **International 'norm structures' and instruments,** viz., human rights codes, urban habitat norms, international labour standards, environmental agreements, UN conventions on disability and on women, peace and conflict (1325 and 1820), have been extensively used by our movements to pursue their goals, and in many different ways. For instance, international agreements and norm structures have been used to pressure national or local governments, and successes at the local level have been used to push for changes at the international norm level. A good example

of this is how domestic workers have worked on labour standards for domestic work at all these levels simultaneously, resulting in a very recent victory: the adoption of an international convention on domestic work in 2011.

- **Health, education, and other service providers.** Movements like that of rural women in Kenya, disabled women, lesbian women and sex workers have challenged and engaged a range of service providers who exclude or marginalise them because of their identity and particular constraints. For instance, disabled women have demanded accessibility from schools, colleges, hospitals and employers; and sex workers have challenged the way HIV/AIDS programmes position them as disease vectors, rather than legitimate and equal beneficiaries of prevention and treatment services.

- **Warring regimes and factions.** Some of our movements have courageously challenged and interacted even with militant, violent actors who have themselves threatened their survival. For instance, the Sudan women's peace movement engaged warring forces and their supporters from the local to the international level to ensure that the women's peace agenda was a part of both the formal peace negotiations and informal peace initiatives at the community and neighbourhood level. The immense significance of this cannot be overemphasised—dealing with the very people who may be responsible for the violence committed on you, for your displacement, for the loss of your family and livelihood and natural resource base, takes a level of courage and determination that even powerful leaders often lack.

- **National, transnational and global policy processes.** Almost all our movements have been involved in policy processes at various levels, and in the creation of new norms. These range from labour standards, sustainable cities discourses, indigenous people's rights and new 'cosmovisions', HIV/AIDS and micro-credit policies, human rights enforcement standards, sex workers' rights, LGBT rights, the framing of the UN convention on disability, negotiating quotas for disabled women in education and employment, to peace negotiations in conflict-ridden or occupied territories.

- **Market forces and the neo-liberal agenda.** The chaos, impoverishment, violence and conflict catalysed (directly or indirectly) by neo-liberal economic policies have compelled some movements to take on market forces and actors in different ways. For some of the movements, neo-liberal policies have had direct impacts—such as the growing 'informalisation' of work, the dislocation or withdrawal of state-supported services, and even, in the case of Argentina, complete economic meltdown. For others, market interests play a powerful but indirect role in shaping their realities: for example, a root cause of the civil war in Sudan is the mineral resources in the South; mineral resources are also the reason for the attacks on the rights and habitats of the indigenous people in Mexico. Some women's movements— such as the Piqueteras in Argentina—tackled these forces directly, taking over abandoned factories and demanding pro-poor economic reforms. Others are engaging them indirectly, as in the case of the domestic workers or Czech mothers, by making common cause with other constituencies affected by the privatisation or dismantling of public services.
- **Other social movements or women's movements.** Surprisingly, some of the movements have had to challenge and confront the very movements that should have embraced and advanced their interests, such as women's movements. Due to factors analysed in those cases, groups like disabled women and sex workers have had to deal with their exclusion or stigmatisation by women's movements themselves. Similarly, the GALANG movement-building process emerged at least partly out of the marginalisation or neglect of the issues of poor lesbian women by the Philippine LGBT movement; and even the Mothers Centers movement emerged partly because of European feminist discomfort with the issues and interests of women isolated by their child-rearing roles.[9] Thus, many of the case studies indicate that these

---

[9] This point is not raised in the case study, but is a personal communication of the late Monika Jaekel, one of the founders of the German Mothers Centers, when she described the origins of that movement to the author in 2003. The Czech Mothers Centers movement was inspired and supported by the German Mothers Centers.

movements have had to engage the mainstream social movements to gain greater visibility and voice, to transform male-dominated movements, to take over movements abandoned by men, and to radicalise movements with a more conventional liberal agenda. In at least one case, however, this 'targeting' has been reversed: in Argentina, it was left political parties and the trade unions that targeted—and later successfully co-opted and demobilised—the movement.

- **Social structures and cultural norms.** An incredibly broad range of deeply embedded structures of hierarchy, cultural beliefs and practices have been confronted and challenged. These include long-standing social structures like racism, patriarchy and hetero-normativity, and discrimination based on caste, ethnicity, ability, nationality and class. The movements have also tackled cultural norms that tolerate violence against women—especially 'deviant' women like lesbians and sex workers—but also simply because they are considered fair game in situations of war and conflict. They have challenged the social justification and acceptance of the victim image or of the exclusion of certain women because of their ability, occupation, ethnicity, etc.

- **Customary and formal legal systems.** Land rights for HIV/AIDS widows, recognition of the rights of disabled or lesbian women, legislation to regulate informal work such as domestic labour, and challenging police inaction in the face of violence against sex workers are all examples of the way many women's movements have tackled both customary laws and the formal legal and law enforcement system in their contexts.

- **Religious institutions and leaders.** The Iranian women's movement has been forced to engage with the national Muslim clergy as well as local imams to challenge their interpretation of Islamic law, and demonstrate that the denial of rights over their children after divorce or widowhood, or loss of citizenship rights if they marry non-Iranian men, have no basis in or sanction from the Quran or Shari'a. The Sudan women's peace movement has similarly had to confront and overcome the narrow roles allocated to women in their communities by religion and custom, and to claim their rights as equal citizens in the peace process.

Strategies

The range of strategies used by these movements presents a dazzling array of incredibly innovative and politically astute methods of pursuing their change agendas. Some appear deceptively conventional on the surface, but are applied towards very radical feminist and social justice goals. Given the plethora of strategies visible in the case studies, it is impossible to analyse all their dimensions. This section will present a typology of their organising strategies and interventions.

All the movements used **multi-faceted strategies** that reflected the complex way in which they framed their issues and their theories of change. None had a uni-faceted strategy or depended on some single 'magic bullet' approach, even if they had begun that way. This is an important lesson for those who believe that a single intervention—such as credit or income-generation or quotas—can grow automatically into a 'movement', or create broader transformative changes in women's lives. This is the background against which we must view the inter-linking strategies used by our movements, which are described below and depicted in Figure 7.6.

Internal movement building strategies

- **Feminist popular education** of various kinds is a fundamental building block in virtually all these movements. They have recognised that mobilising and organising women, and building a collective political agenda for the movement are not possible without raising the affected women's consciousness, awareness of their rights, self-esteem, awareness of the social, economic and political structures and power relations that oppress and exploit them, thereby unleashing women's latent revolutionary potential and desire to act for change. Many movements may not term this process feminist or even popular education, but in essence, it is what they have done or are doing. And everywhere, this consciousness raising is tailored to the political and social contexts and realities in which women are located, and in the language and constructs that are accessible and meaningful to them.

Figure 7.6
Women's Movements' Strategies

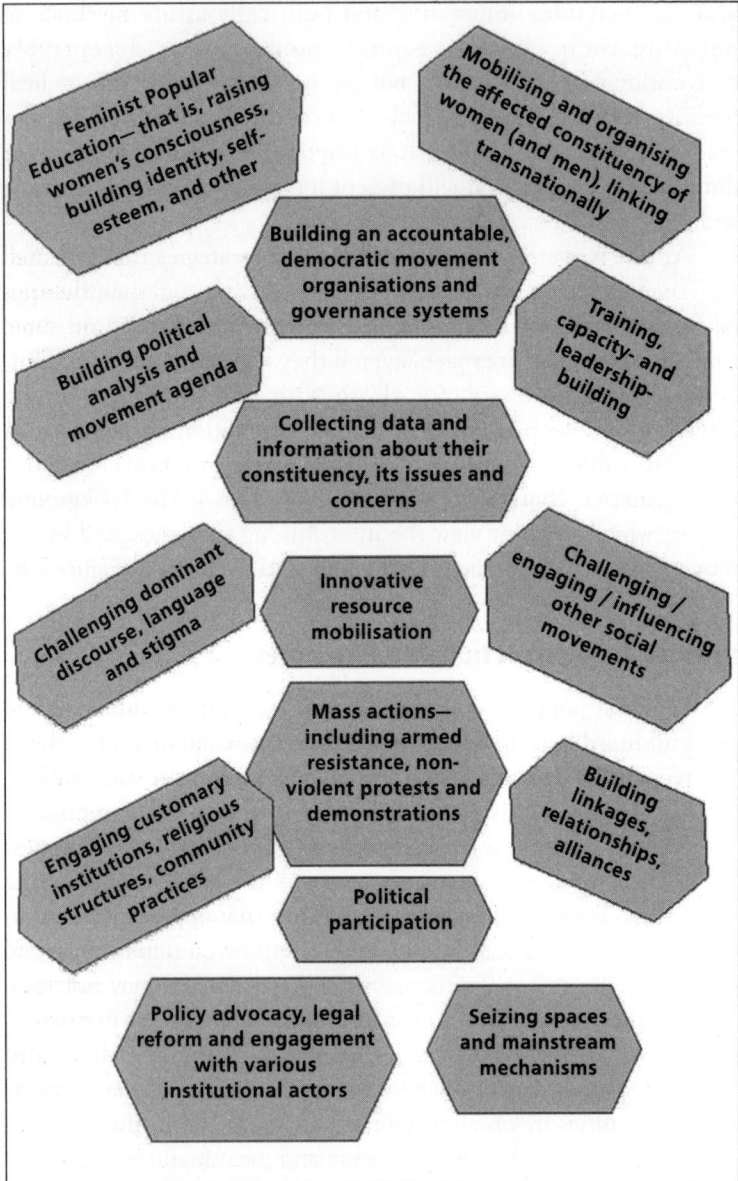

Feminist Popular Education— that is, raising women's consciousness, building identity, self-esteem, and other

Mobilising and organising the affected constituency of women (and men), linking transnationally

Building an accountable, democratic movement organisations and governance systems

Building political analysis and movement agenda

Training, capacity- and leadership-building

Collecting data and information about their constituency, its issues and concerns

Challenging dominant discourse, language and stigma

Innovative resource mobilisation

Challenging / engaging / influencing other social movements

Engaging customary institutions, religious structures, community practices

Mass actions— including armed resistance, non-violent protests and demonstrations

Building linkages, relationships, alliances

Political participation

Policy advocacy, legal reform and engagement with various institutional actors

Seizing spaces and mainstream mechanisms

- This goes hand in hand with **mobilising and organising the larger constituency of women**—or, as the VAMP/SANGRAM case study puts it, 'collectivizing women'. This is just beginning in some of our movements—such as the GALANG group in the Philippines, some of the disabled women's groups, or the Roma women—while for others, it is at a very advanced and sophisticated stage. Some of the case studies show that mobilisation is itself a huge challenge in some contexts—for disabled women, for instance, accessibility issues make it enormously difficult even to organise face-to-face gatherings to build a common identity and awareness. With the sex workers, innate competitiveness and suspicion of outside organisers had to be overcome with patience and persistence. With the poor lesbian women in urban slums, apathy and dependence bred by patronage politics are the barriers. For the Czech mothers, there was no safe space to meet but the sidewalk or a café. Where domestic workers were concerned, it was difficult for these overworked women to find the time. And for the women of Sudan and Iran, ceaseless conflict and a draconian, repressive regime posed immense obstacles to their organising.

- The **forms of organising vary from formal to informal**, and these choices have been made based largely on the political and social contexts in which the movements operate, as well as the nature of their mission and constituency. Thus, while the Iranian regime has not been able to identify a single organisation or leader that controls the entire movement and could therefore be targeted for repression, the sex workers, Dalit women, Czech mothers, domestic workers and Kenyan women present layers upon layers of mobilisation, organisation and leadership. Some movements—most notably that of indigenous women, mothers centres and disabled women—have also linked transnationally to strengthen their regional and global presence and advocacy.

- What is important, though, is that our case studies demonstrate that **women are capable of mobilising and building movements under even the most hazardous circumstances**. This belies the notion of 'enabling and disabling' conditions for movement-building mentioned earlier in this chapter. The movement cases

in fact seemed to assert that movements can and have been built
despite—and sometimes almost *because of*—such conditions!

- **The development and refinement of their political analysis
  and agenda** has been a key strategic component in all these
  movements. Our case studies demonstrate the evolution of the
  women's thinking about the social, political, economic and
  cultural basis of their subordination, about the nature of the
  power dynamics that exclude and marginalise them, about the
  non-material as well as material bases of their exclusion and
  oppression, and the sophistication of their political agendas have
  grown and been refined along with their analysis.

- **Strengthening their own organisations and governance
  structures** seems to be a key part of their internal strategies. As
  they have grown and expanded, many of these movements have
  attempted to create democratic, accountable and representative
  participation, decision-making and governance systems. There
  is clearly a conscious attempt to tackle and eschew the
  centralisation of power and the exclusionary tendencies of
  mainstream structures.

- **Training, capacity-building and leadership development** have
  been critical to this process of building democratic organisations
  and accountable governance. Several movements have placed
  great stress on ensuring leadership training opportunities for all
  their members. Political participation—both in formal roles as
  elected representatives and in other political spaces—has also
  been used to influence the institutions they engage or enter.

- It is interesting to note that none of the movements studied
  were/are entirely dependent on external funding or donor-driven.
  Many have used **innovative strategies for raising resources,**
  including membership fees, paid services, leveraging their own
  spaces, and financial and other resources, and contributions in
  kind (see, for instance, the Solidarity Fund for Kosovar Roma
  Refugees, home-based care provision by Kenyan women, self-
  supported Mothers Centers, Dalit women's pooled savings and
  Iranian women's completely self-resourced organising). This
  should not justify the declining priority among major donors for

movement-building approaches, but does indicate that women always find ways of supporting their movements. The question really is not whether movements can be built or survive without external resources, but what they might achieve if they were more richly resourced.

External action strategies

- **Challenging the dominant discourse and language** is a key strategy of the majority of these movements, but has been most critical to the work of the sex workers, disabled women, Dalit women, indigenous women, lesbian women, violence survivors, and mothers. Each of these struggles has attempted to challenge and change the way they themselves, their social role and their issues are depicted by external actors—be they academics, feminists, social activists, the government, the media—and the stereotypical images that grip the popular imagination. Typically, they have overturned public perceptions of these women as helpless victims, deviants, or vamps.

- One way in which this has been done is through **building alternate data and information** (especially through participatory research methods) to challenge mainstream images and analyses of their issues, and to engage policymakers in an informed way. But it has also been a means of mobilising and politicising their own constituents. These movements recognised and deployed the power of their own knowledge, and of engaging dominant knowledge systems on their own terms.

- All the movements in this volume have **built new linkages, relationships and alliances** to strengthen their power, influence and visibility, or gain access to new spaces and processes, gain political leverage, or protect themselves. For Iranian, Sudanese and Mexican indigenous women, for instance, international linkages were vital to protecting their leaders and voices, and to keeping their issues—and their repression—on the international stage. These linkages have also been made with other social movements, sensitising and educating their leaders, sometimes in ways that have helped to revive them—the Domestic Workers Alliance, for instance, helped put new vigor into the American Social Forum and the social movements of that region.

- However, along with building alliances, **challenging / engaging other movements** has been a key strategy for movements like those of disabled women and sex workers. The disabled women's case discusses this in detail, especially the impact of their marginalisation by both the women's movement and the male-dominated disabled people's movement. The sex workers case study analyses their long struggle to gain space within feminist movements in their region, as well as a recognition of their rights.

- The movement case studies are also replete with examples of the use of **policy advocacy, legal reform, and engagement with a range of formal and customary institutional actors.** This ranges from 'educating' local officials and government representatives to grasp their approaches and support, rather than obstruct, their work, to **legal advocacy. Engaging religious and customary institutions and leaders** has also been critical for many movements—lobbying, for instance, for the reform of religious laws and codes, or claiming non-traditional public roles was a vital strategy used by several of the movements (Iranian women, Roma women, Kenyan women, Sudanese women).

- **Mass actions of various kinds** are an obviously critical strategy used by several movements. Sometimes, this has involved **armed resistance** (as in the case of the Piqueteras and Indigenous Women) or **non-violent resistance** like protests, demonstrations, marches, etc. We could even include here the 'No Sex Without Condoms' campaign of the VAMP sex workers collective. The point is that women's movements can and do engage in very militant mass action.

- **Seizing spaces, mechanisms or control** usually exercised by other, more powerful actors is evident in several of the movement case studies. Some examples of this are the Piqueteras taking over factories abandoned by the 'bosses' and their male compatriots; the taking over of outreach and HIV awareness work (normally done by NGOs) with their clients and lovers by sex workers; seizing the right to recognition and reward from the state (the

Czech Mothers instituting a 'Family Friendly Prize' for city officials); and using religious gatherings and meetings to raise women's rights issues (Iranian women). And, of course, seeking election and formal political roles would also be included as part of this strategy.

The above is only a very brief and cursory summary of the hugely diverse and innovative strategies—both internal and external—that women's movements have developed in pursuit of their agendas and visions of change. The case studies themselves offer a much richer analysis of movement strategies.

Achievements and influence

The case studies presented an incredible range of achievements, and numerous spheres in which they have exercised influence on public attitudes, discourse about their issues, and on law, policy and practice. The multiplicity of these impacts are, in a sense, well articulated in the indigenous women's journey:

> The new spaces for participation, the multiple dialogues established with various social actors, and a new approach to the rights of women and the rights of indigenous peoples, have necessarily upset gender roles .... All these organizational spaces—whether independent or governmental—may be conceived of as spaces for the production of meaning, a process that has led indigenous women, intentionally or unintentionally, to reflect on their condition, thereby producing an interchange between gender, ethnicity, and social class.[10]
>
> ... [The] Discourse impacts on feminism and feminists: broadening the comprehension of how to relate gender identity to other identities, such as that of class and ethnicity; recognizing and understanding the resistance of many women to controversial themes in the feminist movement, such as sexuality; dismantling the view of indigenous women as a vulnerable group lacking the ability and power to bring about changes in their own condition; recognizing the need to create alliances with other social movements and to reflect on the role that men should

---

[10] Proyecto Colectivo,'Viejos y Nuevos Espacios de Poder: Mujeres Indígenas, Organización Colectiva y Resistencia Cotidiana'.

have in the struggle for gender equity; and recovering numerous forms of struggle and resistance that are innovative for the feminist movement, above all with a view to the construction of a broader social base, capable of becoming a counterweight to de facto power.

The case studies themselves reflect the impressive range of achievements of these movements, as does the analysis of their internal and external strategies. Nevertheless, the following is a brief review of their impact and influence thus far. The movements in the case studies have:

1. **Mobilised and organised impressive numbers of women** to challenge, resist and transform the socio-cultural, economic and political processes that have exploited, marginalised, excluded or violated their rights in different ways.
2. **Raised the affected women's political and personal consciousness,** and they now operate with an awareness of their rights, their own power and agency, enabling them to become primary actors and leaders in radical processes of social change.
3. **Challenged, advanced and reframed discourse**—such as, what are feminist issues, what is feminism, what is violence, what are the religiously sanctioned rights of women, how we understand the body, ability, new notions of peace, etc.
4. **Enhanced women's space, voice and visibility,** especially for groups that had little presence or influence before these movements began, and constituencies who were often neglected or excluded by even women's movements and other progressive social movements.
5. **Influenced and changed laws, policies and development paradigms,** reshaping labour laws and policies, challenging dominant interpretations of religious codes, ensuring family-friendly urban planning, self-help approaches to home-based care for the ill or childcare, women controlling and managing unemployment subsidies, approaches to customary land and natural resource rights, etc. At another level, policy processes like peace negotiations or the development of international norms on issues like disability and domestic work have been influenced and gendered in powerful ways.

6. **Improved access to justice for women,** not only formally, through courts, but also by transforming public perceptions of the nature of violence against women, and the invisibility of some forms of violence—such as the stigmatisation and legitimisation of violence against lesbian women, sex workers, disabled women, Dalit women and girls, or the subtle forms of violence inherent in the deprivation of inheritance rights and rights over children for women widowed by AIDS or wars and conflict.

7. **New bodies of information and knowledge**—the surveys, data collected and knowledge-building by some of these movements have challenged not only dominant/mainstream constructions, but even feminist understandings. Domestic work as labour, rethinking the role of family and traditional culture and practices, the high levels of militancy of the Piqueteras and their ability to generate jobs and increase production in businesses abandoned by entrepreneurs, the creation of a new framework linking sexuality, violence and poverty—the list of knowledge increments and transformations is impressive.

8. **Claimed and gained concrete new resources and assets for women,** including collective spaces like the Mothers Centers, inheritance rights and land and property for women widowed by AIDS, access to health and other services, especially for women with disability and sex workers, livelihoods and incomes, etc.

9. **Created new skills and capacities for women**—the range of leadership and other capacity and skill-building approaches of the movements has created an entirely new form of power and personal and collective capital for their members.

10. **Changes in customary practices and power relations**—the achievements of the Dalit, Roma, Kenyan, Sudanese and Indigenous women are all examples of how culture has been reclaimed, but also transformed in particular ways, and where real changes have occurred in resistant areas like caste-based or ethnic-based exclusion and discrimination.

11. **Issued challenges to and sensitised other social movements.** This is a key achievement of several of the movements, which have not only transformed (with some resistance) the larger male-

led movements of which they are a part, but also the movements with which they have allied themselves.

12. **Increased public awareness and sensitisation.** Many of the movements have, in the process of their mobilisation and action strategies, gained a high profile, media attention, and implicitly, some degree of sensitisation of public opinion to an alternative viewpoint on important issues like rape, sexual orientation, sex work, and the power and agency (rather than victimhood) of poor or marginalised women.

In conclusion

What are the stories of these movements trying to teach us? What is it, in essence, that these women's movements have accomplished to a remarkable degree, often under seemingly overwhelming odds? A simple but deeply profound answer is offered by Shirin Ebadi, 2004 winner of the Nobel Peace Prize and one of the champions and icons of the Iranian women's movement, who says:

> It's not just about hope and ideas, it's about action ... Our duty is to have a dream, but work everyday for reality.

Reading the experiences of the powerful and amazing movements in the case studies is both humbling and inspiring—they show us the dreams that inspired them, but also the hard everyday work it takes to change reality. In every case, a handful of strong, committed and politically conscious women began these feminist revolutions by saying 'Enough! This must change!' And they show that strong, committed and politically conscious women are everywhere, ready to mobilise and organise their sisters, challenge the status quo and powers that be—including their own brothers! They are ready to confront and resist violence and repression, and claim their place at the policy table as well as in other movements for social justice. The possibilities for change that these movements represent will hopefully inspire more of us to re-dedicate ourselves to building strong, vibrant feminist movements wherever we are located in the world!

References and suggested readings

Alvarez, Sonia. 1998. 'Advocating Feminism: the Latin American Feminist NGO "Boom"'. Available at http://www.mtholyoke.edu/acad/latam/schomburgmoreno/alvarez.html, 2 March.

Batliwala, Srilatha. 2011. *Feminist Leadership for Social Transformation: Clearing the Conceptual Cloud*. New Delhi: CREA. Available at http://web.creaworld.org/items.asp?CatID=1.

——. 1992. *Women's Empowerment in South Asia—Concepts and Practices'*. FAO/ ASPBAE.

Batliwala, Srilatha and L. David Brown (eds). 2006. *Transnational Civil Society: An Introduction*. Hartford CT: Kumarian Press.

——. 2006. 'Shaping the Global Human Project: The Nature and Impact of Transnational Civic Activism', in Srilatha Batliwala and L. David Brown (eds), *Transnational Civil Society: An Introduction*. Hartford CT: Kumarian Press.

Batliwala, Srilatha and Deepa Dhanraj. 2007. 'Gender myths that instrumentalize women: a view from the Indian front line', in Andrea Cornwall, Elizabeth Harrison and Ann Whitehead (eds), *Feminisms in Development: Contradictions, Contestations and Challenges*. London / New York: Zed Books.

Bunch, Charlotte, with Peggy Antrobus, Samantha Frost and Niamh Reilly. 2001. 'International Networking for Women's Human Rights', in Michael Edwards and John Gaventa (eds), *Global Citizen Action*. Boulder CO: Lynne Rienner Publishers.

Butler, Judith. 1990. *Gender Trouble: Feminism and the Subversion of Identity*. London: Routledge.

——. 2004, *Undoing Gender*. London: Routledge.

Carlsen, Laura. 1999. 'Las mujeres indígenas en el movimiento social', *Revista Chiapas*, 8.

Clark, Cindy, Annie Holmes, Lisa Veneklasen and Everjoice Win (eds), 2007. *Women Navigate Power—Stories About Claiming Our Rights*. London: Action Aid International.

Cornwall, Andrea, Elizabeth Harrison and Ann Whitehead (eds). 2007. *Feminisms in Development: Contradictions, Contestations and Challenges*. London / New York: Zed Books.

Crenshaw, Kimberlie. 1989. 'Demarginalizing the Intersection of Race and Sex: A Black Feminist Critique of Antidiscrimination Doctrine, Feminist Theory and Antiracist Politics', Lecture delivered at the University of Chicago.

Edwards, Michael and John Gaventa (eds). 2001. *Global Citizen Action*. Boulder CO: Lynne Rienner Publishers.

Kabeer, Naila. 1991. *Reversed Realities—Gender Hierarchies in Development*. London & New York: Verso.

Kerr, Joanna and Ellen Sprenger (eds). 2004. *The Future of Women's Rights: Global Visions and Strategies*. London / New York: Zed Books.

Meer, Shamim. 2007. 'In Search of Freedom: Thirty Years of Feminist Struggle in South Africa', in Cindy Clark, Annie Holmes, Lisa Veneklasen and Everjoice Win (eds), Women Navigate Power—Stories About Claiming Our Rights. London: Action Aid International.

Molyneux, Maxine and Shahra Razavi (eds). 2002. Gender Justice, Development and Rights. Oxford: Oxford University Press.

Rao, Aruna, David Kelleher and Rieky Stuart. 1999. Gender at Work—Organizational Change for Equality. Hartford CT: Kumarian Press.

Rao, Aruna and David Kelleher. 2002. 'Unravelling Institutionalized Gender Inequality', in Aruna Rao, David Kelleher and Rieky Stuart, Gender at Work. Hartford CT: Kumarian Press.

———. 2005. 'Is there life after gender mainstreaming?', Gender and Development, 13 (2): 57–69.

Raskin, Paul, Tariq Banuri, Gilberto Gallopin, Pablo Gutman, Al Hammond, Robert Kates, and Rob Swart. 2002. Great Transition: The Promise and Lure of the Times Ahead (Boston: Stockholm Environment Institute & Global Scenario Group).

Sen, Gita and Peggy Antrobus. 2006. 'The Personal is Global: The Project and Politics of the Transnational Women's Movement', in Srilatha Batliwala and L. David Brown (eds), Transnational Civil Society: An Introduction. Hartford CT: Kumarian Press.

Vance, Carole S. 1989. 'Social Construction Theory: Problems in the History of Sexuality', in A. van Kooten Nierkerk and T. Van Der Meer (eds), Homosexuality, Which Homosexuality? Amsterdam: An Dekker, pp. 13–34.

Veneklasen, Lisa and Valeria Miller. 2007. A New Weave of Power, People and Politics: An Action Guide for Advocacy and Citizen Participation. Sterling, VA: Stylus Publishing.

8. Clearing the Conceptual Cloud: Feminist Leadership for Social Transformation

Introduction

Over the past fifty years of development history, a series of abstract notions and concepts have entered the development lexicon and the vocabulary of activists. Many of them became widely used buzz-words and mantras long before they were defined or deconstructed—take, for example, concepts like 'participation', 'empowerment', 'civil society', 'movement', or 'rights-based approach'. In the world of feminism, women's rights and gender equality, terms like 'liberation', 'autonomy', 'women's empowerment' and 'gender mainstreaming' became widespread. The concept of *feminist leadership* has also been widely discussed, described and analysed. But the last thirty years of feminist experiments with building alternative organisational forms and leadership practices needs to be interrogated and theorised, particularly in light of the far deeper understanding of power and organisational behaviour that has emerged during this time.

This task assumes urgency, given the widespread use of terms like leadership and leaders, particularly in the context of social justice and women's empowerment; but even more because entire programmes of leadership development, or leadership building, have been framed and launched without adequately analysing the past decades of experience and struggle in creating feminist leadership practices, or re-framing our concepts with the advances made in fields like power analysis and organisational theory. Perhaps this is because leadership is one of those ideas that is considered self-evident, and hardly in need of explanation or deconstruction—or perhaps because it is one of those hard-to-define phenomena that is clearest when it is absent! Or because '… leadership is like the Abominable Snowman, whose footprints are everywhere but who is nowhere to be seen' (Bennis and Nanus 1997: 19).

This chapter is therefore an attempt to pull together existing definitions and concepts around leadership, view these through a feminist lens, place them in the context of social justice and feminist leadership, and then attempt to articulate a new and more rigorous conceptual framework for *feminist leadership*. Hopefully, this will help feminist organisations and capacity builders, as well as donors interested in advancing effective leadership by and for women (such as foundations and women's funds), to look more critically at our current leadership development approaches, and strengthen our practice in this vital arena.

Why does this matter?

Does conceptual clarity about leadership—especially feminist leadership—really matter? If we all know what it is, surely definitions are a matter of semantics? On the contrary, there is a very important reason to try to 'nail the jelly to the wall': if we cannot define and deconstruct leadership, especially the kind of feminist social justice leadership we are talking about, then we have no way of assessing the value or efficacy of the leadership development interventions in which we are engaged. As social justice organisations, women's organisations, capacity-building organisations and donors, we have all invested enormous energy, human resources, creativity and money in building leadership for social transformation. How do we know whether our models are building the kinds of leaders we need, and how do we measure their impact? How do we know what critical but hidden aspects of leadership our approaches are not addressing, and hence are failing to build the very alternative leadership that is their goal? And, most important of all, how do we integrate and advance our approaches by harvesting the learning from the last decades of feminist leadership experience in both organisations and movements around the world? None of these goals can be effectively achieved without clearing the conceptual cloud—without conceptualising the theory and practice of feminist leadership more clearly.

Another imperative for creating more clarity is that leadership is a *means*, not an end. We build leadership capacity and skills *for* something, *to do* something or *change* something, and not because leadership is a product or service for consumption. This is especially true in social justice contexts. Without understanding clearly the concept and practice of leadership for feminist social transformation, and how the two are related, we are walking down a blind alley. Worse, we are making assumptions about the links between the two that may or may not be valid.

Indeed, a critical analysis of the material on leadership development in the social justice context is rife with assumptions, although few of these are explicit. For example, there is a ubiquitous assumption that strong, coherent leadership—and strong, competent individual leaders—will inevitably strengthen and enhance the impact of social change organisations, interventions and movements. But there is documented evidence of social movements with highly dispersed and non-individualistic leadership that have achieved remarkable results—the Piqueteros and Piqueteras of Argentina, for example, or the campaign to ban landmines. So perhaps strong leadership is a useful, but insufficient condition for effective change.

Finally, we need greater clarity and a more analytical approach to leadership in order to distinguish between the different forms, models and styles of leadership, the diverse purposes to which it is applied, and the ideological frameworks that inform its practice. This is where we move beyond the descriptive—looking merely at what leadership *is*—towards the normative, which is concerned with what good leadership should be. This is critical in the context of *feminist* leadership, since our concern is not merely with capacitating more women to play leadership roles, but to lead differently, with feminist values and ideology, and to advance the agenda of feminist social transformation in a way that other forms of leadership do not and cannot. Such clarity would also enable us to build feminist leadership capacity in non-feminist women and men!

So, for all these reasons, it is time we confronted the ambiguity and at least attempted to deconstruct what leadership might mean to those of us committed to feminist social transformation.

Nailing the jelly to the wall:[1] defining abstract ideas

Defining and unpacking abstract ideas is a challenge, but not an impossible one. Over the past two decades, great strides have been made in deconstructing a number of abstract but vital social realities, and in finding ways to measure them. Perhaps the most historic was the concept of 'human development', pioneered by the late Mahbub ul Huq at the UNDP, as part of his struggle to counter the highly economistic approaches to development advanced by the Bretton Woods institutions. The Human Development Index (or HDI), for all its shortcomings, became a widely accepted proxy for the level of disparity / equity in a society. It has grown to be one of the most powerful advocacy tools in the world, and evidence that creating an accessible and dynamic, but not *simplistic*, measure of an abstraction like human development is very useful in the 'real' world.

Along similar lines, creative researchers and activists have developed frameworks for assessing such complex and abstract phenomena as world values (the World Values Survey—see www.worldvaluessurvey.org), corruption (Transparency International's Corruption Perception Index—see www.transparency.org), and democracy (Freedom House's Democracy surveys [www.freedomhouse.org] and the Polity project series—see www.systemicpeace.org/polity/polity4.htm). All these different methodologies have attempted to capture social and political phenomena through concrete indicators, since they reveal the inherent challenges involved in measuring and concretising abstract ideas that are experienced and seen in reality.

Finally, a plethora of feminist researchers and innovative thinkers have for decades developed frameworks and indicators for translating the reality of gender discrimination into manageable and compelling data and assessment tools—for example, we have frameworks for assessing the status of women, violence against women and gender disparities. Surely pinning down the concept of leadership for feminist social transformation is equally feasible!

---

[1] With grateful thanks to my friend and former Ford Foundation boss, Michael Edwards, who reminded me of this very useful phrase when he used it in his famous essay on civil society.

A study of all these different frameworks and measurement tools reveals that coming to grips with abstract ideas involves attempting to fix, with as much clarity and precision as possible, at least four key dimensions:

1. **What is it?** Defining the concept as clearly as we can;
2. **What is in it?** Unpacking the core components of the phenomenon;
3. **Where is it?** Locating the sites where the phenomenon occurs; and
4. **What does it look like?** Analysing the key characteristics of the phenomenon in practice.

This chapter will address these four questions. We hope the conceptual framework we present here will help you to look at how leadership works in your contexts, and understand the changes that need to be made to make it work as it should.

I. Defining leadership

[There are] almost as many definitions of leadership as there are persons who have attempted to define the concept.

Stogdill 1974: 259

Always, it seems, the concept of leadership eludes us or turns up in another form to taunt us again with its slipperiness and complexity. So we have invented an endless proliferation of terms to deal with it . . . and still the concept is not sufficiently defined.

Warren Bennis, 1959

These are unavoidable truisms. After sifting through literally hundreds of definitions, I found that they fall into two categories: definitions of *leader/s*, which mainly focus on the attributes and practices of effective leaders, and definitions of *leadership*, as a process and a practice. These definitions come largely from the management and organisational development fields. I also found that in the recent past, the 'feminine style of leadership' has become popular in the corporate world, as larger numbers of women entered companies and began to demonstrate that they could produce results and profits through different means from the testosterone-driven male style the 'boys' had used (competitiveness, aggression, etc.). And while some of these essentialise women and seem to build on gender stereotypes about women's ways of working and dealing with others, they do recognise indirectly that gender construction processes result in women negotiating interpersonal and collective processes differently, and possibly more effectively.

Boxes 8.1 and 8.2 provide a selection of mainstream definitions of leaders, and some provocative and interesting definitions of leadership; they help to get us thinking about the content and characteristics of leaders and leadership more generally, and about how these diverge or converge with feminist definitions. Reviewing these definitions, it is striking that the vast majority are of Northern/ Western origin, barring the ones from Chinese philosopher Lao Tse, and that they are overwhelmingly male. Most recent scholarship on leadership and leadership development also comes out of management schools and management research, and hence tends to focus on the accomplishment of corporate goals and the effective management of organisations and systems. The definitions of 'feminine leadership' recognise that women bring different qualities to leadership, with greater attention to collaboration, cooperation, collective decision-making, and, above all, relationship-building. But these come hazardously close to essentialising women (and axiomatically, men too!) and playing into long-standing gender stereotypes, even if unintentionally.

These definitions also reveal some common threads, viz.:

- The individual as leader, and the leader as (usually) a man.
- The leader as hero, and leadership as heroism.
- The leader as decision-maker.
- The leader as an embodiment of character and integrity.
- The leader as a provider of vision, mission, goals and strategy for the enterprise, and motivating others to share those goals.
- The capacity to influence, inspire and motivate others, directing others' behaviour and actions.

A composite of these core ideas would yield a definition of leadership along these lines:

Box 8.1
Definitions of Leaders

As for the best leaders, the people do not notice their existence. The next best, the people honor and praise. The next, the people fear; the next, the people hate.

The superior leader gets things done with very little motion. He imparts instruction not through many words but through a few deeds. He keeps informed about everything but interferes hardly at all. He is a catalyst, and though things would not get done well if he weren't there, when they succeed he takes no credit. And because he takes no credit, credit never leaves him.

Lao Tse, 604–531 BC, in *Tao Te Ching*

The first job of a leader is to define a vision for the organization …. Leadership is the capacity to translate vision into reality.

Warren Bennis

Be willing to make decisions. That's the most important quality in a good leader.

General George S. Patton Jr.

Managers have subordinates—leaders have followers.

Murray Johannsen

If your actions inspire others to dream more, learn more, do more and become more, you are a leader.

John Quincy Adams

A leader takes people where they want to go. A great leader takes people where they don't necessarily want to go, but ought to be.

Rosalynn Carter

I am looking for a lot of men who have an infinite capacity to not know what can't be done.

Henry Ford

… a set of actions and processes, performed by individuals of character, knowledge and integrity, who have the capacity to create a vision for change, inspire and motivate others to share that vision, develop ideas and strategies that direct and enable others to work towards that change, and make critical decisions that ensure the achievement of the goal.

Box 8.2
Definitions of Leadership

Leadership is an intangible quality with no clear definition. That's probably a good thing, because if the people who were being led knew the definition, they would hunt down their leaders and kill them.

Scott Adams, *The Dilbert Principle*

Leadership revolves around vision, ideas, direction, and has more to do with inspiring people as to direction and goals than with day-to-day implementation. A leader must be able to leverage more than his own capabilities. He must be capable of inspiring other people to do things without actually sitting on top of them with a checklist...
Leadership is a function of knowing yourself, having a vision that is well communicated, building trust among colleagues, and taking effective action to realize your own leadership potential.

Warren Bennis

Leadership is a combination of strategy and character. If you must be without one, be without the strategy.

Gen. H. Norman Schwarzkopf

Leadership is not a person or a position. It is a complex moral relationship between people, based on trust, obligation, commitment, emotion, and a shared vision of the good.

Joanne Ciulla

Leadership is a process of giving purpose (meaningful direction) to collective effort, and causing willing effort to be expended to achieve [that] purpose.

Jacobs and Jaques

Leadership is influence—nothing more, nothing less.

John Maxwell

Leadership is about articulating visions, embodying values, and creating the environment within which things can be accomplished.

Richards and Engle

One of the hardest tasks of leadership is understanding that you are not what you are, but what you're perceived to be by others.

Edward L. Flom

If you want to build a ship, don't drum up the men to gather wood, divide the work and give orders. Instead, teach them to yearn for the vast and endless sea.

Antoine de St. Exupery

The obvious lacuna in this definition is the absence of any politics, context, or vision about the nature of the 'change' that leadership seeks to bring, as though the *purpose* of leadership does not alter its *nature*. This is the gap that sociologist James V. Downton filled when he articulated the concept of *transformational leadership* (1973), a style of leadership 'where one or more persons engage with others in such a way that leaders and followers raise one another to higher levels of motivation and morality'. James MacGregor Burns, a political scientist, scholar of political leadership and American presidential biographer, further developed Downton's work (MacGregor Burns 1978), and their ideas have some resonance with the emerging thinking on feminist leadership.

Burns contrasted Downton's concept of transformational leadership with *transactional leadership*, which accepts the goals, culture and structure of the existing organisation or enterprise, and is essentially based on conventional motivation, reward, punishment and compliance; change is achieved incrementally, and the motivators are *extrinsic*. In contrast,

> Transforming leadership ... occurs when one or more persons engage with others in such a way that leaders and followers raise one another to higher levels of motivation and morality. Their purposes, which might have started out as separate but related, as in the case of transactional leadership, become fused. Power bases are linked not as counterweights but as mutual support for common purpose .... transforming leadership ultimately becomes moral in that it raises the level of human conduct and ethical aspiration of both leader and led, and thus it has a transforming effect on both (MacGregor Burns 1978: 20).

While feminists would question the use of terms like 'moral' and 'morality', and even of 'leader and led', these advances in thinking on leadership models help us to recognise how, depending on cultural context and history, dominant models and practices of leadership are deeply embedded within us, even if we are feminist women— and men—seeking to change our own practice. One recent and useful analysis of how gender, feminism and leadership come together and affect one another also helps us to place these various definitions in a feminist perspective. In the volume *Women and Leadership* (Lau

Chin et al. 2007), Bernice Lott's introduction offers us three insights into the prevailing approaches to leadership and women:

- That mainstream research and theorisation only engages with the *'feminine'*—not *feminist*—style of leadership;
- Even works *devoted to women's leadership* do not address or discuss feminist leadership; and
- The *attributes of feminine leadership styles are all within the accepted gendered roles of women*, that is, nurturing, caring, sensitive, cooperative, consultative, inclusive, etc. (Chin et al. 2007: 24–27).

The definitions of 'feminine leadership' given in Box 8.3 illustrate Lott's points quite clearly.

Lott asserts that it is critical to make a distinction between feminine and feminist leadership, since the former does not engage with gender power and women's lack of access to formal positions of authority. She proposes, very sensibly, that both terms— 'feminism' and 'feminist'—have to be understood more clearly before clarity can be achieved on feminist leadership. So let us turn now to how feminists have defined and understood the notion of leadership.

Defining feminist leadership

The search for definitions of feminist leadership is more challenging than one would imagine.[2] As a feminist labour scholar recently wrote, 'The exact term "feminist leadership" proved to be scarce in the literature that discusses women in leadership positions' (Mitchell 2004: 2). Indeed, I found the results of my early web-based research equally disappointing. Others who have worked consistently on unearthing definitions, ideas and information about feminist leadership find that while some data exists about feminist leadership in different domains (in grassroots groups, community work, business

---

[2] The dilemma was captured in the plaintive plea of a Canadian graduate student I found during my web research: 'I have to do a term paper on feminist leadership and I can't find a single definition—can someone help?'

Box 8.3
Definitions of 'Feminine' Leadership

.... feminine leadership is the key to transforming organizations, communities and us. Long-term change has to happen in a new model where values such as integrity, compassion, listening, receiving and a win-win approach to negotiation play key roles. Feminine Leadership inspires authenticity, caring and sharing, a new leadership style and feminine ways of doing business.

www.feminine-leadership.com

The feminine leadership style emphasizes cooperation over competition; intuition as well as rational thinking in problem solving, team structures where power and influence are shared within the group ... interpersonal competence; and participative decision making.

Marilyn Loden (1985)

Feminine leadership is a social demand coming from the economic world. The McKinsey Quarterly report claims that feminine talent in organizations has competitive value, it's not about 'best practice'. The statistics of the report show the necessity of incorporating feminine values and talents for the companies to be more competitive and innovative. Many European female Directors are setting standards to incorporate feminine talent that otherwise would be lost to society and to the economies of their countries. The egalitarian presence of women's positions in the organizations is an indicator of progress and the opposite is perceived as an indicator of social delay.

European Union, European Directive 2004/113/EC, 2004

... Feminine Leadership is a new social paradigm that allows the emergence of the feminine talent ... Feminine leadership is a social commitment, not a tendency for women only. It represents a new paradigm, answering many of the questions that are being posed in this historic moment.

www.literagofemenino.com, Universitat Pompeu Fabra, Barcelona

The 'feminine leadership' style, characterized by cooperation, participation, sharing of power and information, teamwork, energizing others, enhancing self-worth of others, etc., is a leadership style of the future.

Nina Poloski

Sacred feminine leadership is not about women taking over control from men. It is not about replacing patriarchal hierarchy with matriarchal hierarchy. It's not about passivity. Rather, it is about contributing sacred feminine attributes [unconditional love, being, holding space, serving, facilitating, allowing] to the human psyche, so that the doing and the being, the outer and the inner, are balanced. And, while it may be generally easier for women to contribute sacred femininity and men to contribute sacred masculinity [doing, achieving, analyzing], a dynamic balance within each person is what is actually required.

Carol Hiltner

management and teaching), it has not been fully explored or developed as a feminist construct.

This does not mean that feminists have not interrogated and analysed leadership as a concept and practice, or that it has not occupied an important place in feminist debates in different parts of the world. On the contrary, our research reveals that since the dawn of early modern—or 'Second Wave'—feminism in the 1970s and 1980s, feminist thinkers and activists have addressed the question of leadership very actively (Hartmann 1999),[3] believing that '... leadership is a crucial make or break issue for feminism' (*Quest* 1974).

Much of the early feminist work on leadership emerged from North American feminists, and occurred within larger discussions of power and of alternative, non-patriarchal, non-hierarchical structures and organisations (see, for instance, Bunch and Fisher 1976). Southern feminists were perhaps less focused on leadership *per se* at this time, but equally engaged in experiments with alternative structures and processes, and with deep analyses of the gendered nature of power in the social, economic and political realms. And in both the North and the South, there was widespread research and analysis of women's exclusion from power and authority in the public realm, with accompanying advocacy campaigns to increase women's access to political power, and for greater representation of women in leadership positions in government, business and civil society.

Consequently, feminist approaches towards and definitions of leadership were often indirect products of their struggles to examine their own relationship to and practice of power, to advance gender equality in positions of power in the public and private sectors, and to create feminist structures that would not reproduce the patriarchal models that dominated most societies and cultures. There was a very vibrant search for theory and practice in alternative ways of using and applying power, new, non-hierarchical organisational forms, and thus, new ways of leading.

---

[3] Early feminist journals like *Quest: A Feminist Quarterly*, carried discussions of feminism's intersections with leadership from as early as 1976; the writings of Crater 1976; Masterson 1976; and St. Joan 1976 provide interesting glimpses into early Western feminist thinking on leadership issues.

Unfortunately, much of this earlier feminist analysis is invisible to us because it is not available online or in management or scholarly social science journals—it is located in the libraries of universities or independent women's studies centres, in unpublished reports of meetings, or in individual women's personal archives of the debates and discussions around the subject in the 1970s and 1980s. The definitions given in Box 8.4, therefore, have been culled from both online and offline source material, spanning at least thirty years of feminist thinking about leadership.

Several important factors must be borne in mind when we examine these [and other] definitions of feminist leadership.

The above definitions are by no means a comprehensive or representative sample of the full diversity of feminist thinking. We cannot homogenise the feminist discourse—and hence definitions— of leadership, as though there was one single global conversation about it. In fact, there were debates and experiments all over the world, on every continent, with new forms of organisations, movements, and leadership structures and practices, with marked differences in concerns and frameworks. In the South Asian context, for instance, the 1980s and early 1990s saw a much stronger focus on transforming gender power relations through building collective power, and far less on leadership, which became either a given, or an invisible element that did not receive much emphasis (see, for instance, Kumar 1993; Shah and Gandhi 1990). Having been much involved in these debates and activism, I cannot recall, for instance, any 'leadership building' courses for Indian women in the 1980s or 1990s—but plenty of 'awareness building' and 'empowerment' programmes and interventions. Also, there was greater concern with creating *collective leadership* models, rather than individual 'heroines'[4] who would inevitably succumb to the politics of domination and control.

There were also contestations and resistance from the grassroots, Black, indigenous, Southern, and otherwise marginalised voices, to the definitions and approaches of what they considered mainstream,

---

[4] An ironic term used by many of us in India in the 1980s to signal our criticism of the single-leader model of leadership.

Box 8.4
Definitions of Feminist Leadership

Leadership from a feminist standpoint is informed by the power of the feminist lens, which enables the feminist leader to identify injustices and oppressions and inspires her to facilitate the development of more inclusive, holistic ... communities. Feminist leaders are motivated by fairness, justice, and equity and strive to keep issues of gender, race, social class, sexual orientation, and ability at the forefront .... The elements particular to a feminist leadership construction include a focus on both individual or micro-level and societal or macro-level social justice concerns, a desire to bring marginalized voices to the center of the conversation, and a willingness to take risks as one strives to enact a transformative agenda.

Tracy Barton (2006)

... feminist ... leadership is ... women and women's organizations sharing power, authority and decision-making in our common pursuit of social, legal, political, economic and cultural equality.

DAWN Ontario (http://dawn.thot.net/feminism11.html)

[S]ociety has tended to mystify leadership skills as somehow belonging only to a few people who are then seen as better than everybody else. But if we view leadership skills as something that many people have to varying degrees—skills that can be built upon, supported, and enhanced because they are needed in the world, not in order to make one person superior—then we might have a better way of dealing with leadership.

Charlotte Bunch (Institute for Women's Leadership 2002: 16)

We are not interested ... in leadership for leadership's sake. We are interested in bringing women's talents to bear, along with men's, in addressing major social, political, and economic concerns.

Mary S. Hartmann (Institute for Women's Leadership 2000: 9)

[T]he question is not whether we should have leaders, but how we develop all women as leaders .... Leadership as a function of growth is also, then, the process of building confidence, not only so that others will follow, but also so that others will attempt leadership themselves ... it is especially important that leadership be considered a form of stewardship.

Flora Crater (1976)

If you want to do something big, it's not just you. You have to have people with you who see the common goal or objective. I think the most important thing in taking initiatives is to make people part of it so that all of them will feel that they are responsible .... If you work to make something grow and to share the results with others, then the thing in itself has a life .... So I understand that leadership

is related to the possibility of creating solid initiatives that last. You can go away, and the structures or whatever you have created remain, they are there.
Jacqueline Pitanguy (Hartman 1999: 167)

There is a difference between women's leadership and feminist leadership, because the latter has a particular political standpoint. Nevertheless, it is important to increase the number of women in leadership, period, regardless of their politics .... Studies have shown that women tend to lead more inclusively. They have been peace-makers and reached across ethnic lines. Leaders are born in part, but leaders must be fostered; many people get discouraged from trying to be leaders. Women have led a lot, but their leadership is not recognized.
Charlotte Bunch (Institute for Women's Leadership 2002)

[In building Feminist Leadership] I saw the need to work at two levels: first, building women's self-esteem in order to strengthen their leadership, and second, giving women the skills, resources, and access to decision making which would enable them to have more power to make a difference in their own communities. In other words, leadership for change.
Peggy Antrobus (1999)

Transformational leadership is leadership concerned with causing social change; feminist transformational leadership is concerned with achieving gender justice. For any kind of feminist transformational leadership, leaders need to undergo a process of personal transformation, consciousness-raising, and internalization of feminism.
Peggy Antrobus (2000)

Patriarchy, reflected through all the structures and institutions of our world, is a system that glorifies domination, control, violence, competitiveness and greed. It dehumanizes men as much as it denies women their humanity. So we need leadership that will explore and expose these links and challenge patriarchy. The only leadership that does this is feminist leadership.
Peggy Antrobus (2002)

Words like 'sacrifice', 'altruism' do not settle well with many feminists because these qualities have been abused by society .... My argument is that we can make ourselves powerful by celebrating our very own strengths and not letting it be judged by the normative values of the male world .... Why not suggest that leaders are those who can lead communities to well being and peaceful living? Leaders are those who make sacrifices, who are altruistic and look after others? .... Unless we do that, and raise our own consciousness of the quality and content of feminist leadership, putting ourselves in the place of men in a male driven and designed political and cultural space is really quite pointless if not invalid.
Devaki Jain (1995)

[G]ood leadership—leadership that serves both women and men, poor and rich, and the powerless and powerful—is inclusive, participatory and horizontal ... leadership should be about capitalizing on the ideas and skills of as many individuals as possible .... A good leader is also conscious that the processes— the means by which she carries out her objectives—are just as important as the objectives themselves.

Afkhami et al. (2001)

In modern leadership theory, the leader plays [a] star role (takes the lead, becomes the head), all others become bit players, supporting characters, and extras in the play, the theatrics of leadership. Modern leadership is by definition hierarchical, male and phallic spectacle. Feminist leadership is more circular, bottom up and less male.

David M. Boje (2000)

To create something that replaces and surpasses you, that has a life of its own because there are many people who will be drawn into it and who will give leadership to it as a group, even. The point is that wherever we are as women, wherever we are situated in our lives, we can advance a feminist agenda if we stop thinking about how to be leaders and think rather about how to be doers, how to be agents if you move on or go away. To me, that has always been the measure of leadership.

Gerda Lerner (1995)

Feminist leadership [is] oriented to a different arrangement of the human order: re-distribution of power and re-distribution of responsibilities. Fighting societal inequalities. Changing economic and social structures, beginning with transformation of psychic structures. Bridging personal freedom with collective freedom. Aiming at cooperation instead of competition .... In feminist leadership equality, mutuality and absence of sex role behavior should be visible. Feminist leadership should promote (or even rehabilitate) emotionality and the values of relationships. Feminist leadership renounces external paraphernalia of power and their influence.

Admira Toolkit (http://www.zenska-mreza.hr/prirucnik/en/ en_read_management_leadership_8.htm; accessed 10 October 2008)

Some people claim that feminist leadership and good leadership are synonyms. In a sense it is, as long as the beholder also claims that feminism, considered as a set of values, is THE *good set of values .... Others think that feminist leadership is a kind of contradiction in terms, feminism being contrary to power and feminist equality contrary to leadership itself .... On behalf of the subject we renounce both positions, and define feminist leadership as leadership congruent with feminist principles.* (emphasis mine)

Admira Toolkit (n.d.: http://www.zenska-mreza.hr/prirucnik/en/ en_read_management_leadership_8.htm) privileged, elite feminists. Albino and Caldwell-Colbert (2007) are among the feminist leadership scholars who address the issue of how women's social diversity influenced the feminist construction of leadership:

> The distribution of power and seeking egalitarian relationships are complex goals of feminism that necessitate that we attend not only to gender, but also to other systemic forms of oppression and privilege. The inclusion of varied life experiences and literature reflecting the impact of ethnicity, race, class and gender are especially important in our constructing feminist leadership and considering its practical enactment.

Much of this rich diversity of debate and innovation remains hidden or inaccessible to a work like this document because of language barriers,[5] blinding us, for instance, to the powerful critiques and conceptualisations of Latin American feminists, or to the rich discussions and debates that were not recorded or documented; or if they were, because they are not available online or in some set of identifiable institutions or archives. These factors have inevitably biased the discussion in favour of the recorded and largely 'online' history of feminist thought on leadership in the English language, and consequently, towards the work of Western/Northern feminists and feminist knowledge centres that worked in English.[6]

Bearing these qualifications in mind, let us focus on several important features of the definitions:

- It is striking that many of them are descriptions of *a set of attributes and behaviours, values and practices.* They are often constituted of adjectives and verbs like inclusive, participatory, collaborative, nurturing, empowering, consensus building,

---

[5] For example, the huge body of Latin American discourse on the subject, which is in Spanish or Portuguese, or the thinking of non-Anglophone European feminists, which is available only in German, French, or Spanish.

[6] Much of what is presented below is the result of CREA's research at the Center for Women's Global Leadership at Rutger's University, the first international feminist centre to focus on the theory and practice of feminist leadership, and to dedicate itself to the development of feminist leadership in women's movements worldwide.

valuing and respecting others, and valuing growth and development.

- But more importantly, we see that the definitions deal with *power and politics,* dimensions that are almost invisible in the mainstream definitions of leadership, even feminine leadership.
- Some of the definitions also hint at the critical issue of *feminists' own use and practice of power when they occupy leadership positions.* This is a very sticky and uncomfortable point, but one that has become increasingly central to the challenges that feminist organisations are dealing with today, especially in the context of sustaining their organisations and movements, and in making way for young women's voices and leadership.

Drawing upon these richly layered interpretations, a composite definition of feminist leadership would be something like this:

> Women with a feminist perspective and vision of social justice, individually and collectively transforming themselves to use their power, resources and skills in non-oppressive, inclusive structures and processes to mobilise others—especially other women—around a shared agenda of social, cultural, economic and political transformation that ensures equality, peace, justice and human rights for all.

II. What's in It? Unpacking Feminist Leadership

Unpacking the content of feminist leadership would not be possible without the pioneering and innovative leadership development work of feminist women's organisations and capacity builders around the world. We are indebted to a long list of trailblazers in this field: The Center for Women's Global Leadership (CWGL); Development Alternatives for Women in a New Era (DAWN); Women's Learning Partnership (WLP); Just Associates; Gender at Work; International Women's Rights Action Watch (Asia Pacific); GROOTS International; MADRE; ADMIRA; The Disabled Women's Network (DAWN) Ontario; the Forum of Women's NGOs in Central Asia; and CREA (Creating Resources for Empowerment in Action). In addition, several women's movements around the world have taught us a great deal with their approach to broadening, deepening and democratising their leadership base, and these insights have informed and enriched the analysis in this section. For example, movements such as the Domestic Workers Alliance of the USA, the Mothers Centers of Western and Eastern Europe, the indigenous women's movements of Latin and Meso America, the One in Nine Campaign, the disabled women's movements, the Iranian women's movement, and several others have done innovative work in building truly feminist approaches to leadership.[7]

Based on our analysis of these and other feminist definitions and thinking on leadership, and feminist leadership capacity building programmes and strategies, it is clear that feminist leadership for social transformation contains four essential components, which might be termed the 'Four Ps', viz.:

1. Power
2. Principles / values
3. Politics / purpose
4. Practices

It will be useful to explain and examine the content of each of these components, particularly in relation to the leadership development modules and approaches that are widely in use today.

1. Power

Leadership is first and foremost about power—it is about holding power, exercising power, and changing the distribution and relations of power, in multiple forms and settings. Feminist leadership means functioning with a greater consciousness not only of others', but of one's own power, while intentionally moving away from the way leadership and power have intersected in mainstream organisations and structures, and from feminists' ambivalent historical relationship with power. The DAWN Ontario framework on feminist leadership analyses the challenge thus:

---

[7] For more information on the leadership development approaches of these movements, see the case studies of these movements, downloadable in English, French and Spanish at http://awid.org/library/changing-their-world2.

Within feminist organizations, leaders work from a vision of shared power, providing opportunities for all members to develop and use their leadership skills. This idea may feel unfamiliar at first, as we often think of leaders in the traditional sense: a handful of people with high-ranking positions who have claimed the most power within their organization. Power is not shared in these structures, because being successful means always competing to be 'number one'.

It is not surprising, therefore, that a number of feminist leadership development programmes prioritise power analysis in their curricula, enabling participants to deconstruct and examine the different forms and ways in which power operates in the social context. Unfortunately, most of the other leadership development programmes aimed at social change activists—including women activists—tend to take a more instrumental and managerial approach, placing greater emphasis on mechanical management and resource mobilisation skills, but barely touching upon the fundamental concepts and dynamics of power. However, even feminist leadership programmes rarely address the internal power dynamics of women's organisations and movements. These are serious omissions, since the most overriding goal of feminist leadership is not creating well-managed organisations that maintain the social status quo; rather, they work to transform the relations of power in society, and to create alternate models of power within their own structures. Consequently, it will be useful to focus this section on strengthening our own understanding of power, and the different ways in which it operates within and between individuals, groups and systems.

Dimensions of power in leadership

Veneklasen and Miller—two practitioner-scholars who have greatly advanced our understanding of power from a feminist perspective—provide an enormously helpful starting point by identifying the three realms in which power operates (2002: 51):

- **the public** (where it is visible, such as the power of the government, military, police, judiciary, corporations, etc.);
- **the private** (within institutions like the family, clan, ethnic

group, or in marriage, friendships, and other relationships); and
- *the intimate* (the power—or powerlessness—that we feel within ourselves, expressed usually in terms of self-confidence, self-esteem, control over our bodies, etc.).

This framework takes the first feminist step of acknowledging, naming and analysing two important spheres of power that affect women's lives deeply: the private and the intimate. Even more importantly, this helps us to recognise the vital issue of the power within us, thus drawing upon feminist notions of the *agency* that even the most seemingly powerless and marginalised women have. Recognising the intimate realm of power means we are not empty vessels tossed around by the forces of power operating *upon* us, but that we possess power too, although we often do not recognise this, or use it negatively or reactively, to resist or subvert the forces acting on us. This is an important idea to hang on to as we begin to tackle the dimension of power in feminist leadership.

Veneklasen and Miller also talk about the 'three faces of power', which they identify as *visible, hidden* and *invisible* (2002: 46–48)—these closely intersect with other power frameworks that identify *direct, indirect* and *agenda-setting power* (Foucault 1976; Gaventa and Cornwall 2001; Lukes 2005). Since these forms of power play a critical role in sustaining patriarchal privilege and subordinating women, it is vital to unpack and understand them clearly:[8]

- *Visible power* is the one we are most familiar with, and have all experienced. It determines who participates—and who is excluded from—decision-making in the public realm; decisions, for instance, about what a country's development priorities should be, or how the village council's budget will be spent. Visible power is held by political leaders (elected or not!), the police, military and the judiciary; it is also held by the heads of multinational corporations, of clans and tribes, of social

---

[8] I would like to thank Jethro Petit of the Governance and Participation Unit, Institute for Development Studies, Sussex, UK, and Just Associates 'Power of Movement' workshop in December 2009 for contributing greatly to my own clarity on power.

movement organisations like trade unions, or in the leadership of NGOs and women's organisations. **Direct power** is similar, although it operates in both the private and the public realms, and determines how power, privilege and opportunity are allocated, and who is given the authority to control resources, other people, or access to knowledge and information. A good example of this for women is the direct power held by male heads of households, and the gender division of labour and decision-making power, which dictates that women will perform certain household and production tasks that are critical for household survival, but will not have the right to equal wages, control over their income, inheritance rights, or even control over their bodies in terms of their mobility, relationships, sexual expression, or reproduction. Visible or direct power also explains phenomena like son preference, or how the interests of powerful economic and social groups (by virtue of their assets / wealth, position, gender, race, class, ethnicity, or caste, for instance) are able to dominate political systems, at the cost of poorer people.

- **Hidden power**—sometimes called **agenda-setting power**—is about who influences or sets the agenda *behind the scenes*, and the barriers and biases that determine which issues can be addressed, whose voices are heard, or who is consulted on a particular issue. Again, hidden or agenda-setting power operates in both the private and the public realms. In the public realm, for instance, we see hidden power operate when violence against women in conflict is not considered as critical an issue as the loss of territory or military personnel. Hidden power is also evident in the nexus between political leaders and fundamentalist lobbies with whom they have close, but covert, links, so that the latter are able to influence political decisions and policies—such as changes in school curricula, or laws governing reproductive rights—without any visible power or legitimacy. Within families, we also see how 'good women'—those dutifully carrying out the patriarchal agenda and protecting male privilege—often enjoy behind-the-scenes power to influence male decision-makers, without any formal authority.

- **Invisible power**—or **indirect power**—is in many ways the most insidious and problematic of all to challenge and confront, because it is the capacity to shape people's self-image, self-esteem, social attitudes and biases, without there seeming any apparent role in doing so. The media and marketing / advertising industries are classic purveyors of such invisible power. The media exercises invisible power by constantly making choices about what issues to highlight and what to ignore, and by constructing images and shaping meaning in lasting ways. Everyday's television news, for instance, is instilling in us a sense of what the most important issues of the day are—but what they ignore and do not cover in the news is equally significant. These decisions are also deeply gendered, as many feminist analysts have pointed out (see Joseph and Sharma 2006 [1994]). By making some issues visible and others invisible, they shape our sense of social, economic and political priorities in profound ways, which we ourselves are barely aware of! To understand the power of the media, we have only to consider the widely held image of the man-hating, family-breaking, hard-as-nails, promiscuous feminist. Most people have never met this creature in real life because she doesn't exist— she is a media creation, but one that has taken such a powerful hold of people's imaginations everywhere, that few women who believe in gender equality and women's rights are willing to call themselves feminists! Similarly, the advertising industry exercises invisible power by shaping meaning and creating new norms about what is good, desirable, positive, or bad, regressive, negative—the almost universal desire for fair skin and thin bodies among Southern women, for instance, which in turn affects their sense of self-worth, is testimony to the invisible power of these forces.

These facets of power remind us that while leadership is primarily associated with decision-making power, it is about much more than that. As Devaki Jain argued over a decade ago,

> Leadership as a concept is much stronger than and different from the concept of decision-making. Participation in decision-making does not necessarily include, or address, the power hierarchy. One could be part of a decision-making process and not be powerful enough to influence

that decision. Leadership, on the other hand, has a hierarchical significance. The demand from everywhere, whether from women, the Platform for Action in Beijing, or the Human Development Report, is for participation, for fixed shares in decision-making. That is not enough. To make effective demands for change, there is a case for the feminist movement to claim leadership and claim it because of its ethics and not only its gender (1996: 7).

At the highest level, therefore, the goal of feminist leadership is two-fold:

1. To challenge visible, hidden and invisible power wherever it operates, and especially where it constructs and reinforces women's subordination in both gross and subtle ways, or furthers discrimination against women; and

2. To construct alternative models that amplify visible, direct forms of power to the maximum extent possible, and gradually eliminate—or at least minimise—invisible and hidden power. In other words, *feminist leadership will strive to make the practice of power visible, democratic, legitimate and accountable, at all levels, and in both private and public realms.*

Let us now look more closely at power within leadership roles. Here, it is useful to first make a distinction between the *intrinsic* and *extrinsic* power of leadership, mirroring feminism's long-standing slogan that the personal is political.

- *Intrinsic power—or intimate power—*is the force of the personality traits, charisma, talents, capabilities, knowledge, and experience that the individual leader has, which have been acquired through the circumstances of her life, and are hence unique to her. This could also be termed the role of the SELF, of our psychic structures, experiences and attributes in a leadership role. Recognising that we bring both negative and positive qualities, and a willingness to examine and address our negative traits are vital components in feminist leadership, since by tackling the personal effectively, we are also enabling ourselves to better tackle the political goals of equality, human rights and justice.

- **Extrinsic power,** or the authority that comes to a feminist leader from outside herself, includes
  a. the **assigned authority** she is given by others (for example, a board of directors or trustees, the people who elected her the leader, etc.);
  b. the **positional authority** that her leadership role gives her (hiring, firing, managing people and finances, representing, raising resources, making strategic decisions, etc.);
  c. the **earned authority** that she gains by using her assigned and positional authority carefully and fairly, by sharing her power with others, by acting inclusively, and because of the personal attributes, experience and skills—or **intrinsic power**—that she brings to her role. There is a lot of evidence showing that the best feminist leaders are those who convert their assigned authority into earned authority in a short space of time, so that their leadership is supported by all those engaged in the enterprise with them, and not just by a set of external actors!

At the organisational or movement building level, feminist leadership must also wrestle with five key **expressions of power** attendant in such processes (Rowlands 1997; Veneklasen with Miller 2002):

- **Power to**—refers to the agency and capacity to act that leadership must leverage, within itself and in others, to create change. It is about the strategic skills, experience, insight, etc., that can be marshalled and mobilised towards the transformative agenda that has been adopted. *Power to* is the recognition of what we, the change makers, bring to the table—the *intrinsic* power described above.
- **Power over**—derives from direct power and positional / assigned authority, the control (direct or indirect) over human and other resources within the process, and the way such control can very quickly slip into domination; also control over the use and deployment of resources, decision-making, etc.;
- **Power with**—the effective empowerment and enabling of all those engaged in the transformative process to create solidarity,

mutual support systems, safety nets, etc. (This is the power that tests whether leaders are acting as individual heroes / heroines with followers, or as initiators and sustainers of collective processes of change with a number of fellow-travellers);

- **Power within**—this is often the source of the sustainability of feminist organisations and movements, since this relates to intrinsic power, but also to the capacity to regenerate oneself and one's strategies in response to the challenges and reversals that feminist change processes inevitably unleash. The power within also includes, in Naila Kabeer's classic term, those 'intangible resources' (1994)—such as knowledge, access to information, influence, contacts, etc.—that can be leveraged for the cause or organisation, and make up a distinct characteristic of leadership; and

- **Power under**—in many ways, this is the most complex but pervasive expression of power in women's organisations, and helps us to understand why people who have experienced abuse, oppression and trauma often become abusive, authoritarian and oppressive themselves when they gain power (especially power to and power over). Steven Wineman, a psychologist, developed this concept as a result of his work on survivors of conflict, trauma and violence. He posits that *power under* emerges from *powerless rage*, which unleashes both the destructive power of sabotage and subversion that is often unconsciously deployed by those who have experienced severe oppression or trauma, and the constructive power to confront and overcome injustice (2003: 47–118). Internally, survivors of trauma and violence find it difficult to transit from being objects / victims of oppression to subjects and agents of change; they are unable to hold and exercise power non-oppressively. Since feminist organisations are often created, led and staffed by women, many of whom are survivors of various traumatic or oppressive experiences, the *politics of powerlessness* creates behavioural patterns that affect organisational functioning in profound and disturbing ways:

We have known for a long time that tendencies toward domination and top-down practices don't just exist in mainstream society, but also

---

Box 8.5
The Zanzibar Experience

An excellent example of the destructive capacity of *power under* is what many seasoned African feminists call the 'The Zanzibar Experience'—a promising meeting that turned into a nightmare of pain, anger and recriminations. In 2003, a group of feminists met in Zanzibar to plan the African Feminist Congress. Thirty-five of them met on a Monday, and soon discovered that assumptions each woman had made about the others' unarticulated individual and organisational politics were not holding up—in other words, there was a lot of *powerless rage* playing itself out in the process. By Thursday, back-biting, hostility, personal attacks, challenging each others' motives, and its resultant chaos reigned, and half the participants had left in tears or bitterness. The Congress didn't happen, and the participants learned the difficult lesson that theory and practice do not always go together. On the positive side, the Zanzibar experience led African feminist leaders to realise that one of the first steps to effective feminist leadership is to acknowledge that we need to create basic rules of engagement to govern how we treat each other, and to handle our own destructive tendencies. The African Feminist Charter (www.africanfeministforum.org/Charter), the first such code of conduct in the feminist world, was the powerful gift of the Zanzibar debacle.

---

within progressive ... movements and organizations—that we internalize these tendencies and carry them with us, no matter how honestly and deeply we believe in egalitarian principles and values. As products of a society organized around domination, the struggle to create equal power relations is always internal as well as external. I am suggesting that the same is true regarding powerlessness, and that we need to pay the same kind of scrupulous attention to power-under within social change movements that is needed to struggle against tendencies toward power-over. In fact, domination and powerlessness are two sides of the same coin, and are interrelated not only between individuals but also within individuals in ways that are critical to examine and understand (Wineman 2003: 48).

Power in organisations

Leadership is practised, for the most part, in organisational settings. Having unpacked a whole range of concepts about power, it is now necessary to understand the dynamic of power within organisations in order to address how feminist leadership can create genuinely different structures to achieve their goals. So it is important to understand organisations more clearly. An organisation is defined as *'a social arrangement which pursues collective goals, controls its own performance, and has a boundary separating it from its environment'* (see http://en.wikipedia.org/wiki/Organizations). Organisations can be either *formal* (legally constituted and recognised entities like cooperatives, trade unions, companies, foundations or NGOs) or *informal* (not legally constituted, but structures created for the fulfillment of some purpose or goal—such as a farmer's group, women's savings and credit groups, collectives, etc.).

Organisations—whether formal or informal—are microcosms of the social environment from which they emerge. But most of us assume that unlike social structures like the family or clan, which are replete with gender and other biases and hierarchies, organisations are rational, logical entities where stated values, goals and policies will be operationalised in all its processes. Unfortunately, research in organisational behaviour has shown that this is simply not true—organisations, after all, are created and run by human beings, and human beings are not entirely rational! What is more, organisations emerge from social institutions in which a wide range of power imbalances and inequalities are embedded. Rao and Kelleher note, for instance, that

> Organizations swim in a sea of societal norms, which not only influence organizational behavior but often operate below the level of consciousness .... They constrain organizational efforts to challenge gender-biased norms both in the society and in the organization ... [but] The building blocks of many of our organizations are gender biased in ways that are quite invisible (2008: 5–6).

Consequently, another social scientist, Geoffrey Wood, argues that despite the formal norms and values that we may create for our organisations, we are not always able to leave behind our familial and social conditioning when we enter our offices (1994). Wineman would probably add that we are also unable to leave behind the early experiences of powerlessness that damage our self-esteem and disable us from using our *power within* constructively. To make the point, Wood asks: 'What social and cultural distance does an official have to travel from home to work every day?' (ibid.). This question applies equally to any of us in our diverse endeavours. We clearly bring to organisations—whether at a leadership level or otherwise—the biases, conditioning, experiences with power, and all sorts of psychic baggage, *as well as* our aspirations, high-minded goals and good intentions.

This is equally true for feminists, but harder to address since we see ourselves as agents of transformation of the inequalities created by others, by mainstream ideologies and institutions such as patriarchy. Indeed, there are now more open discussions, in both international and domestic spaces,[9] on the fact that feminist organisations and feminist leaders have not always succeeded in creating environments that are markedly different from those of male social justice activists. A range of issues—'the founder syndrome', misuse or abuse of power, lack of space for younger women's agendas and leadership, and so forth—have emerged much more openly in recent times. Perhaps much of this is because of our failure to 'walk the distance', or recognise our own internalised experiences with power. Feminist leaders are usually more conscious of and sensitive to their visible power than to their hidden and agenda-setting power, that is, to their power *for* and *to*, not their power *over*. But unless we get past this, there is little chance that our leadership will be transformative, or even particularly feminist.

In order to move towards more effective and transformative engagements with our power, and create more effective organisations and movements, it is useful to examine the concept of the *'deep structure' of organisations and movements* (Rao et al. 1999; Rao and Kelleher 2000: 75), where most of the indirect and hidden power and *power under* is located, and from where direct and visible power is resisted, sabotaged, or subverted.

Deep structure is a vital organisational concept, and refers to

---

[9] This has been an increasing topic of discussion at successive AWID forums, for instance, and in national-level women's conferences.

the hidden sites and processes of power and influence, the implicit culture, the informal values and systems of reward and recognition, all of which have an enormous impact on how people and organisations actually function. Deep structures are, in a sense, like the elephant in the room—we all know they're there, but we do not know how to name them and tackle them analytically or practically. To illustrate the point, some common dimensions of organisational deep structures is presented in Figure 8.2.

Feminist organisational development practitioners have found that deep-seated resistance to organisational change, especially towards more gender equal and just practices, arises from the deep structure, and without specific tools to unearth and transform it, only superficial changes will occur. Within feminist organisations and movements, deep structures are even more complex, especially where there have been attempts to create 'flat' or 'circular' or 'non-hierarchical' structures. Hierarchies and power structures have arisen in these regardless, but operate at the level of deep structure, making them even more difficult to see, address, or transform. As early as 1970, Jo Freeman wrote about 'The Tyranny of Structurelessness' (1970) and the hidden power hierarchies that had emerged in the organisations of the American women's liberation movement of the time, and about the use of 'trashing' to discredit / ostracise / demoralise / disempower someone (1976). At least some part of the 'trashing' process is a manifestation of *power under*, and is a classic deep structure phenomenon that continues till today.

Deep structures are also important because this is where the culture of the organisation is embedded and reproduced, no matter what the formal, stated, or aspired-for culture may be. It is also where people's internalised attitudes and behaviours are manifested, contributing to the construction of that culture. And the less the organisation's visible structure enables open processing of its members' conflicts, aspirations, ideas and problems, the more these are driven into the deep structure, making it a site of tension, resistance, subversion and sabotage. In other words, the more open, transparent and accountable an organisation, the shallower and less destructive will the deep structure be.

Figure 8.2

Some Facets of the 'Deep Structure' of Organisations

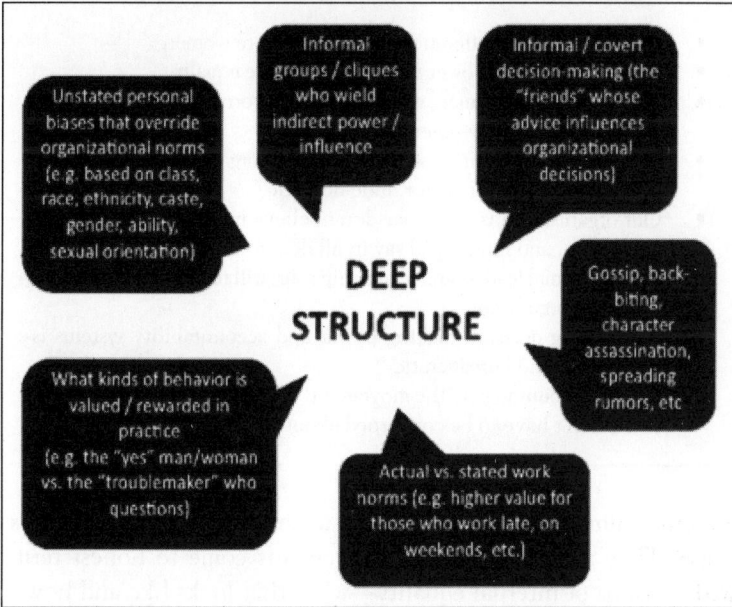

Informal groups / cliques who wield indirect power / influence

Informal / covert decision-making (the "friends" whose advice influences organizational decisions)

Unstated personal biases that override organizational norms (e.g. based on class, race, ethnicity, caste, gender, ability, sexual orientation)

DEEP STRUCTURE

Gossip, back-biting, character assassination, spreading rumors, etc

What kinds of behavior is valued / rewarded in practice (e.g. the "yes" man/woman vs. the "troublemaker" who questions)

Actual vs. stated work norms (e.g. higher value for those who work late, on weekends, etc.)

Despite the experiences and challenges that feminist organisations and movements have faced, and the recognition, if not naming, of the problems lurking in their deep structure, there are a surprising number of myths that survive about them—idealised notions about their superior handling of issues of power, facilitated by the deep structures that submerge and hide the problems. Although some may seem clichés, the more widespread ones are worth noting.

A key task of feminist leadership development programmes is therefore to arrive at a much clearer understanding of organisations and their deep structures, and to examine and surface deep structure dynamics in order to build more transparent, accountable and democratic ways of dealing with power in our organisational and movement structures. Leadership development programmes must strengthen inputs on organisational behaviour, culture and organisational power dynamics, including—especially—the deep

---

Box 8.6
Popular Myths About / Within Feminist Organisations

- Women will lead differently because they are women
- Women will share power more readily, more equally
- Because we're all women, we don't have to worry about power within the organisation/movement
- Because we are feminist women, we / our organisations cannot be oppressive, exclusionary, or undemocratic
- Our organisation is 'flat'—we don't believe in hierarchy, we are all equal here, and have equal say in all decisions
- Having formal leaders and leadership roles will reproduce patriarchal organisational forms
- Formalising decision-making power and accountability systems is patriarchal and bureaucratic
- We are accountable to 'the movement' (Which one? Where? How?), so we don't have to be concerned about accountability

---

structure dimension, and equip participants with tools to address these. They also have to help participants come to honest terms with notions of internal equality—what that looks like and how it works in practice, and perhaps also get past fears of tackling power arrangements more openly.

2. Principles and values

It is a moot point whether principles and values should have preceded politics and purpose in a document on feminist leadership. Regardless, they are critical to our discussion because leadership does not occur in a moral or social vacuum—it is always informed by values, whether explicit or not; and values are not held only by progressive leaders, since even autocrats, warlords, terrorists and dictators create a moral justification for their tyranny and violence. Thus, leadership embraces the values and principles consonant with its mission and purpose, or which have framed or catalysed that purpose.

It is useful to begin by distinguishing between values and principles; and we need to discuss values before principles. *Values*

are the ethical norms that guide behaviour; principles are norms that guide action. Obviously, they are not mutually exclusive—there is not only a good deal of overlap between them, but many principles derive from values. For instance, equality and equity are both values and principles; but functioning in democratic, transparent and accountable ways are principles derived from the value of equality. Similarly, the value of gender equality guides the actions for empowering women.

Principles and values are particularly important in conflict situations, whether the conflict is within an organisation, or the organisation is dealing with the effects of conflict in the external environment—such as a political crisis or war. This is precisely when it is tempting to jettison principles and values in order to deal with the short-term crisis; which is why feminist leaders must ensure that their organisations and movements develop sound and explicitly articulated principles that can inform strategic choices during precarious times. But building consensus about values and principles is itself a challenging task. Some feminist leaders stand vehemently for equal legal rights for women or women's right to choice, but are deeply uncomfortable supporting gay rights movements; others will gladly march with allies in demanding democratic governance, but avoid instituting the same principles in their own organisational structures. The value dimension is therefore not only rhetoric for creating a moral high ground, but also an active, alive instrument of feminist politics.

There are several core values and principles that feminism has embraced throughout history, with some variation based on culture and context. Table 8.1 attempts to capture some of these in a simple form to advance our discussion, although it is not intended to be an exhaustive list.

Another way of articulating core values and principles is through naming the 'non-negotiables' that feminist leaders and their organisations will protect and advance. An example of such non-negotiables, listed by key feminist leaders and feminist leadership development experts at a recent workshop (CREA 2008), are presented below.

Table 8.1 Feminist Values and Principles

Values	Principles
Equality, equity and inclusion for all, regardless of gender, race, religion, age, ability, ethnicity, class, caste, nationality, location, or sexual orientation	Equality under law; Equity and equality in policies;Transform all social relations of power that oppress, exploit, or marginalise women and men on the basis of their gender, race, religion, age, ability, ethnicity, class, caste, nationality, location, or sexual orientation
The human rights of all peoples to achieve their full potential, as long as it does not impede or constrain the rights of others	Enforcement of the full body of human rights through existing and new international instruments; Against fundamentalisms of all kinds
The basic right and entitlement of all people to food, shelter, health, education and livelihood	Economic justice, including equitable access to productive resources, employment, and basic services for all
Physical security and integrity, freedom from violence or coercion in any form, and the **right to choice** in reproductive and sexual life	Zero tolerance for gender-based and other forms of violence; Freedom of choice in sexual and reproductive life
Peace	Non-violence; stand against all forms of war, conflict, militarisation,
A healthy planet	Sustainable development; Ecologically sound practices in personal, organisational life; for public policy that promotes sustainability
Honour diversity and difference	Against religious, ethnic, racial, and other fundamentalisms
Democracy, transparency, accountability	Voice and vote for all people; Participatory, transparent and accountable governance at all levels and in all institutions, private and public; Right to public information; Associational freedom and right to freedom of expression
Changing the use and practice of power	Sharing power, consultative, collective, transparent and accountable decision-making

Source: Batliwala 2008: 11–12.

Feminist leadership—some 'non-negotiables'

- Feminist leadership *must* include an active participatory attitude and inclusion at all levels of the organisation. This applies particularly to the integration of people/women from marginalised groups.
- Feminist leaders must have extensive knowledge of the issues with which the organisation engages.
- Feminist leadership is sustainable only when women are able to balance all aspects of their lives.
- Decision-making must be transparent for a viable and vibrant leadership to flourish. This involves a clear, shared decision-making process that pools the strengths of participants and allows everyone to have some power, and provides an atmosphere that facilitates every person's strengths. Each person in an organisation must have some authority, as well as tools, information, responsibility and accountability.
- The organisation's membership at large must understand their roles and be involved in certain decisions, and in the evolution of the organisation's structure.
- Feminist leadership must ensure that the same rights apply to all, and that these rights are indivisible. Organisation members must have full knowledge of the organisation's philosophy and agenda, and should be able to choose, as much as possible, how they work within the organisation, and how much influence they have in decision-making.
- Feminist leadership must be used to intervene in structures of power that keep the world unjust; it must challenge multiple oppressions, but gender justice must be a priority.
- Leadership is a process, a goal, a practice and a means.
- A feminist organisation needs an affirmative vision of change that takes it forward, rather than focusing only on oppression.
- Feminist leaders need to constantly challenge and rethink organisational structure.
- There must be space for leaders of all generations, and we must embrace diversity, inclusiveness and mutual respect.
- We must act as feminist transformational agents, and understand

that people who hold [formal] power are not necessarily the best leaders.

Since our politics is driven by these values, principles and non-negotiables, our practice of power has to be transformed by them. Feminist leaders and organisations can use this normative framework in several ways, for example:

- to **articulate their values and principles in more specific, contextualised ways** to reflect the culture and socio-political environment in which it operates;
- to **translate them into *policies*, and more importantly, *practices*,** within their organisations and movements;
- to **resolve problems and conflicts** in organisational life;
- **build more inter-sectional and less fragmented strategies** in order to address multiple sets of principles; and
- **build its advocacy agenda and alliances** according to these values and principles.

Feminist organisations and leadership development programmes must address these critical priorities. The value dimension, as stated earlier, is key to sound feminist leadership—not as rhetoric for seizing the moral high ground, but as an active, living demonstration of feminist politics.

III. Politics and Purpose

A key component of feminist leadership is its *politics and the nature of the mission* (that is, purpose) that guides it. By *politics* is meant the analysis of socio-economic realities, and the ideological lens that informs that analysis (for example, profit and free enterprise, public good, gender equality, social justice, etc.). And *purpose* refers to the longer-term vision and mission for change that emerges from that politics.

Feminist politics, based on contextually defined and situated feminist ideology (not some universal form of feminism), must inform feminist leadership, and the political agenda it pursues. In other words, ***transformative feminist leadership*** will use the analysis of gender and social discrimination in a particular society, community, or setting as its starting point, and will attempt to transform the structures or institutions it engages towards a more gender and socially equitable architecture in both formal and informal terms. And of course, this politics must begin at home, from within the organisation, movement, or any other location from which it is attempting to change the larger reality.

This of course begs the question: Can feminist leadership occur without a transformative goal? Can it, for instance, be applied or used within a less radical context—such as running a business, managing a service NGO, or administering a museum? Indeed, even within these seemingly less revolutionary and more static settings, the feminist leader is still transforming *something*—perhaps the 'psychic structure' of staff, as the Admira toolkit puts it, or the way staff problems are dealt with, or questions relating to what is an organisational issue and what is not. But for most of us in women's movements, our concern with building feminist leadership is for broader social transformation that puts gender and social equality at the centre of the mission.

Since leadership is a means and not an end, the politics that inform it, and the purpose for which it is practised, are critical. *Leadership development must therefore bring to the surface and equip people to articulate their politics and purpose in clear, conscious ways.* This is where inputs of information, analytical tools, concepts and ideas play a big part—women unfamiliar with the human rights framework, or with feminist concepts like patriarchy, may articulate their politics very differently from those aware of these transformative ideas.[10] *Expanding the repertoire of possibility and intellectual horizons, and exposing participants to new analytical frameworks, information and knowledge to which they may not*

---

[10] This is why these inputs form a critical part of the leadership development approaches of organisations like the Center for Women's Global Leadership, CREA, Just Associates, the Domestic Workers Alliance of the USA, the Forum of Women's NGOs in Central Asia, GROOTS International, International Women's Rights Action Watch (Asia Pacific), MADRE, Women's Learning Partnership, and other avowed by feminist organisation.

*have had access, are thus essential components of building more
transformative politics and purpose through leadership
development. These tools and frameworks can also become
touchstones for strategic decision-making when they face dilemmas
and crises.*

Politics and purpose also distinguishes feminist leadership from
all other forms—including feminine leadership, women's leadership,
etc.—where the leader/s may be female (or male), but does not adopt
a feminist political agenda, that is, an agenda that clearly privileges
and centres women's empowerment and gender equality within its
social transformation goals, internally and externally. Feminist
politics—whether named or not—will analyse both the social order
and the particular changes it seeks through a gender and social justice
lens, and will assume that social justice (such as labour or land rights)
cannot be achieved without centring gender justice within the
process.

4. Practice

And finally, we come to the largest domain of leadership—the
transactional, lived, quotidian realm of practice. This is the
component that constitutes the largest chunk of most leadership
development and training programmes. At the most primary level,
transformative feminist leadership is about ways of doing and enabling
myriad things, which are categorised as the different types of 'work'
these practices fall into:

- **Visioning work**: developing and articulating a theory of change,
  clarifying vision and objectives, determining focus (issue or
  sector) and approach, etc.;
- **Political work**: assessing the political environment and
  opportunities, undertaking social power analysis of the context
  and intervention area, anticipating political reactions, building
  alliances, etc.;
- **Strategic work**: developing and guiding strategies, monitoring
  implementation, evaluating impact, analysing gains and setbacks,
  revising direction and approach, etc.;

- **Relationship work**: this is a critical component of leadership practice, and includes inducting and training others, mobilising constituents / 'target groups' / stakeholders, motivating and sustaining energy and morale, imparting and imbibing passion and commitment, building alliances and goodwill, resolving conflicts and tensions, etc.;
- **Communication work**: which includes internal and external communication systems, creating communication strategies, ensuring quality content, strategic communication when required (for example, the use of the media), use of new technologies to create effective and strategic external communication, use of traditional technologies (folk theatre, song, etc.) where more appropriate, etc.
- **Resourcing work**: finding and sustaining financial and other resources (expertise, materials, information, ideas, etc.) that are critical to the transformation process; this may include some relationship building work with donors and supporters, and skills such as proposal-writing and building networks of contacts to access expertise, information, materials, trainers, etc.; and
- **Managerial work**: seemingly humdrum, but a very critical component of leadership practice, including democratic, transparent and accountable policies and mechanisms for internal functioning, managing financial and legal obligations and requirements, allocating human and financial resources, auditing correct utilisation, reporting to external constituencies and stakeholders, etc.

In examining current feminist leadership development approaches, we have to assess the relative emphasis given to *imparting skills* in the above areas vs. *the normative framework—* that is, transformative power, politics and principles—that must underlie those skills. In other words, we cannot approach skill-building in an instrumental way, or separate them from our ideological position. Skills are not neutral, portable abilities; they are shaped by values and politics, as for example in the way relationships are managed, conflicts are resolved, or salary scales and job descriptions are framed. *Our leadership development modules must therefore advance an approach that does not disconnect practices from power, politics and values.*

What is more, feminist leadership training must enable practitioners to converge the four dimensions of leadership in any setting. Today, much of leadership training is focused on the practice piece, with little attention to equipping practitioners with concrete ways of articulating and practising the other three dimensions. This leads to further intensifying deep structures, as we have seen. One dimension of this is the failure, in many locations, of feminist organisations and movements to secure their future through supporting the growth and advancement of young feminist leaders.

Many long-established feminist women's organisations and movements are beginning to 'age out', either because their leadership has failed to invest in developing younger leaders, or because their culture and environment are unwittingly unwelcoming to younger women. *Without conscious attention to the way practices converge with power, politics and principles, younger feminists tend to be marginalised or even ousted from processes because they challenge established priorities, analyses and ways of doing.* Some leadership development initiatives are now specifically addressing this issue,[11] but must not reproduce the gaps that the older leadership programmes contained. Several young feminist initiatives are in active discussion about these issues, and have attempted to create guidelines for more multi-generational approaches that are well worth integrating within organisational settings.[12]

Sometimes, this means moving out of our own spaces and comfort zones, and going into the spaces of the women we wish to reach, rather than inviting them into ours. Sanushka Mudaliar of AWID speaks of her experience of working with young Southeast Asian women in the garment industry in Cambodia. When activists went into the factories and introduced concepts directly related to their

---

[11] See, for instance, the CREA South Asia Movement Building and Rights Institute, or the CREA-Akina Mama wa Afrika Feminist Movement Building and Advocacy Institute, www.creaworld.org.
[12] See, for instance, the Multigenerational Toolkit produced by the Young Feminist Activism Initiative of AWID, prior to the 2008 AWID Forum in Cope Town.

Figure 8.3
The Self and the Feminist Leadership Diamond

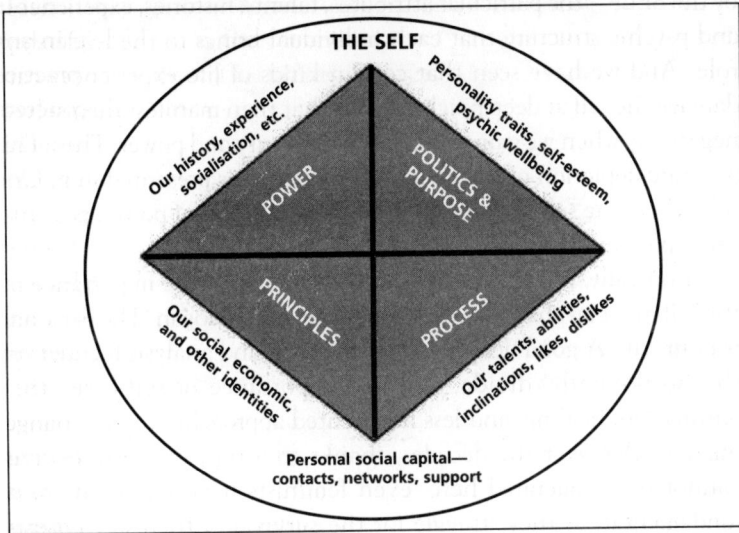

work, the women were galvanised. In Sanushka's words, "When you show them where you want to go, not just what your values are, feminism is electrifying!'[13]

Figure 8.3 captures the interconnectedness of these four elements in a 'diamond' that can also be the basis of an assessment framework for our training approaches.

The role of the self in leadership

When examining the leadership diamond, it is immediately obvious that it should not—and does not—float in the air like a kite without a string. Leadership is practised by people, so the diamond is anchored

---

[13] Experience shared by Sanushka Mudaliar, then manager of AWID's Young Feminist Activism Initiative, at the meeting 'Building Feminist Leadership—Looking Back, Looking Forward', 12–13 November 2008, Cape Town, South Africa. It was organised by CREA, where an early draft of this paper was shared with a cross-section of feminist activists, leaders, and leadership and organisational development experts.

within individuals, whether they are leading alone or together with others. The diamond, therefore, is shaped and transformed in practice by the SELF—the particular attributes, talents, histories, experiences, and psychic structure that each individual brings to the leadership role. And we have seen that certain kinds of life experiences can damage the self at deep psychic levels that then manifest themselves negatively when we gain positions of authority and power. The more accurate depiction of the diamond, therefore, is presented in Figure 8.3, where the self surrounds our implementation of power, politics, principles and practices.

Ironically, it is feminism that first articulated the importance of the self in social change, with the coining of the slogan 'The personal is political'. A good deal of earlier research and analysis focused on the 'work-family' divide, and the importance of self-care, self-affirmation, healing, and less fragmented approaches to our change mission. But over the decades, thanks to a host of pressures that cannot be enumerated here, even feminists have forgotten these fundamentals as they struggle for the survival of their movements and organisations in an increasingly hostile social, political and funding environment.

However, recent research by feminist capacity builders and other organisational development experts has re-emphasised the critical role of the self in both constructing and destroying the best endeavours, and the importance, therefore, of addressing the self in leadership development work (Friedman and Meer 2007; Zimmerman et al. 2010). And as we have seen in examining 'power under', there is also a growing awareness that social transformation must include, if not begin with, transformation at the individual level (Edwards and Sen 2000). The damage caused by the neglect of this dimension, and the importance of self-care and balance, was also a key theme of discussion among feminist movement actors at the 2008 AWID Forum in Cape Town, South Africa (Batliwala 2009).

While the self comprises a wide range of factors—and some that are yet to be named or analysed!—the most important from a leadership perspective are:

- **Personality and self-esteem:** People with low self-esteem tend to be insecure, and are more likely to become authoritarian in positions of authority, threatened by the competencies of their colleagues or subordinates, and less willing to share power. This is often not intentional, but the playing out of subconscious scripts; however, it creates enormous problems in organisations. These are very deep dimensions of the self that need to be addressed and tackled with structured support.

- **History and experience:** Especially experiences with power (both positive and negative), which shape our attitude towards it, and often override our intellectual understanding of it; history also includes the way our experiences in multiple contexts generate insight, political savvy and strategic skills;
- **Personal social capital:** Our individual histories and experiences also generate social capital—personal contacts, connections, support systems, networks—that are part of the unique resources we bring to our organisational role, and these become particularly important assets in leadership positions;
- **Talents, abilities, inclinations:** These are part of the unique package that every individual brings to leadership, and the special gifts that they can leverage in leadership roles (a good sense of humour, for instance, or skilled articulation—the 'gift of the gab'—or artistic or musical skills); and finally,
- **Identities:** The multilayered identities based on our class, race, gender, ethnicity, caste, ability, religion, location, sexual orientation—which in turn shaped our histories and experiences in particular ways, especially of power—such as being a rural Dalit woman, a sex worker, a Muslim woman survivor of communal conflict, a woman with a disability, etc. Similarly, coming from a powerful social class or group also shapes our sense of privilege and the power we invisibly wield in an organisation, regardless of our formal position in the hierarchy. We bring these identities into leadership roles in both subtle and overt ways, and they sometimes determine how we respond to different kinds of leadership challenges.

Recognising the powerful role of the self is critical in the feminist leadership context because women's psychic structures have been constructed not only through the usual institutions, socialisation processes and experiences (like family, school, peers, etc.), but also through the particular nature of the patriarchal structures in which they have lived and the oppressions they have consequently negotiated. So, for instance, women are often less comfortable with holding overt power and more comfortable exercising it indirectly, or with challenging or subverting it (power under) as they have done in most other locations (such as within the family or marriage). This leads to very specific distortions that need to be surfaced, and women often need additional tools to address their internalised—and often unrecognised—dilemmas with the kind of overt authority, responsibility and accountability that leadership roles bring.

On the other hand, leadership development from a feminist perspective has also been extremely transformative for individuals, enabling deep-seated changes in the self that have resulted not only in a sense of self-awareness, empowerment and liberation, but also in new ways of acting for change in the external world. In CREA's own experience, for instance, women undergoing these personal transformations during training workshops have gone on to challenge violence, feudal oppression, and religious fundamentalism in their own families, communities and villages. Feminist leadership development programmes must therefore integrate mechanisms enabling participants to analyse their psychic structure—the SELF— in a safe space, with expert support, and provide longer-term support systems to deal with and overcome the negative baggage within the self, as well as unleash the profoundly transformative potential that lies within it.

IV. Where is It? Sites of Feminist Leadership

Many amorphous, hard-to-pin-down concepts can be grasped partly by locating them within the specific sites in which they occur. In the case of feminist leadership, there are as many locations as there are power structures and institutions that subordinate women:

- **The family, clan, caste, tribe or community.** These are primary sites where feminist leadership for transformation is practised, especially by feminists and their grassroots movements. They seek equality and transformation in these critical institutions where the majority of women must negotiate their lives and their rights.
- **The state** and its various arms. Feminist leadership and movements have traditionally targeted the state, regimes and public policies as key sites that can either enable or disable their empowerment. Legal systems have been particular targets, since they enshrine the socially prevalent systems of gender inequality and discrimination. But government policies, and the creation of enabling mechanisms like gender budgets and national women's commissions, have also been the targets of feminist leadership and activism.
- **The market and private sector.** This is a site where feminist leadership has gained a significant foothold, although feminist leadership principles and practices have also been instrumentalised to advance corporate and market goals (Due Billing and Alvesson 2002). Corporations and management schools have eagerly co-opted many leadership practices of women, feminist and otherwise, and applied them to enhance productivity and motivation.
- **Civil society, women's movements and other social movements.** This is a more familiar site where we have seen feminist leadership transacted. While many civil society organisations—especially those led by men and non-feminist women—have attempted to incorporate elements of the feminine leadership 'style', these are often cosmetic or superficial in nature. On the other hand, gender-sensitive male leaders can sometimes practice feminist leadership principles more authentically and effectively than

non-feminist women leaders, or even feminist leaders who have
not been able to deal honestly with their organisational deep
structures or problems with handling power in more transparent
and accountable ways. The most interesting civil society sites,
however, are those where feminist leaders consciously experiment
with creating organisational structures and systems that
intentionally bring a transformative character to their power,
politics, principles and practice.

• **Cultural and religious institutions.** For many feminist leaders,
  these are critical sites of engagement and transformation.
  Indigenous women in Latin America, Roma women in East
  Europe, feminist Christian women, and even HIV/AIDS activists
  in Africa have confronted the gender discrimination embedded
  in cultural and religious norms, and challenged the re-
  construction of tradition and religious norms to enforce male
  privilege. Mexican indigenous women, for instance, have insisted
  that oppressive elements of pre-colonial indigenous culture be
  acknowledged and discarded in the larger (and male-led)
  indigenous people's movements (Lopez 2007); similarly, Roma
  women are demanding that oppressions arising from patriarchy
  be separated from other cultural expressions in articulations of
  'Roma Culture' (Iszak 2007).

All these are key sites of learning for feminist leadership
development programmes. Specifically, they challenge us to help
practitioners unravel the particular ways in which each site reacts to
feminist power, politics, principles and practice, and equip them with
analytical and practical tools for authentic and transformative
engagements in each location.

V. What Does It Look Like? Feminist Ways of Leading

There are several illustrations of what feminist leadership looks like in practice, and these are worth examining to ground our discussion. One set of principles-in-action and leadership practices emerged out of a study of twenty women leaders from around the world, some openly feminist, some not, but all acting for gender equality, and practising what we would describe, in terms of the definitions offered earlier in this chapter, as feminist leadership (Batliwala and Rao 2002). After in-depth interviews, the study located the following common elements in the way these women transacted their leadership:

- They create and sustain social change strategies that place *changes in gender power relations at the centre.* They see gender justice and social justice as interconnected changes, and feel that male social justice leaders do not always see gender justice as integral to their agendas.
- They are not different just because they are women leaders, but because they are women leading with a *transformative agenda* that connects gender power to social change.
- Feminist leadership requires incredible *agility and resilience* because each step forward creates new and sometimes graver challenges or backlash. This makes feminist leaders stronger and smarter strategists and negotiators.
- The mission of gender equality and social justice is infused into *every job, every activity and every location* (running a journal, an NGO, an academic teaching programme, a grassroots programme).
- The mainstream does not reward—and may even *penalise— feminist leadership.* Pressures come from the family, community, church, party, government, or one's own organisation. So feminist leadership requires risk-taking.
- Feminist leadership means the *ability to influence agendas even without the formal power or authority to do so,* and the capacity to leverage larger-scale changes (in policy, legal rights, social attitudes and power relations) with very marginal resources.

- Many of the leaders in the study did not see themselves as leaders in an individualistic sense, but as *people at the vanguard* of broader processes of change.
- *Feminist leaders are often uncomfortable with their power*. Leadership held a negative connotation for many of them, and many were uncomfortable being characterised as leaders. As one leader said, 'Leadership is a condition that others attribute to you, not you to yourself.'
- Feminist leaders emphasise the *value of collective and multilayered leadership*, the sharing of power and responsibility, and generally reject the male and 'Western' 'lone ranger' model of individual leadership.
- Consequently, feminist leadership is *not a one-way or top-down process*, but leads through consultation, participation and consensus building. These leaders do not preach participation and responsiveness to their constituencies as much as they practice it. This approach, they felt, is both a weakness and a strength. It is slower—leading to shorter-term losses—but deeper, leading to longer-term gains.
- For feminist leaders, good leadership is about *relationship building*—within their organisations, with their constituencies, and with both allies and opponents. They invest time and energy in building a broad range of relationships, and see no short-cut to this.
- They bring *'the feminine universe'* into their organisational practice—a resource that male leaders lack or are afraid to use in their workplaces. They use women's traditional nurturing roles and relationship skills in their leadership practice.
- They are concerned with the *empowerment and transformation of men*—particularly from oppressed and excluded groups—as well as of women. They work for gender and social equality, not just for women's empowerment.
- Feminists are *introspective and critical about their own leadership* and the failings or shortcomings of their own movements and organisations. Feminist leaders emphasise the importance of constant self-examination with regard to power and its effects. They acknowledge the corrupting possibilities of

power, especially formal power—egotism, arrogance, authoritarianism, selfishness—and create mechanisms to check their own use and abuse of power.

- They create **innovative organisational structures and governance practices** to bring their transformative agendas into their own organisations. For instance, they create spaces and opportunities for other leaders to emerge—for example, giving younger staff real organisational power—because they believe feminist leadership must enable the emergence and growth of other leaders, rather than holding on to power and control for oneself.

DAWN Ontario offers these insights into struggles in the practice of feminist leadership principles, to provide an image of how things can look when these struggles are successful, and neatly summing up the implementation of the feminist values and principles we outlined earlier:

> We may expect that feminist groups will be problem-free, or that we will create inclusive environments by virtue of our collective work. As women, we must acknowledge that we come from different experiences of leadership, and that our practices are informed by traditional, hierarchical structures. Sometimes we repeat the very practices we dislike, even when we are trying to do things differently. We may encounter other challenges, including women who bring destructive behaviors stemming from issues or a lack of power within our personal lives into our organizations. As feminists .... we need to examine the structures we have come from, and consider how our experience informs our current practices.
>
> Within equality-seeking organizations, we may expect that our feminist members will not struggle with issues of power. Leaders need to be aware that power dynamics happen in any organization, and that some women are supportive while others are more comfortable with conflict. For example, a woman may gain power through manipulation, claiming disempowerment when she cannot have things her way. We may become so afraid of conflict that we stop challenging, allowing individual women to take power away from our organization. This does not serve our collective interest, as our work toward equality and inclusion becomes lost within our own practices. We may feel

uncomfortable with power struggles, but we are more at risk when we do not challenge exclusionary or destructive behaviors. Feminist leaders challenge destructive patterns that emerge, while continuously drawing on the skills and talents of women in our group.

Leaders of feminist equality-seeking organizations are accountable not only to our members and service users, but to the global movement for peace, equality and justice. We typically expect our leaders to ensure that our organization's finances are in good order, projects are on track, and public relations are effective. Feminist leaders are also responsible for ensuring that the perspective and analysis of our equality-seeking organization is brought to the larger feminist community. Women in leadership roles need to take every opportunity to build links with other women and women's organizations that share our agenda for equality and inclusion. We need to consider how we are accountable to our group and community, and if our service and advocacy work is effective or appropriate to the needs of women. As feminists, we must always remind ourselves of the larger reasons why we are drawn to equality-seeking work, and of our desire to transform our organizations and communities into safe, equitable, and inclusive places for all women.

... Within the feminist practice of leadership, leaders are members of a team of women working toward a common goal of equality and inclusion. Each woman on the team has a unique skill or ability that is valuable to our common efforts. This does not mean that our roles and responsibilities are identical, but that our contributions and participation are equally valued. Whether a woman chairs a meeting, or prepares the food for a meeting, her contribution is important in advancing our equality-seeking work ...

Members of equality-seeking organizations choose our leaders. As willing followers and supporters, we invest power in our leaders. We entrust they will share their skills and abilities with our group and provide opportunities to develop other women's leadership potential. For example, feminist leaders create opportunities for meaningful discussions where every woman's participation is encouraged. We expect our leaders to mentor others, drawing out the ideas and analysis of every woman in making decisions and creating strategies for our organizations. Feminist leadership is a vehicle for women and organizations to find power to deal with issues, change policies, and transform communities (DAWN Ontario 2008).

The Admira Toolkit on Feminist Leadership Components

(Admira n.d.), developed by examining both the literature on feminist leadership and good practices, summarises the three dominant components of feminist leadership that emerged from their study: skills, norms and values, and personal characteristics (the 'self'). The detailed attributes and dimensions of each are:

Skills

- Learning ability, dealing positively with criticism, curiosity, receptiveness or susceptibility.
- Empowerment, recruiting competent people, making use of diversity, creating conditions for empowerment, delegating.
- Cooperating, networking, oriented at stakeholders, connecting and attuning, not being defensive, oriented at internal cooperation.

Norms and values

- Guiding vision, a forceful own vision, being inspiring, capacity to conceptualise, transforming ideas into action.
- Open engagement, visible emotional involvement, passion and compassion, commitment with people, societal involvement.
- Being a moral authority, actively [practising] morality, being recognised as a moral authority, applying moral standards.

Personal characteristics

- Locus of control, internal locus of control, self-knowledge, self-consciousness, autonomy.
- Credibility, congruity, being trustworthy, authenticity.
- Emotional intelligence, able to handle own emotions, introspection, optimism, empathy.

There are several common threads running through these descriptions of what feminist leadership looks like: first, they resonate with the four dimensions of the feminist leadership 'diamond'—power, politics and purpose, principles and values, and practice. They also point to the embedded dichotomy of aspiration vs reality: the way things *should be done* by feminist leadership, and the realities that derail the aspiration because of the baggage of history, culture, experiences of power and pain that we bring to the process. But most importantly, they stress the need for concrete tools and mechanisms to ensure that feminist leadership is practised in the best possible way, recognising that many of us need these to overcome our own fear of power, internalised ways of using—and misusing—power, and that creating appropriately democratic and transparent structures can help us achieve our aspirations for truly feminist enterprises.

The messiness and embeddedness of our own experiences of power and powerlessness is beautifully deconstructed in Gender at Work's excellent documentation of their action-learning programme with three South African social change and human rights organisations, entitled 'Change is a Slow Dance'. Gender at Work facilitators worked to help the staff and leadership of these organisations to deepen their capacity for improving gender relationships and power inequalities, both within the organisation and in their programmes. In one case, of an organisation founded by women survivors of violence in Pietermaritzburg, there was a critical moment when the leadership team recognised how their own need for victimhood—and their entrapment in the politics of powerlessness—was damaging their leadership practices and blocking the organisation's growth. During one workshop with the Gender at Work team in Cape Town, when this realisation struck them, they undertook a powerful symbolic act of liberation from this negative force: they went to the top of Tabletop Mountain and threw their victimhood over the side (Bell and Gany 2007: 53). The idea of the 'feminine universe', which echoes Knight's point on celebration, ritual, joy and sadness, is also a very interesting dimension, and points to the role of transformative feminist leadership in breaking the 'private-public' and work-family divides that have characterised modern organisations (Rao and Kelleher 2000).

These live examples and insights lead us to think about the extent to which our feminist leadership development programmes help practitioners develop greater clarity and access concrete tools and mechanisms for their own leadership practice, and be particularly attentive to the architecture and dynamics of power in their organisational or movement contexts.

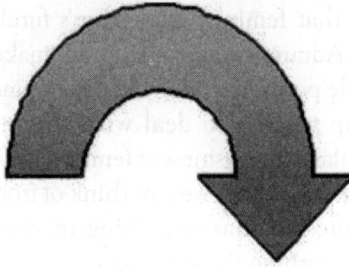

Conclusions

This chapter has attempted to provide a framework for unravelling the complex and generally amorphous concept of leadership, and to illuminate the concept and practice of feminist leadership. The goal of the chapter, however, was not to provide solutions and recipes, but food for thought for those of us engaged in building, strengthening and advancing feminist leadership for social transformation. It has sought to deconstruct the concept into some hopefully useful components, based on an extensive review of literature—scholarly and popular—on leadership, organisational behaviour theory, power analysis, as well as on feminism and feminist leadership.

While this framework has hopefully nailed the jelly to the wall more firmly than before, it is still tentative, and intended only to advance our debate. There may be many flaws and gaps that need to be filled, or dimensions of leadership that have not been incorporated.

We also hope that this framework will inform, challenge and support those of us engaged in feminist leadership training and development to look more critically at our approaches, and identify components that are currently missing, weak, or in need of revitalisation in our curriculae and pedagogy.

It is also a beginning in creating a structure and more sensitive indicators to track and assess the impact and usefulness of leadership development programmes—a very important goal at a time when donors are increasingly reluctant to fund leadership development because of the difficulty in establishing that it does, indeed, make a difference.

Perhaps it is most appropriate to conclude this chapter with a crucial reminder: that feminist leadership's fundamental attribute should be, as the Admira toolkit insists, to 'make waves'. In other words, there is little point in leadership development programmes if they do not equip women to deal with the messy, frightening, dangerous but exhilarating business of feminist social transformation. For every great feminist leader we can think of from anywhere in the world, past and present, has one thing in common: she led by challenging and disturbing the status quo.

Feminist leadership must make waves.

References

Admira. n.d. *Management & Leadership: Feminist Leadership*, Section 8. Available at http://www.zenska-mreza.hr/prirucnik/en/en_read_management_leadership_8.htm.

Afkhami, Mahnaz, Ann Eisenberg and Haleh Vaziri. 2001. 'Leading to Choices: A Leadership Training Handbook for Women', *Women's Learning Partnership for Rights, Development and Peace* (WLP) (Bethesda MD).

Albino, Judith and Toy Caldwell-Colbert. 2007. 'Women as Academic Leaders: Living the Experience in Two Perspectives', in Jean Lau Chin, Bernice E. Lott and Janice Sanchez-Hucles (eds), *Women and Leadership: Transforming Visions and Diverse Voices* (Oxford: Blackwell Publishing), pp. 69–87.

Antrobus, Peggy. 1999. *In Conversation with Charlotte Bunch and Marianne DeKoven*, 'Talking Leadership: Conversations with Powerful Women' (New Brunswick: Rutgers University Press), pp. 29–44.

———. 2000. 'Transformational leadership: Advancing the agenda for gender justice', *Gender and Development*, 8 (3): 50–56.

———. 2002. 'Feminism as Transformational Politics: Towards possibilities for Another World', *Development*, 45 (2): 46–52.

Barton, Tracy. 2006. 'Feminist Leadership: Building Nurturing Academic Communities', *Advancing Women's Leadership Online Journal*, 21.

Batliwala, Srilatha. 2008. 'The Power of Movements: Clarifying Our Concepts', in AWID, *Changing Their World: Concepts and Practices of Women's Movements* (AWID), pp. 11–12.

———. 2009. 'Feminism's Coming of Age: Celebrating Diversity and Power', *Development*, 52 (2).

Batliwala, Srilatha and Aruna Rao. 2002. 'Women, Leadership and Social Change', Unpublished report of a Sounding Study conducted for the Ford Foundation, July, pp. 11–18

Bennis, W.G. 1959. 'Leadership theory and administrative behavior: The problem of authority', *Administrative Science Quarterly*, 4: 260.

Bennis, Warren and Burt Nanus. 1997. *Leaders: Strategies for Taking Charge* (New York: Harper Collins).

Boje, David M. 2000. *Postmodern Leadership Theory*. Available at cbae.nmsu.edu/~dboje/teaching/338/postmodern_leadership_theory.

Bunch, Charlotte and Beverly Fisher. 1976. 'What Future for Leadership?', *Quest: A Feminist Quarterly*, II (4): 2–13.

Bell, Jenny and Fazila Gany. 2007. 'Justice and Women (JAW)', in Michel Friedman and Shamim Meer (eds), *Change is a Slow Dance*, Gender at Work, October.

Crater, Flora. 1976. 'Leadership, Growth, and Spirit', *Quest*, II (4): 60–66.

CREA. 2008. 'Building Feminist Leadership: Looking Forward, Looking Back', Workshop held at Cape Town, South Africa, 12–13 November.

DAWN Ontario. 2008. *The Feminist Principle of Leadership*. Available at http://dawn.thot.net/feminism11.html (accessed October 2008).

Downton, James Victor. 1973. *Rebel Leadership: Commitment and Charisma in the Revolutionary Process* (Basingstoke: Macmillan).

Due Billing, Yvonne and Mats Alvesson. 2002. 'Questioning the Notion of Feminine Leadership: A Critical Perspective on the Gender Labelling of Leadership', *Gender, Work & Organization*, 7 (3): 144–57.

Edwards, Michael. 1998. *Nailing the Jelly to the Wall: NGOs, Civil Society and International Development* (London: Edwards Associates). Available at www.futurepositive.org/docs/JELLY.doc.

Edwards, Michael C. and Gita Sen. 2000. 'NGOs, Social Change and the Transformation of Human Relationships: A 21st Century Civic Agenda', *Third World Quarterly*, 21 (4): 605–16.

Foucault, Michel. 1976. *The History of Sexuality, Part I* (London: Allen Lane).

Freeman, Jo. 1970. *The Tyranny of Structurelessness*. Available at www.struggle.ws.

———. 1976. 'Trashing: The Dark Side of Sisterhood', *Ms. Magazine*, April: 29–51, 92–98.

Friedman, Michel and Shamim Meer (eds). 2007. *Change is a Slow Dance*, Gender at Work. Available at www.genderatwork.org/learning-center.

Gaventa, John and Andrea Cornwall. 2001. 'Power and Knowledge', in Peter Reason and Hilary Bradbury (eds), *Handbook of Action Research—Participative Inquiry and Practice* (London: Sage Publications), pp. 70–80.

Hartmann, Mary S. 1999. *Talking Leadership: Conversations with Powerful Women* (New Brunswick: Rutgers University Press).

——— (ed.). 1999. 'Jacqueline Pitanguy: In Conversation with Charlotte Bunch and Barbara A. Shailor', in *Talking Leadership: Conversations with Powerful Women* (New Brunswick: Rutgers University Press).

Hiltner, Carol. 2007. 'An Invitation to Sacred Feminine Leadership', Paper presented at the Global Leadership Forum, Novosibirsk, Russia.

Institute for Women's Leadership. 2000. 'Are Leaders Made or Born? Educating Women for Leadership', National Dialogue on Educating Women for Leadership 1, New Brunswick, Institute for Women's Leadership.

———. 2002. 'Power for What? Women's Leadership: Why should you care?', National

Dialogue on Educating Women for Leadership 1, New Brunswick, Institute for Women's Leadership.

Izsak, Rita. 'The European Romani Women's Movement: International Roma Women's Network', Case study prepared for AWID, October 2007. Available at www.awid.org.

Jain, Devaki. 1995. 'Why Women? Is There a Special Quality in Women's Leadership?', Unpublished paper, available at the Center for Women's Global leadership, Rutgers University.

———. 1996. 'Women and Ethical Leadership', in Bella Abzug and Devaki Jain, *Women's Leadership and the Ethics of Development*, Gender in Development Monograph, Series 4, UNDP, August.

Joseph, Ammu and Kalpana Sharma. 2006 [1994]. *Whose News—the Media and Women's Issues* (New Delhi: Sage Publications).

Kabeer, Naila. 1994. *Reversed Realities: Gender Hierarchies in Development Thought* (London: Verso Press).

Kumar, Radha. 1993. *The History of Doing—An Illustrated Account of Movements for Women's Rights and Feminism in India, 1800–1990* (New Delhi: Kali for Women).

Lau Chin, Jean, Bernice E. Lott and Janice Sanchez-Hucles (eds). 2007. *Women and Leadership: Transforming Visions and Diverse Voices* (Oxford: Blackwell Publishing).

Lerner, Gerda. 1995. 'Leadership: Feminist, Spiritual, Political', *Woman of Power*, 24 (44).

Loden, Marilyn. 1985. *Feminine Leadership or How to Succeed in Business Without Being One of the Boys* (New York: Times Books).

Lopez, Marusia. 2007. 'Las mujeres en el movimiento indigena de Mexico: Nuevas Rutas para Transformar el Poder' (Women in the Indigenous People's Movements of Mexico: New Paths for Transforming Power). Case study prepared for AWID (Association for Women's Rights in Development), December, available at www.awid.org.

Lukes, Steven. 2005 [1974]. *Power: A Radical View* (London: Palgrave MacMillan).

MacGregor Burns, James. 1978. *Leadership* (New York: Harper Collins).

Masterson, Lorraine. 1976. 'Feminist Leaders Can't Walk on Water', *Quest*, II (4): 29–40.

Mitchell, Lisa. 2004. *Feminist Leadership in the Private Sector: Somewhere Out there?* (New Zealand: Labour Studies Department, University of Waikatu).

Quest, A Feminist Quarterly. 1976. 'Leadership', II (4).

Rao, Aruna, Rieky Stuart and David Kelleher. 1999. *Gender at Work: Organizational Change for Equality* (Bloomfield CT: Kumarian Press).

Rao, Aruna and David Kelleher. 2000. 'Leadership for social transformation: Some ideas and questions on institutions and feminist leadership', *Gender and Development*, 8 (3): pp. 74–79.

———. 2008. 'Unravelling Institutionalized Gender Inequality', Occasional Paper,

Gender at Work. Available at www.genderatwork.org/learning.

Rowlands, Jo. 1997. *Questioning Empowerment—Working with Women in Honduras* (Oxford: Oxfam).

Shah, Nandita and Nandita Gandhi. 1990. *The Issues at Stake: Theory and Practice in the Contemporary Indian Women's Movement* (New Delhi: Kali for Women).

St. Joan, Jackie. 1976. 'Who Was Rembrandt's Mother?' *Quest*, II (4): 67–79.

Stogdill, Ralph M. 1974. *Handbook of Leadership—A Survey of Theory and Research* (New York: Free Press).

VeneKlasen, Lisa with Valerie Miller (Debbie Budlender and Cindy Clark [co-eds]). 2002, *A New Weave of Power and Politics—An Action Guide for Advocacy and Citizen Participation* (Oklahoma City: World Neighbors).

Wineman, Wineman. 2003. *Power-Under: Trauma and Nonviolent Social Change'* (Cambridge, MA.). Available at www.TraumaandNonviolence.com, pp. 47–118.

Wood, Geoffrey D. 1994. *Bangladesh: Whose Ideas? Whose Interests?* (London: Intermediate Technology Publications)

———. 1994. 'Social Dimensions of Governance', World Bank / Bangladesh National Institutional Review.

Zimmerman, Kristen, Neelam Pathikonda, Brenda Salgado and Taj James. 2010. *Out of the Spiritual Closet—Organizers Transforming the Practice of Social Justice* (Oakland CA: The Movement Strategy Center).

III. Assessing Empowerment

Introduction

IN this final section, I offer readers several chapters in which I grapple with the complex question of how to assess or measure empowerment, if one was trying to evaluate its impact, or prove that women had been empowered by any particular intervention.

Chapter 9, 'Capturing Change in Women's Realities', is another AWID publication, done in collaboration with AWID colleague Alexandra Pittman in 2010 and 2011. I share here the first part of the paper, which I wrote, and which critiques current approaches to the monitoring and evaluation (hereafter, M&E) of women's empowerment and rights. and gender equality work more generally, especially as promoted or compelled by donor agencies. This was a paper I hugely enjoyed writing, and I will always be grateful to AWID's inspiring Executive Director, Lydia Alpizar, for having the vision to see that a feminist critique of M&E approaches was the need of the hour, and for encouraging me to focus on the spectrum of challenges within this field. Indeed, these issues were waiting to be unearthed, critiqued and articulated on behalf of the thousands of women's organisations around the world who were struggling to fit their work into the square holes of most M&E models, because their donors required it of them. The critique came together so quickly and easily that it was clear I had been storing away all this data about what wasn't working and about women's groups' disaffection with these instruments for a long, long time, unknown even to myself.

When the first version of the paper was shared, at a conference on monitoring and evaluation of women's rights organised by the Oak Foundation in Geneva at the end of 2009, the applause and endorsement of the analysis was overwhelming. Several participants came up to me and said, 'Thank you! You've put together everything we've been feeling and didn't know how to say about why these M&E

systems aren't working for us!' The paper builds a strong critique of why most M&E models are by and large inadequate, inappropriate, or ineffective in capturing the changes wrought by women's empowerment interventions and processes. It particularly underscores their inability to capture and accurately interpret the backlash and reversals that are inevitable when women are the key actors and subjects of empowerment, and patriarchal structures and institutions its targets.

Following this, I offer a couple of shorter articles that were not written precisely to explore how we assess empowerment, but actually do so in different ways. They are also personal favourites, in which I articulate some sets of ideas that had taken hold of me for some time, or which break some new ground.

The first, 'Gender Myths', was co-authored with feminist filmmaker Deepa Dhanraj, and was based on a longer paper that had included Geetanjali Misra as a co-author. This longer version had been written for a path-breaking conference organised by eminent feminist scholar and thinker Andrea Cornwall—who was kind enough to write the foreword for this book—at the Institute for Development Studies in Sussex, on 'Gender Myths and Feminist Fables'. Andrea had initially approached me to write a paper, situated in the Indian context, for this conference. The brief was to focus on some key ideas advanced by feminists that had either been co-opted and depoliticised by the state or other development actors (what she termed 'gender myths'), or that continued to be fondly upheld by feminists themselves long after their value had proved questionable (what she called 'feminist fables'). Since at this point I had been working outside India for quite a few years, I decided that rather than go it alone, I would invite two India-based women who worked from a feminist perspective, but with widely differing experiences, to join me in writing the piece—and Deepa and Geetanjali were kind enough to agree.

Later, when the paper had to be cut down for publication in the IDS Bulletin, I used the sections which had caused the greatest controversy at the conference, written by Deepa and myself, and which seemed to offer the most provocative ideas for a wider audience. These sections essentially questioned the way in which empowerment was being assessed and instrumentalised by the state. It is ironic that some of the ideas in this paper are no longer considered that provocative—for instance, the idea that micro-credit is not a magic bullet for empowering women, and brings a host of new challenges into women's lives, is now widely accepted. But at the time, it was considered heresy, including by eminent feminists, as though we were questioning women's right to receive these precious economic resources.

Chapter 11, 'When Rights Go Wrong', is a piece I love because in some ways, it was not written for anyone but myself. Although it was commissioned for an anniversary issue of the journal *Seminar*, the topic was left entirely to me—I chose to write about this because I had been feeling strongly that like the donor-imposed M&E frameworks, the so-called 'rights-based approach' had become yet another externally imposed framework. My own grassroots work with very poor urban and rural women had convinced me that the global project of framing and articulating human rights was far from complete, and that the ways in which empowered women articulated and claimed their rights was mediated by local culture and political realities, and should not be dismissed because it did not take the forms (such as litigation) that rights advocates promote. This is another paper that caused an outcry in some circles—my good friend and human rights advocate Sunila Abeysekara, for instance, was appalled by its arguments and simply said, 'Really, Sri, how could you? How could you advocate the use of patriarchal customary systems that have always devalued and discriminated against women when we have fought so hard for rights-based laws?' Sunila is of course right, but that's not what the paper is actually advocating at all—I invite readers to draw their own conclusions.

Choosing the closing chapter of this book—a collection of one's writings on empowerment—is quite a daunting task! Should it be something weighty—and lengthy? Or something that has been highly popular, like the conceptual framework on women's empowerment or women's movements? Should it be a personal favourite? Or ... should it be a piece that was a turning point of some kind in one's own journey of exploring this fraught and amorphous and challenging notion of empowerment—a 'eureka' moment in one's own growing understanding, an epiphany? Well, this last criterion is what swayed me in making my choice.

And so I close this book with 'Walk Beside Us'— an adaptation of a presentation I made in April 2002 to former US Vice President Al Gore, at a seminar series organised for him at the Kennedy School of Government at Harvard University, where I was a Research Fellow at the time. A few of us were asked to address the question: 'What is the role of governments, and what is the role of civil society groups, in addressing gender inequality?' Rather than answer the question with my own views and ideas, I decided to frame the response with the voices of the poor but empowered women in the urban slums and rural villages that I had worked with and learned so much from. It also addresses an issue that has become increasingly important in today's context, when more and more governments and donors are turning women into the new magic bullet that will raise the quality of life of their households, and increase their income to become consumers in the global marketplace, absolving the state and the private sector of all responsibility. The new mantra is 'invest in women and girls'—not because they have been historically marginalised, deprived of equal rights, and exploited, but because with a tiny amount of money by way of a loan, or a little bit of schooling, they will transform their entire communities.[1] In other words, women and girls are the most cost-effective solution to poverty and underdevelopment!

'Walk Beside Us' demonstrates that this simplistic approach will never work, because empowered women without responsive and accountable states and supportive civil societies will reach the limit of their capacity to change the world very quickly. They cannot be made solely responsible for social, economic and political transformation while state and non-state actors sit idly by. Women understand this very well.

I choose to close this book with this piece because it contains the visions, insights and voices of the women whose own journey of empowerment has been the raison d'etre of my work, its purpose and

---

[1] See Nike's 'Girl Effect' video as an example of this approach—http://www.girleffect.org/.

meaning. Throughout my life, it has been women like Sundaramma, as much as the great social science scholars and thinkers of the world, who have taught me the most powerful lessons about empowerment and its myriad pathways—and about the responsibilities of other actors to support the process, and its results, in various ways. Many other grassroots teachers stand alongside her: Sakina, Medina, Lakshmi and Mehrunnissa from Mumbai's women pavement and slum-dwellers federation, Mahila Milan; Baijubai, Shalubai and Paranjapebai from the Mandwa Rural Health Research Project in coastal Maharashtra; and Mahadeviamma, Nagamma, Renukabai and Gowramma from the Mahila Samakhya Karnataka project districts. It seems entirely fitting that I conclude this book with Sundaramma's words, rather than mine.

9. Capturing Change in Women's Realities*
(with Alexandra Pittman)

Introduction[1]

Over the past few decades, great strides have been made in developing ways to capture a whole range of abstract but vital social realities, and particularly in trying to quantify them. These efforts have been the result of the realisation that we must devise ways of checking whether the policies, resources and strategies applied towards building more equitable, sustainable, rights-affirming, inclusive and peaceful societies are working effectively or not—whether they are producing the changes we wish to see. This demands ways of measuring and tracking both the people and the processes involved in change.

While the attempt to assess changes in social realities certainly has been a positive development, measurement has become something of a power unto itself in modern times. Indeed, one of the hallmarks of modernisation has been the creation of a range of instruments to measure virtually everything—the size of sub-atomic particles, the health of economies, the rate at which blood is pumped through the heart, the level of democracy and transparency in different countries. Measurement has become such an integral part of our approach to the world that we no longer question its value or relevance. We assume that measurement is a good thing, something that enhances our ability to track change, growth, health and success.

---

* Prepared for AWID (Association for Women's Rights in Development), October 2010.

[1] This section, and many parts of this paper, draws extensively on my earlier work, in particular 2003, 2006, and 2010.

This assumption has naturally entered the world of social change as well—Edwards and others attribute this to the permeation of the capitalist business model into the domains of philanthropy and international development assistance (Edwards 2008). Consequently, it is not only assumed that the processes, outcomes and impacts of social change *should* be assessed, but that they *can* be assessed.

In other words, it is taken for granted that the instruments we have at our command for measuring such change are adequate, effective and sensitive. More problematically, it is assumed that change measurement enhances our ability to *make or accelerate positive change*. We need to interrogate all of these assumptions—to determine when and what kinds of measurement are actually useful in comparison to those that may be meaningless or even detrimental to social change. Such an interrogation has become especially urgent with the burgeoning demand, particularly from donors, for increasingly elaborate monitoring and evaluation (hereafter, M&E) systems of the social change projects they support. Social change organisations and activists are spending substantial amounts of time and energy filling in sophisticated LogFrames and compiling various kinds of data that are thought to effectively track change.

In this paper (Batliwala and Pittman 2010a), we examine these assumptions in the context of women's rights, gender equality and women's empowerment work, where M&E approaches create particular kinds of challenges. Part I provides a critique of current M&E frameworks and approaches as experienced by women's organisations and movements worldwide, and attempts to articulate some principles and attributes to engender our M&E approaches. Part II [not included in this volume] offers an analysis of a large number of M&E frameworks and tools, along with some of their strengths and weaknesses in assessing women's rights and gender equality processes and impacts.

While we are aware that M&E frameworks and tools are often not freely chosen but required to meet donor or other needs, we nevertheless hope that this document could be used as a platform to help women's rights organisations and activists reflect on their M&E systems, critically assess the systems they are currently using and make improvements, and negotiate with donors and others on how to best measure their performance. Most of all, we hope it will help women's rights actors to shift their attitude towards M&E from an externally-imposed necessity to an internal learning system that is central to strengthening their organisations and movements.

Clarifying our concepts

Throughout this paper, we frequently use the terms monitoring, evaluation, frameworks, approaches, tools and methods as concepts that are critical to our analysis. It is important, therefore, to define and clarify these to avoid confusion and conflation of meanings. As such, we begin by making a distinction between **monitoring** and **evaluation**.

In the context of social change work, **monitoring** is an ongoing programme management activity, assessing the implementation of activities and progress made towards meeting outcomes (organisational, programmatic, or policy-related) for the purposes of measuring effectiveness and efficiency. Monitoring is done on a frequent and regular basis to determine whether work is proceeding according to plan, and if sudden or unexpected shifts or reversals have occurred that must be attended to in order to proceed towards intended goals and objectives. In practice, monitoring systems generate information that will feed into longer-term programme or project evaluations.

Evaluation aims to assess the overall impact of a social change intervention[2] against an explicit set of goals and objectives. Evaluation involves the systematic collection and analysis of data to help us discover if, how and why a particular intervention or set of interventions worked or did not. Evaluations are conducted less frequently than monitoring, as they are more comprehensive and aim to capture the big picture of impact at particular moments in time. Evaluations can be conducted before (formative),[3] during

---

[2] Interventions can be programmatic, policy-focused, or project-based.

[3] Formative evaluations are conducted when programmes are in development or in the mid-term when making strategic decisions about the inclusion or exclusion of a particular strategy or process. These evaluations focus on assessing the effectiveness of programme processes and different delivery mechanisms or strategies.

(developmental)[4] and after (summative)[5] an intervention is implemented for the purposes of programme, project, or policy improvement, knowledge building, or learning.

Frameworks (typically referred to as M&E frameworks in this paper) are the broad conceptual structures that attempt to pull together a set of ideas about how a change intervention should be tracked and how its effects should be measured or assessed.

Approaches are more specific and usually identify what elements are important to measure in a certain context, as well as provide direction on how to measure it (explicitly or implicitly referencing appropriate methods). Underlying the approach are certain beliefs or hypotheses, at times explicit or not, about what constitutes effective performance, impact and change. In this sense, both frameworks and specific approaches shape how our work is monitored or evaluated, and as a result shape what we can say about impact.

A **tool** is a specific assessment or measurement technique that is used within broader evaluation frameworks and approaches, to generate concrete data or evidence about the results of an intervention or change process.

In any M&E process, different data collection **methods** are used, and methods can be common to many different frameworks and approaches. For instance, quantitative methods, such as surveys, help generate statistical evidence, while qualitative methods like interviews, focus groups, mapping, and so forth help gather richer, more nuanced information on individual and collective struggles, experiences and interpretations of the change process.

With these definitions in place, let us move into our analysis of M&E in the context of women's empowerment and gender equality work.

---

[4] Summative evaluations occur at the end of a given intervention or project cycle, focusing on analysing the overall impact that a programme has had, as well as detailing the strengths and weaknesses of the programmes, policies, campaigns, organisations, etc.

[5] Developmental evaluation focuses on assessment in rapidly changing environments. The focus is on creating evaluation teams with strong relationships and the ability to adapt evaluation questions and tasks as programmes and contexts evolve (see Quinn Patton 2009).

Two steps forward, one step back

Women's empowerment and gender equality initiatives have been under increasing pressure to measure their impact over the past two decades. At the same time, donor support for certain kinds of women's empowerment or rights work has decreased, at least partly, because they are considered too slow, amorphous, or intangible. There is growing evidence, in fact, that the lion's share of investment in gender equality has shifted to a handful of 'magic bullets' like microfinance and political representation (see, for example, Batliwala 2010; Dichter 2003; Rankin 2001), precisely because the results of these interventions are far easier to assess. The challenges of measuring change—that is, of monitoring and evaluation (M&E)—in the context of gender relations, and the social relations within which they are embedded, are somewhat more challenging for several reasons, which are discussed below. The greatest challenge is well summed up in the words of a seasoned Indian activist:

> When you work for women's interests, it's two steps forward—if you're really smart and very lucky!—and at least one step back. In fact, it's often two or three steps back! And those steps back are, ironically, often evidence of your effectiveness; because they represent the threat you have posed to the power structure and its attempt to push you back. Sometimes, even your 'success stories' are nothing more than ways the power structure is trying to accommodate and contain the threat of more fundamental change by making small concessions.[6]

This quote eloquently articulates a universal truth: transforming gender power relations is the last frontier of social change. While changes in the social power relations of North-South, developed-developing, race, class, caste, ethnicity, sexuality, ability, etc., are also difficult to achieve, patriarchal norms are *embedded and normalised within each of these power structures*, such that challenging and transforming them is a doubly daunting task. Since gender power is integral to both public and private institutions and relationships, shifting it in one domain does not guarantee that it has been uprooted

---

[6] Personal communication with Sheela Patel, Director, SPARC, India, in 1987.

in another. However, investors in women's empowerment who demand 'proof' of positive change generally want evidence of a smooth progression, rather than a picture of the messy reality—the steps forward and the steps back—that is closer to the truth.

Why do we measure change?

Any critique—gendered or otherwise—of M&E frameworks must begin with the basic question of why we monitor or evaluate at all. *In theory*, at least, M&E is motivated by at least five basic objectives:

- **To learn** how change happens, what strategies and interventions worked and what did not, in order to refine our policies, strategies and interventions for more effective and impactful change—most of all, to grapple with both progress and reversals and build more effective change strategies as a result;
- **To analyse our role in the change process**—that is, either to attribute credit or locate our contribution to change and to identify cause-effect relationships;
- **To empower our constituencies**—to engage stakeholders in analysing change processes so that they are also empowered and strengthened to sustain, extend and expand change;
- **To practice accountability and build credibility**—to our donors, constituencies, other activists, and the public at large, and to build our legitimacy, credibility and transparency; and finally,
- **To advance our advocacy for social justice**—to demonstrate how change has advanced social justice goals and mobilise broader support for our change agenda.

In practice, however, M&E is more likely to be done because:

- **Donors require it** to ensure their funds have been utilised correctly and to demonstrate the impact to their own constituencies (their governing bodies, contributors, governments, etc.), thereby showing that they are supporting effective work, the 'right' kind of work;
- **To sustain or obtain more funding** or to compete for new grants or contracts—donors are more likely to invest in organisations

with a proven track record of work (manifested in the form of concretely measured results); and/or,

- **To support public fund-raising or advocacy work** by showing how successful particular approaches or interventions have been.

These sorts of pressures convert measurement from an activity designed to *aid learning* into one that *evaluates performance*. They consequently distort the purpose and potential value of our M&E work. A feminist M&E approach would therefore be motivated primarily by the first set of objectives, rather than the second.

Current M&E practice—what isn't working for women's rights organisations

Over the past year, the Association for Women's Rights in Development (AWID) has undertaken a critical review of a wide range of current M&E frameworks and approaches, particularly those that are in wide use among women's organisations. We have gathered and analysed over fifty frameworks and tools to assess their strengths and limitations. We have also reviewed the growing critiques of the assessment frameworks and tools that are currently dominant in the development sector (see, for instance, Bakewell and Garbutt 2005). In addition, we have had in-depth discussions on M&E with a wide range of women's organisations and leaders around the world, including a large number of those who won the Dutch Government's MDG3 Fund grants, and partners and allies of our 'Where is the Money' initiative (see http://www.awid.org/Our-Initiatives/Where-is-the-money-for-women-s-rights). What follows is a summary of the key challenges in current M&E systems, identified through our own analysis as well as by women's rights organisations and activists.

Specifically, we found that very few M&E frameworks or approaches actually enable us to understand *how change happens or how gender relations have been altered*. However, this is necessary if we want to identify the most effective interventions for shifting the complex social power relations that mediate women's access to resources and rights, security and autonomy. Linear frameworks in particular tend to primarily focus on measuring performance against predetermined goals and activities, so that the only thing one can say at the end of a project cycle is whether those goals were achieved or not, but not *how* real change was achieved. Many frameworks and tools thus measure performance, rather than impact or change. This is ironic, since an implicit objective of most M&E exercises is to discover the right 'formula' for change, so that it can be reproduced or replicated in other locations and contexts.

The second and related challenge is to know *what* to measure, particularly in relation to the *assumptions or theory of change* underlying the intervention or programme. There seems to be a growing trend of questioning even long-standing indicators for their inability to tell us what is really happening on the ground in people's daily lives. This dilemma is now being acknowledged even in 'hard' fields like economics, where seemingly invincible measures like GDP have prevailed for a long time (see Box 9.1). Within the domain of international aid, where the goal is to catalyse positive change that promotes human rights, economic development, peace and social justice with gender equality, M&E approaches are supposedly created to highlight lessons and the relevant interventions necessary to guide further action. In practice, however, M&E approaches and their indicators take on a life of their own, often dissociated from the theory of change, becoming an end in themselves rather than a means. There is a widespread feeling among aid recipients—governmental and non-governmental—that measurement is used more as a tool of enforcement and accountability to the donor than as a means of understanding and learning what works, and for changing strategy if necessary (see Bornstein 2006; Helleiner 2000).

In this context, we must also question whether our frameworks *confuse or conflate short-term change with sustainable change*. Women's rights organisations and their allies from around the world—such as the activist quoted earlier—have learned that while power structures often accommodate some degree of challenge and may appear to change, ultimately deeper transformations in the status quo do not necessarily occur. In some cases, a strategy that has worked in the past may not work again even in the same context, given the prior change that has been achieved.

We have also seen that women's movements and other social

Box 9.1
Why GDP Won't Do

The Commission on the Measurement of Economic Performance and Social Progress was set up by French President Nicholas Sarkozy in 2008, headed by Nobel Prize-winning economist Joseph Stiglitz and supported by fellow Nobel Laureate Amartya Sen and several others. The Commission has concluded that highly esteemed indicators of economic growth, such as GDP, can be misleading; they believe new indicators incorporating a notion of *lifestyle* and *national well-being* are required (see Commission Report, http://www.stiglitz-sen-fitoussi.fr/en/index.htm). Indeed, Stiglitz writes in a hard-hitting piece entitled 'The Great GDP Swindle':

> In our performance-oriented world, measurement issues have taken on increased importance: what we measure affects what we do. If we have poor measures, what we strive to do (say, increase GDP) may actually contribute to a worsening of living standards. We may also be confronted with false choices, seeing trade-offs ... that don't exist (Stiglitz 2009a).
>
> It is time for our statistics system to put more emphasis on measuring the well-being of the population than on economic production (Stiglitz 2009b).

President Sarkozy established the Commission because of his conviction that current economic measures often indicate levels of economic progress that are far higher than citizens' actual experience, particularly since these indicators tend to hide high levels of inequality and disparity within societies.

movements with a strong gender equality focus are sometimes more successful in creating sustained change. However, *most existing M&E tools are not designed for tracking movement building or movement impacts.* They have been developed to measure the work of individual organisations and often single projects or interventions. We are yet to design frameworks and approaches that can capture the results of larger-scale women's empowerment processes that build collective power and deeper change, including accounts of success as well as challenges and backlash.

Women's and feminist organisations are increasingly critiquing the inherent narrowness and *inappropriateness of existing M&E systems for multilayered formations, such as transnational or regional networks, coalitions, membership-based organisations, and re-granting organisations, like women's funds*. Our recent study of M&E challenges faced by recipients of the MDG3 Fund awards (Batliwala and Pittman 2010b) describes in detail the multiple assessment challenges faced in these complex organisational architectures, involving many actors (and organisations) working at different levels and locations. Often, the agency responsible for assessing and reporting progress and impact to their donor has to collate and synthesise information from all of these levels and present them as though they were part of one single change intervention. The entity receiving the grant is also required to tease out and establish its own contribution to the change process, using tools that are simply not designed to handle this level of complexity. Many of these 'INGO' (international or transnational NGOs) structures are facing serious funding challenges because it is harder for them to prove their value, given the current assessment tools. They are also questioning the high level of accountability demanded of them when their donor partners—such as bilateral agencies—are not accountable in any concrete way for the way they choose to allocate their resources (AWID/Mama Cash/HIVOS 2009: 8).

The linearity of many tools—especially widely used methods like the Logical Framework or 'LogFrame'—*have been problematic* because they flatten change processes into cause-effect relationships that cannot capture and measure complex social changes, and may even mislead us about how these occur. The LogFrame has, for this reason, been described as the 'simple linear' theory of change model, since it attempts to establish one-dimensional causal chains. The assumptions underlying each part of the LogFrame—that x intervention led to y effect, which led to z change—are also limiting because they cannot incorporate the many other change dynamics and factors that may influence an intervention. In a SIDA study of NGO experiences with the Logical Framework Approach,

> … one NGO respondent commented that the focus is often the logical framework [LFA]—to look at the expected achievements laid out in the matrix—rather than the work itself. As a result the emphasis of

monitoring and evaluation systems based on the LFA is often upwards accountability to the donor, to show whether the intervention is delivering the outputs and impact as proposed (Bakewell and Garbutt 2005: 10).

Recent attempts have been made, however, to make the LogFrame both more modest and less flat—a major bilateral, for instance, has put 'risks and assumptions' into the frame and limits measurement to 'verifiable indicators'. Many women's organisations are discovering some of the advantages of using this tool—such as the ability to track smaller positive steps that raise morale and measure performance (Batliwala and Pittman 2010b). Nevertheless, the tool is at best a supplement to other methods that better accommodate complexity and challenges from both within and throughout the change process.

A hugely important factor, particularly for activists working in the developing world, is the *political assumption of stable and equitable socio-political contexts that underlies many M&E frameworks*. These are macro-political assumptions about the way the world and society works—that democratic rights, law and order, an impartial judiciary and police, due process and access to redress, rights of association, civil liberties, an independent media, etc., are inevitably present and surrounding change processes in a larger safety net. In reality, few of these conditions can be presumed to exist in many of the contexts where women seek radical change. The contextual realities are more likely to include a growing number of attacks on women human rights defenders and the growing incidence of femicide (Guatemala), violent removal of democratically elected regimes by juntas of various kinds (Honduras), weakness or impotence of even democratically elected regimes (Pakistan), violent extremist movements antithetical to women's rights (the Taliban, Islamic and Hindu extremists in India and Pakistan, Iran), humanitarian and natural disasters (in 2009 in India, China, Philippines), wars and civil conflicts (Sri Lanka, Sudan, Congo, Cote d'Ivoire), rogue states and leaders (Zimbabwe), suspension of civil liberties and most rights (Honduras, Zimbabwe, China), mass displacement (Darfur, Congo, Sri Lanka), ecologically and economically-induced migration (India), human trafficking (Russia, Eastern Europe, Indonesia, Philippines, India, Sri Lanka), revival of barbaric and primitive penalties for 'errant' women like whipping, stoning and honour killings (Nigeria, Pakistan, Indonesia, Saudi Arabia), and populations devastated by global pandemics (Botswana, South Africa). These are the catastrophic realities in which legions of women's rights actors operate—abnormalities that are all too normal in much of our world. How many M&E approaches actually enable or allow these factors to be represented as integral elements affecting a project or intervention? If they do not, then these are very fundamental flaws, which deeply affect any change intervention aiming to transform their realities; this is particularly the case since women everywhere are more severely affected by these forces than men.

Similarly, most tools do not allow for *tracking negative change, reversals, backlash,* unexpected change, and other processes that push back or shift the direction of a positive change trajectory. How do we create tools that can capture this 'two steps forward, one step back' phenomenon that many activists and organisations acknowledge as a reality, and in which large amounts of learning lie hidden? In women's rights work, this is vital, because as soon as advances seriously challenge patriarchal or other social power structures, there are often significant reactions and setbacks. These are not, ironically, always indicative of failure or lack of effectiveness, but exactly the opposite—this is evidence that the process was working and creating resistance from the status quo as a result (see Box 9.2). Of course, not all negative changes are signs of progress— they may also provide evidence that our strategies are ineffective or that women need to build greater collective power. Interrogating the forces pushing back or complicating change is critical, and yet this does not really find a place in our current M&E frameworks and approaches. Many women's groups are afraid to even report these backward steps since they could impact their funding flows, losing valuable learning insights for all.

Some women's rights activists and their allies consequently propose that *we need to develop a 'theory of constraints'* to accompany our 'theory of change' in any given context, in order to create tools

for tracking the way that power structures are responding to the
challenges posed by women's rights interventions.[7]

Box 9.2
Why Tracking Negative Shifts Matters

Impact evaluations of micro-credit programmes for women's economic
empowerment in India, where this is a dominant form of investment in
women, have found some interesting facts: the more successful the
programme is in raising women's income levels, the more likely are male
earners in the household to shift responsibility for the household's
economic security onto women, who earn less and work less regularly,
while also taking control of women's income (Nirantar 2007). Women
themselves report increased violence as a result of tensions around their
new-found economic power, especially where lending schemes exclude
men.

In another Indian case, a violence-against-women intervention[8] was
declared a failure because the impact evaluation found that the expected
outcome—viz., increased reporting to and filing of complaints with the
police—did not occur. A deeper enquiry found that the focus on police
and legal remedy was the problem—women were afraid of the police,
whose record in committing atrocities on poor women, including rape,
ensured that no woman would voluntarily seek their help in dealing with
violence from other men.[9] Instead, women had developed community-
level strategies that were beginning to have some impact, but those could
not be measured through the indicators identified, such as police
complaints.

For similar reasons, *tracking less tangible but vital gender equality
interventions is quite difficult with current M&E instruments*. For
instance, women's organisations engaged in building capacity through
training and other means (including research and knowledge
building, challenging dominant perspectives and discourses, changing
public attitudes, playing support roles to other movements or

---

[7] Discussion of considerations for monitoring and evaluation at the AWID/Mama
Cash/HIVOS meeting (2009).
[8] Project details cannot be shared to protect the identity and confidentiality of the
organisation.
[9] Personal communication with Nandita Shah, Akshara Centre, Mumbai.

networks, engaging in policy advocacy, shifting public attitudes through campaigns and consciousness-raising with women, etc.), all find it quite challenging to show the impact of their work. Consequently, they are compelled to measure their *processes, outreach and outputs* (number of training programmes held, number of participants, publications, attendance at rallies and meetings, etc.), rather than the *results* of the process. Many such organisations, especially those working at the global level, have found it very difficult to receive adequate levels of funding, since they are asked to demonstrate impact in ways that are untenable for them. We have yet to create effective M&E tools for this critical range of activities and strategies, which is the core work of thousands of women's organisations worldwide.

Several *false binaries and dichotomies* are embedded within or underlie many M&E approaches—for example, 'quantitative-qualitative', 'subjective-objective', 'macro-micro', 'success-failure', and so forth. These create problematic hierarchies and reveal positivist and reductionist biases rather than immutable tensions. Subjective information, for instance, can be far more telling in measuring change in women's lives than supposedly 'objective' data; at the same time, dismissing the anecdotal as too 'micro' often negates potentially powerful lines of inquiry about change processes. But it is not only hardheaded evaluation specialists who carry these biases—women activists are also guilty, although possibly at the other end of the spectrum. We have witnessed vehement assertions that 'the kind of work we do cannot be measured or quantified—it is very nuanced. We can only tell stories about it, we can't provide hard data.' These stances not only negate the fact that many dimensions of changes in women's status and rights *can* be quantified, but also reinforce the sense that women's empowerment processes are difficult to monitor or evaluate. But if one is motivated by the desire to demonstrate that even the most abstract interventions can have measurable impact, then women's organisations may hold the key to producing incredible innovations.[10]

---

[10] Report of the Results Assessment workshop conducted by HIVOS with Indian partners in 2004.

Women's rights activists frequently encounter a *disjuncture between change measures and time frames*, for the simple reason that the changes we are trying to track may not be visible within the time frame in which we are required to assess. As the veteran activist for the rights of women in the informal sector and founder of SEWA, Ela Bhat, once told me, 'It takes ten years to build an organization, twenty years to build a movement, and thirty years before you see lasting impact.'

For example, the MDG3 Fund grants, with their short time frame of three years, are nevertheless using yardsticks suitable for a much longer project timeline. Many MDG3 Fund grantees find that there is a lack of clarity about short vs. medium and long-term changes in the current M&E reporting processes. This problem gets compounded in multilayered architectures: women's funds, for instance, must demonstrate what they are accomplishing in specific (and usually fairly short) time frames to their donors, and so are forced to pass the pressure on to their grantees.

This brings us to another critical issue—*the problematic assumptions embedded in most M&E methods regarding the capacity of their end-users*. In most cases, it is M&E specialists or other 'experts', rather than women's rights activists, who have developed many of the current tools, which require high levels of training and competence for effective use. More importantly, they tend to assume that their logic and conceptual underpinnings are universal, rather than culture and region-specific. In reality, the majority of women's rights workers, especially in Southern cultures and grassroots contexts, think about change—and its assessment—quite differently (see Box 9.3). Activists from the Pacific, for instance, say that even the use of boxes, as opposed to circles, create problems in their region where people's visual literacy do not easily grasp shapes like squares and rectangles. They may narrate stories of profound and far-reaching change and use concentric circles to make connections between interventions and their results, but struggle to understand and fill in a LogFrame or use SMART indicators.[11] There is also growing

---

[11] Personal communication with activists from the Pacific Islands and Maori groups in New Zealand.

awareness that even activist-developed and supposedly 'bottom-up' tools (several of which are included in Part II of this document) are too complicated for grassroots use. The need is for simple and user-friendly, but culturally sensitive and nuanced, tools that can be used by a broad spectrum of actors without requiring intensive capacity building.

There is a *lack of clarity in the donor community around M&E, especially in the context of women's empowerment work*, which then permeates the relationships with grantees and partners, creating tension. Our research and conversations with women's organisations reveal the perception that donors need to do more homework on M&E in order to become more aware of the complexities and of the possibilities and limitations of various tools, becoming active partners in the search for more relevant and sensitive approaches. As one donor representative at a recent AWID gathering said,

> [in social change work] ... none of us know what we are doing ... we are all flailing around. Donors get to impose [M&E models] but they don't know what they're doing either. What's worked for us is ... the conversation and face to face interaction ... the site visits and dialogue is where we place the emphasis, instead of expecting all the answers in the report.

Women's organisations are also frustrated by the *lack of a genuine and ongoing negotiation space with some donors to discuss what is happening with their assessment systems*. There is a sense that once a framework has been negotiated, it becomes a very rigid tool with little space for modification, even if the users discover that it is not working well or that new dimensions need to be added. This is the nature of social change work, particularly women's empowerment work: Even if we think at the beginning of a process that we know what should be tracked or measured, these are ultimately educated guesses and our indicators may actually prove inadequate and inappropriate in the second or third year of the project. But the bureaucracies within which even sympathetic and supportive donors work may not allow this kind of flexibility—so everyone is trapped.

This problem is also linked to *the sense that M&E is used punitively*—in other words, that if the indicators chosen at the outset turn out to be inappropriate and the data generated reflects poorly on the project / implementing organisation, it negatively influences funding decisions. Many activists feel this belies the rhetoric about evaluation being for learning and improving change strategies, since resources often disappear if the assessment does not show their work to be a 'success'. Few donors, it is felt, stay the course and join grantees in learning how change works and in making mid-course corrections—including in the M&E design—so that some kind of lasting impact can actually be made. But donor agency representatives are under tremendous pressure: to show that they are supporting 'winning' strategies and organisations, or to discontinue support to seemingly amorphous women's empowerment approaches that do not show quick, visible and quantifiable results.

At the same time, our research reveals that *lack of a strong culture of assessment and the tendency of both donors and women's organisations to treat M&E as an afterthought* is a serious challenge in the present environment (Batliwala and Pittman 2010b). Many women's rights activists are acknowledging the fact that there is a negative attitude towards M&E within their organisations—probably because of all the challenges and limitations listed here—or at least, a tendency not to see it as a central and integral component of their work. M&E is often viewed as donor-driven—too often because it is—rather than an essential learning device. Locating and prioritising M&E as a core activity, instead of as an 'add-on', is rare within women's rights organisations, and even among many donors. As one activist put it, 'there is no M&E *culture* in women's groups'; so many are, in fact, doing it to satisfy donor requirements rather than to interrogate their work and retool their strategies. M&E must be rescued from these dynamics and repositioned in women's rights work as a critical element of our accountability to our constituencies, our politics and ourselves. We need to create a *culture of assessment and learning* within our organisations and movements.

On the donor side, *M&E gets shortchanged in terms of resources and emphasis*. While some give a lot of importance to M&E in grant negotiations, others tend to treat it as a postscript initially, but later place a lot of emphasis on it, creating both frustration and resentment on the grantee side. Donors are also unable or unwilling to bear the cost of good M&E—to invest resources in supporting grantees to create well-integrated and effective assessment systems, or to hire the expertise that may be required—but do not hesitate to demand a 'results orientation' as though no staff time or organisational costs are involved in this. While good assessment is not always expensive, the levels or kinds of information some donors ask for requires a lot of staff time, capacity and resources. The attitude that organisations should deliver this data without needing extra resources has to change—tracking and measuring women's empowerment and advancements in gender equality can involve serious costs if it is to be done well.

Finally, many *current assessment methods are neither gendered nor feminist* in their principles or methodology, nor are they sensitive to or designed for the particularities of the power shifts and challenges generated by women's rights interventions. While approaches like Theory of Change and Making the Case work quite well in many of our contexts, others are rather linear and limited. As some M&E analysts have pointed out, even gender analysis frameworks—of which there are several—are not necessarily the same as feminist evaluation (Podems 2007). We therefore need to unpack, explore and construct the core principles and elements of a feminist approach to evaluation.

Given these myriad and serious challenges, it is crucial to re-fashion our existing tools and frameworks to overcome their more serious shortcomings, and strengthen their capacity to adequately capture the complexity of gender equality work and the social dynamic within which it occurs.

Towards feminist M&E

It appears that at the centre of our struggle to produce better evidence in women's rights and gender equality work is the difficulty of pinning down the sometimes amorphous, shifting and always multifaceted manifestations of gender oppression. It is often like the elephant in the room—everyone knows it is there, but to measure its contours and create evidence of its presence is not quite so easy. But at another level, we have made remarkable and enormous progress: we have created excellent and extensive sets of indicators for measuring the status of women—life expectancy, infant and child mortality rates by gender, literacy and education levels, employment and work participation rates, political participation and representation, etc., to cite but a few examples. We have ensured that gender-disaggregated data is available in most national and global statistical systems, something that was unheard of just a few decades ago. Multiple gendered assessment frameworks have also been developed over the past decades (see Batliwala and Pittman 2010b: Part II; and http://www.awid.org/Library/AWID-s-Wiki-on-Monitoring-and-Evaluation).

Why, then, is there still a sense that no M&E approach currently available is quite right—that there is always something we cannot quite capture or that we cannot generate evidence for in the given formats? Why has our research failed to find any existing M&E framework or approach that women's right activists, researchers, advocates and donors declare as ideal and comprehensive?

The answer might lie in returning to the analogy of the elephant: our existing instruments—whether quantitative or qualitative—tell only part of the story; they describe only the part they can measure, but believe that they are measuring the entire elephant. And some of these approaches—such as the gender indices used in national and global statistical assessment, like the Gender Development Index (GDI), are far too gross and too 'macro' to be used for the kinds of work most women's rights activists and advocates are engaged in, or for the levels at which they operate. For instance, a grassroots intervention will likely not be able to identify changes in female literacy in a three or five-year project cycle. Perhaps because of this complexity and multifacetedness, our work requires the deployment of several different frameworks and tools to capture all the aspects of change, as well as the resistance and backlash that may result from our interventions.

Women's rights work is engaged in a complex dynamic of change that often engages both the formal realm of law, policy and resources, as well as patriarchal and other oppressive social structures, cultures, beliefs and practices. The Rao and Kelleher (2002) model (see Figure 9.1) describes four dimensions for unpacking the different domains in which gender power structures operate. The model is extremely useful in highlighting the complexity of the change work that women's rights organisations undertake. As it stands, many of the current M&E tools are actually designed to gauge change primarily in the formal domain, rather than the harder-to-measure realms of cultural norms and practices.

Figure 9.1
Domains of Change in Gender Power

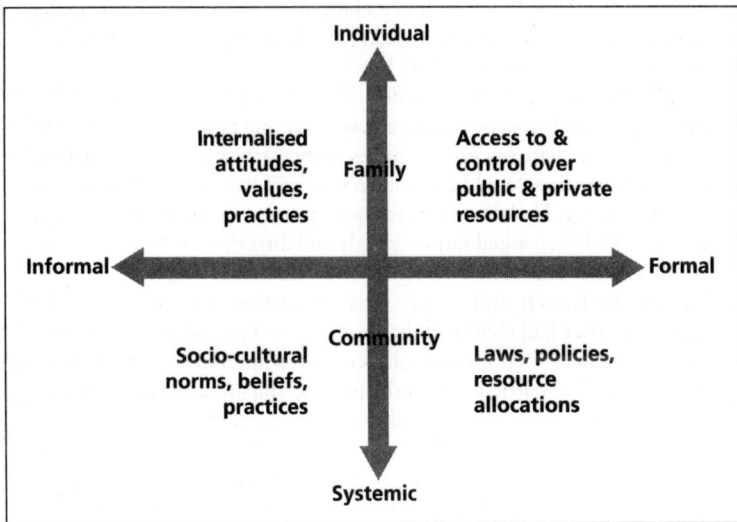

Finally, women from our constituencies are a great, untapped resource in helping us to identify and create more effective indicators for assessing change and impact. Box 9.3 gives some examples of why this is so. We need to work more closely with our constituencies in building our M&E systems to find more creative and often unseen ways of tracking the effects of our—and their—interventions in the change process.

So we must accept that the ideal feminist M&E framework has yet to be created, and that among the wide repertoire of tools currently at our disposal, no single one can serve the assessment needs of every organisation, intervention and change process. The

Box 9.3
Why Women's Inputs are Crucial

A women's empowerment project of three years was undergoing a mid-term evaluation. The evaluation team held meetings with the grassroots women's groups that had been organised through feminist popular education techniques. When the women identified greater strength and confidence as one of the ways in which the process had empowered them, evaluators asked for examples. One woman, a landless agricultural labourer, said, 'Three years ago, when the landlord in whose fields I work addressed me, I would answer him looking down at his feet. Now, I answer with my eyes on his chest. Next year, I will be strong enough to look him right in the eyes when I speak to him.'

Additionally, a study of gender relations and the status of women probed men and women's relative autonomy and power with respect to control over private resources. The researchers struggled to come up with the right question to address women's control over private assets—for example, house, land, livestock, equipment, etc. During the pre-test, the question had been asked rather crudely and directly—'Who has control over the following?' The researchers knew they had not got at the truth because both men and women respondents were confused by the question—they had identified the legal owner or patriarch of the family. The researchers then conducted focus group interviews with a set of women who had participated in the pre-test and discussed this question with them. One wise woman in the group asked with some amusement, 'What are you trying to understand?' The researchers replied, 'Who really has control over this asset.' 'Oh!' she said, 'In that case, all you have to ask is: if there is an emergency and you need money quickly, what can you sell or pawn without asking anyone's permission?' The question was changed accordingly and the study yielded not only accurate, but astonishing results. The vast majority of women identified their personal jewellery as the only asset they truly controlled. And the men said the only asset they controlled was their wife's jewellery (Batliwala et al. 1998: 149)!!

challenge, then, is to determine how we can move forward more effectively with the tools and frameworks we already have. We believe that one strategy is to articulate some principles that can guide our assessment and learning processes, especially in a feminist social change context.

Some principles for feminist assessment

The following principles are based not only on our own research and the work of some feminist evaluators, but also on the feedback we have received from practitioners engaged in gender equality and women's rights work from the local to the global levels in diverse regions and contexts around the world (for a more complete guideline and articulation of principles, see Batliwala 2011). This is not a complete list, but an attempt to articulate some of the key insights that have emerged so far.

- Feminist M&E means choosing and using *tools that are designed to unpack the nature of gender inequalities and the social inequalities through which these are mediated.* Not all tools are designed to do this since they may not disaggregate issues by gender at all. Our tools of choice will treat gender and social inequalities as systemic and embedded in social structures, and will be able to examine the way the interventions being assessed are addressing the structures.
- *No single assessment framework can adequately capture all dimensions of gendered social change processes*; consequently, we must seek to *create M&E systems that combine different approaches and tools* in the most appropriate manner for our specific needs. Similarly, no single tool can assess all the components of a feminist change process.
- Changes in gender power do not go unchallenged—*our tools will enable the tracking* and appropriate interpretation *of backlash against and resistance to change* (that is, not as failures of the strategy, but as evidence of its impact and, possibly, effectiveness).
- *Our tools will not seek to attribute change to particular actors, but to assess who and what contributed to change.*
- *Our approaches will challenge and transcend the traditional hierarchies within assessment techniques*—for example, between the evaluator and the 'evaluated', 'subjective-objective', 'quantitative-qualitative', etc.—and will combine the best of all existing tools to create better evidence and knowledge for all.
- *Women's voices and experiences will inform and transform our frameworks and approaches.* Experience shows that women are

often the best sources for sensitive indicators of hard-to-assess dimensions of changes in gender relations (see Box 9.3); so rather than reduce these to 'anecdotal' evidence, our tools will find ways of privileging these perspectives in our assessments.

- *Recognising that change must occur in both the formal realm of law, policy and resources, and in culture, beliefs and practices,* our tools will track changes in both these domains at the individual and systemic levels.
- *Acknowledging that while changing gender power structures is complex, our assessment tools must combine simplicity and accessibility. We will attempt to create approaches that can bridge this paradox.* We recognise the cultural biases of many existing frameworks and tools and will attempt to modify them to the diverse settings in which we work.
- *We will undertake M&E primarily for our own learning and accountability,* and not because it is required by donors or other external actors. Accordingly, we will prioritise M&E in our work and proactively promote the frameworks, approaches and tools of our choice with donor partners.
- *Consequently, we view M&E as a political activity,* rather than as value-free, *and will deploy this as part of the change process in which we are engaged.*

Building our M&E system

Given that there are several distinct components in feminist social change work, we must choose the best frameworks and tools available for each of these discrete, but central parts of our work:

- **Assessing how change happens**: Systems that help us to understand the pathways through which change happens, as well as make explicit the assumptions that underlie the change we seek;
- **Assessing plans and activities**: Tools to measure the effectiveness of our implementation (for example, have we done what we planned in the time we set for ourselves, and if not, what happened?);

- **Assessing strategies and interventions:** Tools that track and examine the efficiency of our change interventions, to see if they are working (for example, if we are deploying a particular awareness-building strategy, is it the most effective means for changing recipients' understanding of the issues?);
- **Assessing our contribution to changes in formal systems and resources at both the individual and systemic levels, quantitatively and qualitatively** (see the Rao-Kelleher model): Tools that can gauge actual desired changes that have occurred in the domain of policies, laws, rights, institutional arrangements and resource allocations that benefit our designated constituency, issue and arena, and trace our contribution to this in a convincing way;
- **Assessing our contribution to changes in cultural norms, attitudes and practices at both the individual and systemic levels, quantitatively and qualitatively:** Tools that can unearth and make visible the way that embedded patriarchal and other oppressive cultural norms—such as tolerance for violence against women—have changed with convincing evidence, including our role in this change;
- **Assessing reversals and backlashes that have obstructed the change process,** and how we have managed and responded to those; and,
- **Assessing the sustainability of changes achieved:** We cannot rest on the laurels of small victories or treat them as evidence of longer lasting change. We need ways of conducting longer-term assessments to gauge how sustainable changes are, especially in the face of backlash. These tools should help separate short-term effects from longer-term change.

* * *

Despite current M&E shortcomings and drawbacks, today we have a wider range of frameworks, approaches and tools—and far more choice—than was available to our feminist predecessors just a couple of decades ago. The challenge is whether we have the creativity and flexibility to build assessment systems in new ways—to create M&E

architectures that go beyond the scope of any one tool or method. Many of us are already doing this in practice. We hope that this paper will further support these processes and generate new approaches that push us closer towards capturing changes in the lived realities of women throughout the world.

References

AWID/Mama Cash/HIVOS. 2009, 'Resource Mobilization Strategies for Women's Organizing and Women's Rights: A Stakeholders Meeting', Amsterdam, 30 November–1 December.

Batliwala, Srilatha. 2003. 'Can Civil Society Be Measured? A Review of Challenges and Approaches', Hauser Center for Nonprofit Organizations (Harvard University) Working Paper Series, March.

———. 2006. 'Measuring Social Change: Myths, Assumptions and Realities', *Alliance Magazine*, 11 (1): 12–14.

———. 2010a. 'Feminist Leadership for Social Transformation: Clearing the Conceptual Cloud' (Creating Resources for Empowerment in Action [CREA]).

———. 2010b. 'Women's Empowerment in 21st Century India', in K. Shiva Kumar et al. (eds), *Handbook of Population and Development* (New Delhi: Oxford University Press).

———. 2011, 'Strengthening Monitoring and Evaluation for Women's Rights: Thirteen Insights for Women's Organizations' (Toronto: AWID). Available at http://www.awid.org/Library/Strengthening-Monitoring-and-Evaluation-for-Women-s-Rights-Thirteen-Insights-for-Women-s-Organizations.

Batliwala, Srilatha and Alexandra Pittman. 2010a. 'Capturing Change in Women's Realities: A Critical Overview of Current Monitoring & Evaluation Frameworks and Approaches' (Toronto: AWID). Available at http://www.awid.org/About-AWID/AWID-News/Capturing-Change-in-Women-s-Realities/%28language%29/eng-GB.

———. 2010b. 'Learning from the MDG3 Fund Experiment: Results from AWID's Survey of the MDG3 Fund M&E System', unpublished report, AWID.

Batliwala, Srilatha et al, 1998, *Status of Rural Women in Karnataka* (Bangalore: National Institute of Advanced Studies).

Bakewell, Oliver and Anne Garbutt. 2005. 'The Use and Abuse of the Logical Framework Approach—A Review of International Development NGOs' Experiences. A Report for SIDA', INTRAC.

Bornstein, Lisa. 2006. 'Systems of Accountability, Webs of Deceit? Monitoring and Evaluation in South African NGOs', *Development*, 49: 52–61.

Dichter, Thomas W. 2003. *Despite Good Intentions: Why Development Assistance to the Third World has Failed* (Amherst: University of Massachusetts Press).

'Hype and Hope: The Worrisome State of the Microcredit Movement.'

Edwards, Michael. 2008. *Just Another Emperor? The Myths and Realities of Philanthrocapitalism* (New York: Demos—A Network for Ideas and Action, The Young Foundation).

Helleiner, Gerry. 2000. 'Towards Balance in Aid Relationships: Donor Performance Monitoring in Low-Income Developing Countries', *Cooperation South (UNDP)*, 2.

Nirantar. 2007. *Qualitative Study of SHGs and Empowerment*, First edn. Available at http://www.nirantar.net/docs/SHG_ qual_ eng.pdf.

Podems, Donna. 2007. 'Gender and Feminist Issues in Global Evaluation', Paper presented at the AEA/CDC Summer Institute, Atlanta, Georgia.

Rankin, Katherine N. 2001. 'Governing Development: Neoliberalism, Microcredit, and Rational Economic Woman.' *Economy and Society*, 30 (1): 18–37.

Rao, Aruna and David Kelleher. 2002. 'Unraveling Institutionalized Gender Inequality', *Gender at Work*. Available at http://www.genderatwork.org.

Stiglitz, Joseph. 2009a. 'The Great GDP Swindle', *The Guardian*, 13 September, Available at http://www.guardian.co.uk/commentisfree/2009/sep/13/economics-economic-growth-and-recession-global-economy.

——. 2009b. 'Nicolas Sarkozy Wants "Well-being" Measure to Replace GDP'. Available at http://www.telegraph.co.uk/finance/economics/6189582/Nicolas-Sarkozy-wants-well-being-measure-to-replace-GDP.html.

10. Gender Myths: A View from the Indian Frontline

R ELIGIOUS fundamentalism and neo-liberal economic reforms are converting poor grassroots women in India into both agents and instruments in a process of their own disempowerment. Although these forces are not necessarily acting in concert, they are nonetheless reconstructing both gender and other social power relations. While we have analysed this dynamic elsewhere (Dhanraj et al. 2005), in this paper we examine certain gender myths[1]—or rather, myth complexes—that are being used to convert poor women into instruments of both the neo-liberal and fundamentalist agendas in India. The operation of these myths is analysed in the context of a government-initiated rural poverty alleviation programme in southern India, and the constitutionally mandated reservation of seats for women in local elected councils (*panchayats*).

At the outset, we wish to emphasise that we do not offer this critical analysis as academic observers, or deny our own participation in these processes. Indeed, the choice of examples is guided at least partly by our own involvement in these processes, and that of many close colleagues.

We have both been complicit, through our past roles in grassroots activism, feminist training and advocacy, in promoting various gender myths and feminist fables that we have only recently begun to recognise as such. Thus, it is not our intention to point fingers or place blame. This analysis has emerged from a critical re-examination of our own as well as others' past assumptions and interventions. We

---

[1] For the purpose of this paper, we are treating *gender myths* as the 'feminist insights [that] become mythologised as they become development orthodoxy', and feminist fables as assumptions and analyses that informed strategies advanced by feminists themselves. Some of the most problematic of today's gender myths are not single ideas, but a web of interlinking beliefs and views.

believe this is a historical moment when all feminists—whether activists, policy advocates or researchers—must interrogate our past assumptions and strategies, or risk becoming completely marginalised and/or instrumentalised by the forces of resurgent patriarchy, religious fundamentalism and unregulated neo-liberalism.

Gender Myth Complex I

Giving poor women access to economic resources—such as credit— leads to their overall empowerment.
This myth arose out of successful feminist efforts to shift economic resources into women's hands, gain recognition for women's roles in household economies and support women's leadership in local development. Feminist efforts were rooted in empirical data, and an understanding that economic power and access to productive resources would weaken traditional gender and social roles and empower poor women to demand further change. But as these strategies began to demonstrate the wisdom of investing in women's entrepreneurship, they were quickly converted into a new development mantra: poor women became a sound economic and political investment. At the international level, The World Bank, USAID, DFID, and other bilateral and private donors have embraced and enthusiastically promoted the new formula. At the national level, both central and state governments and rural banks have begun to actively promote self-help groups and women's savings and credit programmes through schemes such as DWCRA (Development of Women and Children in Rural Areas), the Indira Mahila Yojana and Swayamsidha. The creation of special Directors for Micro Credit within many provincial Directorates of Women and Child Development tells its own story.

This conceptual legerdemain is neatly summed up by Mary John. She observes that a nation-wide study like Shramshakti (National Commission on Self-Employed Women and Women in the Informal Sector 1988) recorded an enormous pile of evidence of the incredible work burdens stoically borne by poor self-employed and informal-sector working women in India; however, in the hands of neo-liberal advocates, 'these findings are no longer arguments about *exploitation* so much as proofs of *efficiency*' (John 2004; emphasis in original). Poor women were gradually seen as harder working, easier to mobilise, more honest, and better credit risks. They would selflessly work for the betterment of their entire families and communities, and were thus great poverty alleviation agents. Politically, they were soon imagined as loyal voters and excellent anti-corruption vigilantes. Obviously, many of these stereotypes were basically true. But the mythification arose when qualities born out of women's struggle for survival were turned to political and economic ends, rather than the feminist commitment to their empowerment.

In India, one of the most high-profile propagators of this myth was the former chief minister of Andhra Pradesh, Mr Chandrababu Naidu. His affinity for high-tech corporate management systems had earned him the epithet 'The CEO of Andhra Pradesh'. From 1999, his regime launched an economic restructuring project, and Mr Naidu decided to use rural women as the key instruments in his political strategy for staying in power. Since the restructuring project included a major poverty alleviation component to appease the mass of poorer rural voters, who were unlikely to benefit from the de-regulation, improved investment incentives and removal of bureaucratic hurdles that facilitated the urban affluent classes, Mr Naidu's *modus operandi* was to create government-owned NGOs (amusingly called 'GONGOs' in some quarters), administered by elite Indian civil service officers. Mr Naidu made it clear to both his party cadres and government functionaries that implementation of the anti-poverty programme would be *solely* through grassroots women's groups. In the Indian *realpolitik*, this signalled that the only political constituency he was interested in building was women, and he conflated women with 'poor', 'rural' and 'community'.

Thus it was that the largest poverty alleviation programme in the state focused entirely on rural women: the World Bank-funded District Poverty Initiatives Project (DPIP), with a budget of INR 26,000 million (US$ 553 million, UK £333 million) in twenty districts of the state. Headed by hand-picked officers of the elite Indian Administrative Service, the project began with the identification of all formations of women at the village level (Self-

Help Groups, *Mahila Mandals, Bhajan Mandalis²*). Simultaneously, NGOs were asked to conduct training for the women's groups in gender issues, income generation activities, and financial skills such as accounting and bookkeeping.

Although the project was initially designed to enable the women's groups to determine and create local projects based on their own priorities (including building community assets like drinking water pumps), it was rapidly reduced to distributing loans to individual women for income-generating activities on a war footing. Very poor women soon fell out of the net because they could not pay the weekly contribution required to retain membership of the self-help group. In a short while, only women with some stable earning capacity remained in the groups. The project also tried to improve women's access to and relations with markets. For instance, women who gathered and sold tamarind were constantly swindled by middlemen who drove down purchase rates and used falsified weights and scales. An Internet-based system was therefore introduced to check market rates on a daily basis, in order to give women more bargaining power. But many women could not exercise that power since they were heavily indebted to the buyers. The self-help group was simply not a powerful enough structure from which to challenge weights and measures or purchase prices, as a cooperative or trade union might have been—particularly since rights awareness and strengthening the capacity for collective struggle were not part of the organising strategy for such groups.

The project's community organisers also began to press women to take multiple production loans; and the number of hours they were working increased dramatically—there was no other way to keep pace with their mounting debt. Older daughters had to pick up the slack by quitting school in order to perform the domestic subsistence tasks their mothers could no longer do. But if one converted their profits from all these enterprises into wages, not one of them was netting an income above the minimum daily wage. At a workshop on 'Rethinking Micro-Credit', held at the recent World

---

² These are women's clubs and the equivalent of Western choral societies.

Social Forum in Bombay, rural women from different parts of the country spoke passionately about their multiple debt burdens and how repayment had increased their workloads to inhuman levels. Yet, such projects continually cite these women as models of entrepreneurship—not surprising, since the only indicator they use is monthly cash turnover. Meanwhile, men in project villages became sullen and resentful. Women handling such large amounts of money had become a source of humiliation; they neither understood nor acknowledged the women's onerous workload, or the debt-trap. Thus, apart from being overworked and anxious about mounting interest and repayments, women had to deal with this growing hostility (and possibly violence) from men.

Far more problematic, however, was the assumption behind the project's strategy: that once money is handed over to women in the form of loans, they were responsible for improving their lot, and the state's role had ended. At the same time, this munificence would earn the ruling party rural women's allegiance, and secure its political future. Women's political agency has been reduced to the privilege of being agents, consumers and beneficiaries of state-controlled credit and micro-enterprise programmes, with no other resources for improving the condition of their daily lives. There are no investments, for example, in providing cooking fuel, water close to the home, or day care for younger children, so that older daughters can go to school. Women are so preoccupied with earning income to repay loans that they have little time or energy to participate in other public affairs, or organise other issues.

Ironically, this is the same region of India that once saw massive participation by poor women in large-scale political movements (such as the armed struggle in Telengana: see Sen 2000; Stree Shakti Sanghatana 1989) for land, for minimum wages, in protests against the rise in price of basic commodities, and against the sale of country liquor that beggared families while filling state coffers with revenue. How ironic that the women of this same region were converted into passive instruments of the regime's single-point anti-poverty programme, with little or no capacity to negotiate for a different agenda or approach.

It is no wonder, then, that Mr Naidu's Telugu Desam party

suffered a humiliating rout in the May 2004 state elections in Andhra Pradesh. Electoral data showed that both men and women from rural areas had voted almost *en masse* against his party, demonstrating a vehement rejection of his political strategy and policies. Clearly, the poor women of the region had reclaimed their political agency through the ballot box. Since then, the DPIP continues to function, but in a very low-key way. The message sent by women (and men) has not been lost on other political parties, including Mr Naidu's successors.

This kind of narrow approach is not unusual in credit-focused strategies. A decade ago, the staff of the Bangladesh Rural Advancement Committee (BRAC), a Bangladeshi NGO famous for its very large-scale women-focused poverty-alleviation programme, acknowledged the same in a review of the gender impact of their work:

> The evidence suggested that participation in BRAC's programs had strengthened women's economic roles and, to some extent, increased women's empowerment measured in terms of mobility, economic security, legal awareness, decision making and freedom from violence within the family. However, widely acknowledged among BRAC staff was the fact that the imperatives of credit delivery were eclipsing the objectives of social change (Rao et al. 1999: 43).

Programmes to alleviate poverty are obviously rooted in ideological frameworks. The DPIP and the oppressive manner in which it was implemented demonstrate the heavy influence of the neo-liberal paradigm. It was operationalised to ensure that people— for which read women—participated in their economic upliftment in the most apolitical and disempowering way imaginable. As Lucy Taylor argues, the neo-liberal agenda requires the state to keep those 'who have not forgotten their politicised past busy and out of harm's way, distracted from wider political considerations and submerged within the minutiae of issues in their own backyard' (Taylor 1996).

The neo-liberal agenda, Taylor suggests, requires citizens to accept the reformed identity of the state as facilitator, and not key agent, of social and individual betterment. It also demands the twin identities of citizen and individual—that is, the active, socially responsible citizen and the active, socially responsible individual who is in charge of her own destiny. The neo-liberal rules for the new woman citizen, as evidenced in the Andhra Pradesh project, were quite clear: improve your household's economic condition, participate in local community development (if you have the time), help build and run local (apolitical) institutions like the self-help group; by then, you should have no political or physical energy left to challenge this paradigm. These rules sustain a sort of depoliticised activism at the local level—one that inherently does not build upward momentum. It is a matter for celebration that the women of Andhra Pradesh refused to be so diminished and instrumentalised.

Readers may wonder why we are so concerned about this attempt at depoliticising poor women. Isn't it a good thing if poor women gain greater access to productive resources? The answer lies a few hundred kilometres away. It is the experience of the state of Gujarat, which has some of the oldest and largest networks of women's credit and income-generation groups, that challenges such complaisance. It is here that totalitarian, fundamentalist, anti-poor ideologies and their Hindu cadres, largely undisturbed and unchallenged, have waged their violent politics at the grassroots level, culminating in the horrifying and organised carnage of early 2002 against the Muslim minority—the worst since the partition of India in 1947—with Muslim women being particularly targeted.

Despite extensive grassroots-level women's economic empowerment programmes, mostly operated by NGOs who claimed to promote a tolerant, unifying value system, neither Muslim nor Hindu members of these networks seem to have been aware of the approaching carnage, or brought up for discussion the vicious hate campaigns that were afoot for at least one year before the pogroms (Khan 2002). In the very neighbourhoods in which these women lived, the aggressively fundamentalist Vishwa Hindu Parishad had been actively mobilising other women into Durga Vahinis (women's militias), and providing arms training (to defend themselves against the insatiable sexual appetite of minority men). It seems incredible that none of this came to the attention of women in the micro-enterprise or self-employed groups that dot the state, or to the NGOs who organise them. Was this because, as in the BRAC case, they were so narrowly absorbed in their economic activities that they never sensed the political winds blowing through their very villages and neighbourhoods? Or was it because the discussion of larger politics was never included in weekly or monthly women's group meeting agendas?

What we are seeing is a troubling picture. On the one hand, the state and its international allies are promoting not just narrowly conceived self-help programmes for poor rural and urban women, but a model of citizenship and participation that is highly instrumentalist, dissipating women's political agency. On the other hand, fundamentalist organisations and political parties are actively mobilising women of all classes to advance their agendas. It is frightening indeed to contemplate the fact that in India, the only force currently interested in empowering poor women as political actors is the Hindu fundamentalist movement.

Gender Myth Complex II

If women gain access to political power, they will opt for politics and policies that promote social and gender equality, peace and sustainable development. Thus, quotas or other methods of ensuring high proportions of women in elected bodies will transform these institutions. Women will alter the character of political culture and the practice of public power (United Nations 1995).

It is not hard to understand how this fable came into being (sometime in the 1970s, we think). Male domination of public power and politics had led to the destruction of life, humanity and the earth itself. Even in so-called 'liberal democracies', the notion of democracy itself had been reduced, as the late Claude Ake pointed out, to a minimalist version, where the main privilege enjoyed by citizens is that of some protection from state power (Ake 1996). As feminists from the North and the South began to expand and deepen their understanding of the roots of gender discrimination, they argued that women's access to power and decision-making authority in the public realm was as critical to achieving gender equality as changing power relations in the private sphere of households (UN Beijing Declaration and Platform for Action, Strategic Objectives G.1 and

G.2). Looking back, and again, having been part of this process, we believe there were several implicit and explicit assumptions underlying this analysis, including:

- That the transformation of both the *position* and *condition* of women (Young 1988)—that is, meeting both their practical and strategic needs—could only be achieved and sustained in macro terms through political change (enabling policies, legislation, and the protection and enforcement of women's rights).

- That women representatives in local, national and global political bodies would advance the cause of gender equality and women's rights, and sustain the momentum for such change over time.

- That a critical mass of women in political institutions would also initiate policies of development and international relations that would advance social and economic justice and peace, by fostering and promoting non-violent conflict resolution, sustainable and socially just development, access to and protection of the full body of human rights, and placing people and the environment above profits.

- That a critical mass of women in political institutions would transform the very *nature of power* and the *practice of politics* through values of cooperation and collaboration, holding power in trusteeship (power on behalf of, not over), and acting with greater transparency, honesty and public accountability. In other words, there was a belief that women would *play politics* differently and *exercise power* accountably.

With the wisdom of hindsight, we can see how these assumptions reflected our then limited understanding of citizenship, and of how citizenship was constructed in not just gendered ways, but through other categories of social power. We assumed that citizenship was a fixed and bounded terrain, rather than that 'like power relations, citizenship rights are not fixed, but are objects of struggle to be defended, reinterpreted and extended' (Meer, with Sever, 2004: 2). We believed that once women had access to political power, they would act for greater justice and equity.

The push for getting women into politics became strong and

visible in many parts of the developed and developing world by the mid-1970s, and by the 1990s, several European countries, the USA, and developing countries such as India, the Philippines, South Africa, Uganda, Brazil, Chile, Mexico, and many others had large numbers of women in their political parties and governing institutions at various levels. In some contexts—notably India and South Africa— 'pull' factors like quota systems were used; in others, such as the USA and some parts of Western Europe, 'push' strategies (mainly pressure from women's movements) worked effectively to increase the number of women elected representatives. Over time, feminist struggles to promote women's greater representation and participation in politics were picked up and encapsulated into modules and templates by international donor agencies and other institutions, which began to promote the new 'good governance' agenda, particularly in the South.

It would be a grave disservice to thousands of courageous women to say that all the assumptions about their impact on public policy, politics and power have been belied. But the experience of the past two decades forces us to confront some troubling realities and recast our vision for transformation through political power. The most worrying phenomenon at the present time is that the expanding space for women in politics has been seized far more effectively by right-wing, conservative, and fundamentalist parties and agendas. In the USA, for instance, while the Democrats boasted of having fielded the largest number of women candidates for both Congress and Senate, Republicans are rapidly closing the gap (Center for American Women in Politics 2004). Although American women have been more progressive voters (the 'gender gap' in US parlance), tending to vote for more liberal and progressive candidates and parties, this trend is gradually shifting. Christian fundamentalist groups, with their close affiliation to conservative political agendas, have successfully mobilised poor and middle-class grassroots American women voters in the Bible belt and 'middle America', not the progressive movements or parties. In the 2004 US elections, in fact, fewer women voted for progressive John Kerry when compared to those who had voted for Al Gore in the 2000 election. Conservative forces have polarised women and the general public by re-shaping issues such as abortion rights, and focusing on the 'average' grassroots women the progressives have neglected or taken for granted.[3]

In South Asia, the mass mobilisation of women by religious fundamentalists, including the fielding of women political candidates, is nothing short of frightening. In India, the extremist Vishwa Hindu Parishad has launched special training camps for young Hindu women to act as 'Protectors of the Faith', including training in the use of swords and other weapons. Muslim fundamentalists in neighbouring Pakistan and Bangladesh use very similar rhetoric to muster women's support. The Tamil Tigers in Sri Lanka had rallied Tamil women to their cause, and even constructed an image of the 'Pudumai Pen' or *new woman*—who would raise militant children and selflessly dedicate them to fight for the cause.

Let us look more closely at the Indian case to see how it challenges this gender myth. Fundamentalist organising of women first became evident in the late 1980s, when the media flashed images of thousands of Hindu women across the country joining the marches and the symbolic carrying of construction material to the Babri Masjid. This was the ancient mosque that was eventually destroyed by Hindu fundamentalist mobs in 1992, purportedly to rebuild the Ram temple that had allegedly been destroyed when the mosque was built. The images of women's participation became more aggressive during the anti-Muslim riots in Bombay in 1993: hundreds of Hindu women made petrol bombs that their men then hurled on Muslim shanties. The pinnacle, however, was reached before, during and after the anti-Muslim pogroms in Gujarat in early 2002, when thousands of Hindu women, both poor and middle class, actively supported the attackers, joined in the looting of Muslim shops, and marched in massive numbers in the political rallies and processions that were held in support of the state's fundamentalist regime. Before the 2004 Indian general elections, there were four women chief ministers of various Indian state governments, the highest number

---

[3] It was interesting to note, for example, that African American women were the single largest constituency opposed to the war on Iraq, yet have never been significantly mobilised by any progressive movement in the USA after the civil rights era.

since Independence—and *all* of them were members of the ruling Hindu nationalist party, or its close allies.

To dismiss these phenomena simply as a result of false consciousness, or the instrumentalisation of passive women by shrewd and sinister leaders, is a grave mistake. The defeat of the Hindu nationalist regime in the 2004 general elections was not by a wide margin, and should not cause complaisance. Seen from close up, women's participation in these movements is far from passive or blind, but very much through their active agency. As we have argued elsewhere (Dhanraj et al. 2002), the fact is that fundamentalist movements have created a genuine *political space and role* for women. They have given them the possibility of being real political actors, and an active sense of being the architects of a momentous social and political project. Regrettably, this is something that none of the so-called 'progressive' forces have done on the same scale or with the same deadly sense of purpose—not other political parties, nor the labour movement, nor radical social movements (including feminist women's movements). It is unfortunate, but true, that currently Hindu fundamentalists are the most effective and deliberate in deploying mass mobilisation strategies, and have the most conscious programme of women's mobilisation within them. And progressives, rather than waking up to this fact, continue to instrumentalise women as convenient, passive tools whenever a mass protest or event requires their presence!

Meanwhile, India boasts of over one million elected women in its village and town councils, about a quarter of whom are from the poorest communities. This is thanks to the passing of the 73rd Amendment to the Constitution of India—in which, incidentally, Indian feminists had little role. The Amendment made it mandatory for 33 per cent of all positions in local councils to be reserved for women. There were also reservations for Dalit and tribal people. This was brought about by well-intentioned Gandhian advocates and bureaucrats who envisaged a form of local governance and decentralisation that would transform rural India, a social revolution that could redress centuries of marginalisation for both Dalits and women, orchestrated by the State.

The discourse on the impact of this unprecedented structural change, the largest scale experiment of its kind anywhere in the world, is banal at best. It is also quite polarised, between gloomy stories of women representatives' subordination, co-option or subversion on the one side, and cheering protagonists on the other, who dismiss criticism or any analysis that is less than laudatory. Both positions are often derived from anecdotal evidence and ideological positions, rather than a serious inquiry into what is happening on the ground. There are, of course, some large-scale and highly quantitative studies, but these fail to capture many of the complexities and nuances of the reality. They tell us little about what this change has meant for elected women and men from poor castes and communities, how they are negotiating their new roles, or about the nature of grassroots political culture and dynamics.

What we have witnessed on the ground—as documented in Dhanraj's film *Taking Office*—is a complex picture, where both patriarchal and feudal/semi-feudal gender and social power relations are being simultaneously challenged, changed, accommodated and modified. A landless Dalit woman labourer is elected to and becomes the Chairperson of a village council in which her upper-caste landlord (or his wife) is also an elected member. Dalit, tribal, and other oppressed caste and minority women and men elected representatives have to negotiate a vast and dangerous minefield of religion, class and caste politics, patronage networks and affiliations, while the social and economic bases of their lives outside the panchayat remain unchanged. We know of elected women who have been placed under virtual house arrest for attempting to challenge budget allocations; they have been beaten up, threatened, bribed and cajoled into supporting dominant caste or class agendas in the councils.

On the other hand, we know many hundreds of women who have triumphed amazingly over these odds and managed to deliver needed resources to their constituency. Indeed, most of the elected women with whom we have interacted are far from passive puppets. They show remarkable resilience in repeatedly trying to exercise their agency, to fulfil their responsibilities, to flex their political muscles, or simply to function autonomously. The problem, we find, is that since most women have entered these institutions without any kind of political or ideological training, skills or experience—they have not been members of a political party or cadre, for example—or have only the limited apolitical experience of their participation in a village self-help group, they are forced to learn and acquire these skills in the most arduous ways and at great cost. We have seen women devote all their time and energy to simply learn how to steer through the maze. But far too many fall victim to their inexperience and the pressure to become corrupt or expedient.

A major handicap is that these women struggle in the absence of any alternative models of power. As Anne Marie Goetz points out, their images of leadership and experience of the exercise of power are gained within the family/household, from the feudal and caste-based social and economic structures they live in, and the few state and non-state institutions they have interacted with in their lives: the school, the local government officers, and maybe rural NGOs and development organisations (2003: 3–5). None of these are exactly models of alternative politics, much less innovative practitioners of power. Feminist activists have attempted to create these alternatives in a few locations—but more often, women's groups are quick to stigmatise these elected leaders for becoming co-opted or corrupted by the dominant political culture, rather than supporting them to create an alternative. Apart from celebrated examples—Indira Gandhi, Benazir Bhutto, Margaret Thatcher, Jayalalitha, etc.—there are growing numbers of 'Women with Moustaches', as Latin American feminists have called them, in politics at all levels today: hard-nosed, tough, aggressive, and sometimes corrupt women politicians. We believe it is much too simplistic to dismiss this as the result of male consciousness masquerading in female bodies. Nevertheless, in a country like India, there are very few successful elected women to serve as mentors or models.

Conclusion

The above analysis of the operation of two major gender myths seems to suggest that a larger project is at work in India—one that is constructing and then utilising women as particular types of social, economic and political citizens.

On the economic front, the myth of women as the most effective anti-poverty agents and the mass-scale creation of women's self-help groups seems to be nurturing a form of depoliticised collective action that is completely non-threatening to the power structure and political order. These groups, forced to focus all their energies on their productive activities, their loan repayments and the survival of their collective, seem to be rendered oblivious to the ideological/political mobilisations going on under their very noses. Lucy Taylor's analysis of the reinterpretation of civil society and citizenship in Chile in the dictatorship and post-dictatorship years, where the 'twin strategies of incorporation and marginalisation' were used, demonstrates not only how self-help groups were the policy instruments of this agenda, but also that this strategy is not unique to India (1996: 780).

We are not suggesting that economic empowerment programmes for women are either disempowering or unmitigated failures. The successes of micro-credit for women are well documented (ILO 1998), and there is little purpose in raising yet another paean to them here. Our purpose, rather, is to highlight the manner in which such interventions are being designed and delivered in increasingly disempowering ways, instrumentalising poor women, and being distorted to serve other agendas.

On the political front, far from women transforming politics, evidence of the reverse is mounting. Particularly disturbing is the way in which fundamentalist parties have fostered women's political participation to advance their agenda. At the grassroots level, we are witnessing both this kind of instrumentalisation and the marginalisation of women elected representatives in multiple ways, in a manner very similar to what is happening in other parts of the world (Goetz and Hassim 2003). As one analysis puts it, 'the system of representation that gives women "*authority*" through holding an elective post has not transformed into actual "*power*"' (Vijaylakshmi and Chandrasekhar 2001).

What is clear, however, is that the myths regarding women's capacity to transform both politics and public power have been central to all these processes. We clearly underestimated the power of existing modes of power and politics to corrupt, co-opt, or marginalise women, or how it would compel or manipulate them to compromise their goals for narrow party interests. And we failed to address the possibility that women would be proponents of reactionary, sexist, racist, elitist or fundamentalist ideologies. Thus, if we combine the mobilisations of women by the fundamentalist agenda, the depoliticised forms of collective action promoted by state-sponsored micro-credit programmes, and the subversion of the agency of elected women in panchayats, what emerges is a deeply problematic and bounded construct of women's citizenship—a construct that must be seriously analysed, challenged and re-framed.

However, this is also a serious learning moment for feminists. We are clearly at a historic juncture where the marginalisation of feminist critiques and corporatisation of feminist strategies forces us to recast our analyses and approaches. This cannot be achieved without looking closely at what is happening to women on the ground. Using the lens of gender myths helps us to unearth the deeper, more fundamental processes of restructuring power and politics that are afoot—the ways in which resurgent patriarchy, neo-liberal economics and fundamentalism are combining to construct a new kind of female citizen. The challenge now is to move towards more nuanced and contextualised approaches that can hopefully begin to confront and contain these formidable forces.

References

Ake, C. 1996. 'Mistaken identities: how misconceptions of relations between democracy, civil society and governance devalue democracy', Keynote Paper for the International Workshop on Government, Getulio Vargas Institute, Sao Paolo, Brazil, November.

Center for American Women in Politics. 2004. *Advisory, The Gender Gap and the 2004 Women's Vote: Setting the Record Straight* (New Brunswick, NJ: Center for American Women and Politics, Rutgers University). Available at http://www.cawp.rutgers.edu/Facts/ Elections/ GenderGapAdvisory04.pdf (accessed 29 January 2006).

Dhanraj, D., S. Batliwala and G. Misra. 2005. 'Fan Action Framework for South Asia', in J. Kerr, E. Sprenger and A. Symington (eds), *The Future of Women's Rights—Global Visions and Strategies* (London: Zed Books), pp 80–96.

Goetz, A.-M. 2003. 'Political cleaners: How women are the new anti-corruption force', Paper presented at the conference 'Gender Myths and Feminist Fables: Repositioning Gender in Development Policy and Practice', Institute of Development Studies, Brighton, 2–4 July.

Goetz, A.-M. and S. Hassim. 2003. *No Shortcuts to Power: African Women in Politics and Policy Making* (London: Zed Books).

ILO. 1998. 'Women in the informal sector and their access to microfinance', Paper prepared by ILO for the Inter-Parliamentary Union (IPU) Annual Conference, Windhoek, Namibia, 2–11 April.

John, M. 2004. 'Gender and Development in India, 1970–90s', in M. Chaudhuri (ed.), *Feminism in India* (New Delhi: Kali for Women and Women Unlimited).

Khan, Z.-I. 2002. 'New evidence that Gujarat pogroms were preplanned'. Available at www.milligate.com/Archives/01112002/0111200291.htm.

Meer, S., with C. Sever. 2004. 'Gender and citizenship: overview report', *Bridge Pack on Gender and Citizenship* (Brighton: Institute of Development Studies).

National Commission on Self-Employed Women and Women in the Informal Sector. 1988. *Shramshakti* (New Delhi: Government of India, Ministry of Human Resource Development).

Rao, A., R. Stuart and D. Kelleher. 1999. 'Building gender capital at BRAC: a case study', in A. Rao, R. Stuart and D. Kelleher (eds), *Gender at Work—Organizational Change for Equality* (Connecticut: Kumarian Press),

Sen, S. 2000. 'Toward a feminist politics? The Indian women's movement in historical perspective', World Bank Policy Research Report on Gender and Development, Working Paper Series 9 (Washington, D.C.: World Bank).

Stree Shakti Sanghatana. 1989. *We Were Making History—Life Stories of Women in the Telengana Struggle* (New Delhi: Kali for Women).

Taylor, Lucy. 1996. 'Civilising civil society: distracting popular participation from politics itself', *Contemporary Political Studies*, Proceedings of the annual conference held at the University of Glasgow, Political Studies Association, pp. 778–85. Available at www.psa.ac.uk/cps/1996.htm.

United Nations. 1995. *Beijing Declaration and Platform for Action* (New York: United Nations Development Program).

Vijaylakshmi, V. and B.K. Chandrasekhar. 2001. *Authority, Powerlessness and Dependence: Women and Local Governance in Karnataka* (Bangalore: Institute of Social and Economic Change).

Young, K. 1988. *Gender and Development: A Relational View* (Oxford: Oxford University Press).

11. When Rights Go Wrong*

O VER the past fifty years of development history, we have seen the repeated distortion of good ideas and innovative practices as they are lifted out of the political and historical context in which they evolved and rendered into formulas that are 'mainstreamed'. This usually involves divesting the idea of its cultural specificity, its political content, and generalizing it into a series of rituals and steps that simulate its original elements, but lack the transformative power of the real thing. Thus good ideas, evolved to address specific development challenges, are altered into universally applicable panaceas. Transferring the correct rhetoric—buzzwords and catch phrases emptied of their original meaning—is a vital part of this legerdemain. This is not to question the transfer and replication of effective interventions for social justice and development, but to challenge the motives behind it and the manner in which it is done.

As the lack of genuine global commitment to poverty eradication and social justice increases, so does the desperation to find magic bullets and quick fixes which, it is hoped, can overcome the lack of political, social and economic will to address the deeper roots of socio-economic transformation at international, national and local levels. The distortion of good ideas and strategies is both a cause and a result of this process.

A good example of this syndrome is micro-credit, originally developed in the South Asian cultural and political context by pioneers like the Self-Employed Women's Association (SEWA) in India and Nobel laureate Muhammad Yunus' Grameen Bank in Bangladesh. Their idea was to give poor women access to credit to unleash their latent entrepreneurial skills and eventually raise their

---

* Previously published in *Seminar*, 569 (January), 2007: 89–94.

household incomes. But in the past decade, micro-credit has been converted into a 'movement', a universal anti-poverty and women's empowerment panacea. It is increasingly force-fed by development finance agencies into every poverty context, regardless of local culture, gender relations, social structure or political history.

Many of the systems developed by the early pioneers have been mechanically replicated without critical reflection on their viability or equivalents in other contexts. No surprise, then, that the results have been so mixed (Rogaly 1996).

The most recent example of this phenomenon is the attempt to push the 'rights-based approach to development', in which many development assistance agencies—private, bilateral, and others— are the leading players. The hard-sell of usually vague and differently interpreted versions of the rights-based approach—indeed, often what the particular donor agency representatives think is the rights-based approach—to all their development 'partners' is creating a situation where rights are going sadly wrong (SIDA 2000: 9).

One fundamental problem is that the rights-based approach has been advanced before addressing some of the very troubling matters at the heart of human rights themselves. In a compelling critique of the evolution of the current body of international human rights,[1] Makau Mutua argues that not only has the current body of human rights been framed from an overwhelmingly European, Rousseauvian perspective of the individual as both the object and the subject of rights, but they have also increasingly become the goal and instrument of a modern-day civilising project in the non-Western world (Mutua 2002). Mutua asserts that the philosophical underpinnings of the current body of human rights have not been evolved through a genuinely multicultural ground-up debate, distilling what is authentically universal from the highest values and ethical frameworks of societies around the world.

---

[1] The Universal Declaration of Human Rights, The Covenant on Civil and Political Rights, the Covenant on Social, Economic and Cultural Rights, The Convention on Elimination of All forms of Discrimination Against Women, the Convention on Rights of the Child, etc., are collectively known as the Universal Bill of Rights.

As a former feminist activist and native of Karnataka, I can strongly identify with this argument: if the values that imbued the revolutionary Veerashaiva movement of thirteenth-century Karnataka had informed the construction of the international bill of rights, the struggle of the international women's movement against the androcism of the earlier rights framework[2] may not have occurred. Women's right to social equality and physical security were clearly articulated by Bhakti Saint Akkamahadevi in several of her vachanas[3] (poems), and gender equality was an integral part of the Veerashaiva struggle. I raise this not out of naïve chauvinism, but to illustrate the rich and diverse sources that have existed—outside the West—for framing universal human rights.

The individual focus of the rights discourse is another inherent problem that has been widely critiqued. This is sought to be corrected by focusing on collective rights, but this does not resolve the core problem of assumed universality. What is more, the experience of indigenous communities attempting to protect their customary rights to forests and land in the face of market forces indicates that collective rights are no more easily asserted or protected from violation than individual rights. Even when they are, it is through instruments of redress that are still alien, far from traditional norms and values, and which raise a host of new problems. Native Americans in the United States, for instance, have successfully asserted their sovereignty over tribal lands through rights-based legal instruments. But with the collapse of customary governance and judicial systems, they are struggling to distribute revenues from gambling casinos—not to mention cope with the predatory external forces they are ill-equipped to confront. In the words of one analyst:

> ... additional problems are now arising in the reservations due to the lack of pre-existent law regarding the issues raised by open gaming and the impending collapse of traditional Indian courts of justice. This is

---

[2] Which, till the mid-1990s, did not recognise rape and domestic violence against women as human rights violations.

[3] Devotional song-poems that contained clear philosophical precepts and condemnation of social evils such as caste and women's oppression.

becoming a major issue as cyber criminals and organized crime are seeing the lightly defended reservation gaming as open territory. [4]

Another problem with the rights discourse—and pertinent to the arguments I will later present in this article—is that the *responsibilities* side of the discourse remains underdeveloped, especially the notion of collective or communal responsibilities (Flynn 2005). Western-influenced rights advocates even in India fear that the notion of responsibilities is too weak, and leads to misuse and renewed oppression by feudal forces; women and oppressed castes in India, for instance, are often reminded of their responsibilities rather than their rights when they challenge their oppressors.

The rights-based approach to the development community speaks of 'rights-holders' and 'duty-bearers', and in theory at least, acknowledges the critical role of informal/customary mediating structures like clan, caste or tribal councils, and that duty-bearers include not only the state and its agencies, but also a range of customary and informal social structures. The rights-based analysis aims to determine what immediate, underlying and structural obstacles there are to realising rights. This includes examining social, cultural, legal and administrative frameworks, which requires studying how people's claims are processed by authorities in the different arenas of negotiation (for example, customary law, religious law, statutory law, constitutional law, etc.) (Moser and Norton 2001). It must also necessarily identify responsible duty-bearers. Not only does this include the state at different levels, but it also comprises the identification of other duty-bearers in society, including the family, community, corporate actors, etc. The capacities and resources of duty-bearers to fulfil their duties should be assessed (Ljungman 2004). Indeed, for most poor and oppressed social groups, the local social structures in which they negotiate their lives, resources and rights are the determining layer through which their individual circumstances are mediated.

On the other hand, many cultures around the world accord a higher place to collective *duties and responsibilities* rather than to

---

[4] See http://www.americanindians.com/article.htm?id=87&Native_American_ Casinos for a discussion of the problems resulting from casinos.

individual or collective *rights*. This is very significant for the implementation of the rights-based approach, which tends, in practice, to define state authorities and agencies as the primary duty-bearers in protecting and promoting rights, and emphasises individual citizens as rights-holders. This is particularly true when donors have promoted the approach, since the visibility and possibility of measuring successful individual claims and implementation of state obligations shifts the focus to these actors rather than less visible—and measurable—mediating structures. The state is also a far easier target (excluding, obviously, states captured by illegitimate and rogue regimes) to pressure for the enforcement of rights than are families, clans and caste structures.

Here, I am not advancing a cultural relativism argument. Rather, I am pointing out a major flaw embedded in rights strategies, and in particular assessments of their impact. They have not yet been adequately developed to gauge what is happening in the sites where most people, particularly women and oppressed and marginalised groups, actually experience the affirmation or denial of their rights, viz., within the family, clan, tribe, caste group, or community council / *jamaat*.

There is also the knotty problem of the hierarchy of rights, wished away as false or politically motivated by rights advocates, but which continues to plague us. Some people's rights, such as indigenous people's right to their traditional territories (the dam-affected in the Narmada Valley, for instance), will apparently sometimes clash with the equally valid right to employment and food security of others (the drought-affected farmers and agricultural labourers in Kutch and Saurashtra).[5] I do not want to get into the debate here of who is ultimately responsible for, or gains from, putting these rights into opposition; I am merely trying to show that there are a large number of complex and unsettling issues at the heart of human rights, and therefore of rights-based approaches to development.

My point is that it is from this very contentious place, with its enormous and unresolved conceptual and strategic conundrums, that

---

[5] See, for instance, Gail Omvedt's arguments in her Open Letter to Arundhati Roy, August 1999, http://www.narmada.org/debates/gail/gail.open.letter.html.

the discourse of the rights-based approach to development has emerged. It is useful to stress, however, that rights-based strategies themselves are much older than this discourse. One could argue, for instance, that all anti-colonial struggles were rights-based, and that a large number of the struggles of marginalised and oppressed groups in our country over the past fifty years—the movements of Dalits, peasants, workers, indigenous people, displaced people and women—were also rights-based struggles for access to and equitable distribution of the fruits of development. So it is important to distinguish between the discourse of rights-based development and movements for realising the right to equality, non-discrimination, economic power, self-determination and participation, which are certainly much older.

The rationale that gave rise to the rights-based discourse somewhere in the late 1990s is important to understand. It was intended to move development out of the realm of a privilege that benevolent regimes might—or might not—provide their citizens, to a right that could be legally enforced, claimed and asserted. It was intended to remove the element of voluntary fulfilment of basic human needs by benign states, what Ake called the 'modest privilege of protection from the power of the state' (Ake 1996), and replace it with the legal obligation of regimes to enable and actualise the basic rights of their citizens. But most of all, the rights-based approach was originally developed by several international activist NGOs in order to link human rights and development, and to foreground the link between poverty and rights.

The rights approach is viewed as being closely allied to the achievement of the Millennium Development Goals of the UN, and the Poverty Reduction Strategies of the World Bank. Advocates of the approach argue that poverty eradication and the right to adequate income, health, education, peace, security and participation in governance should not be a matter of privilege, benevolence or development goals, but the basic right of all human beings. As some rights advocates would have it, the rights-based approach was developed to enable people to fulfil their basic needs by demanding basic rights. Although social and economic rights are obviously at the core, the approach is usually described as encompassing a much broader and more holistic notion of human well-being. Clearly the rights-based approach to development has many important strengths, but there are four basic processes through which it goes wrong in practice.

1. First, the rights-based approach has been framed so broadly so as to almost blunt it of its usefulness, since almost any duty-bearer could claim that rights are being integrated into their policies and actions. Examine the following definition (Box 11.1) of the approach taken from the website of the UN High Commission on Human Rights.

As we can see, this offers a very comprehensive framework and some useful possibilities for those attempting to hold states and other powerful institutions more accountable for implementing equitable and effective development policies and programmes, and progressive legislation. At the same time, it is clear that its elements are more easily embraced and monitored at the level of law and policy, but less so in terms of administrative procedures and practices. Most of all, it would be very difficult to hold communities and traditional social structures, whose hierarchies and authority systems are not controlled by formal law, to account for violations or positive change. In this sense, the rights-based approach is not necessarily more empowering than other strategies in moving from formal to substantive equality, although that is one of its intentions.

The development of gender-sensitive school textbooks, while the dropout rate for girls remains high—due to factors largely unrelated to schools and textbooks—is a good example of this gap. The right to education for all is guaranteed by Indian law and policy, but is in fact mediated by intersecting institutions like the family, clan, caste, gender, economic status, and so forth.

In other words, the rights-based approach as currently articulated by donors does not adequately or explicitly place the analysis of social power, and strategies to shift power relations, at the centre, although its original architects certainly emphasised such analysis. It is also unclear how the rights-based approach is superior to its predecessors— what is its added value over the awareness-building/empowerment/ organising approaches used decades ago in grassroots work? The only advantage appears to be that many traditional NGOs, engaged in poverty alleviation or sustainable development work, and who did

---

Box 11.1
What is the Rights-Based Approach?

A rights-based approach to development is a conceptual framework for the process of human development that is normatively based on international human rights standards and operationally directed to promoting and protecting human rights ... Essentially, a rights-based approach integrates the norms, standards and principles of the international human rights system into the plans, policies and processes of development ... The norms and standards are those contained in the wealth of international treaties and declarations. The principles include equality and equity, accountability, empowerment and participation. A rights-based approach to development includes the following elements: an express linkage to rights, accountability, empowerment, participation, non-discrimination and attention to vulnerable groups.

Rights-based approaches are comprehensive in their consideration of the full range of indivisible, interdependent and interrelated rights: civil, cultural, economic, political and social. This calls for a development framework with sectors that mirror internationally guaranteed rights, thus covering, for example, health, education, housing, justice administration, personal security and political participation.

Rights-based approaches focus on raising levels of accountability in the development process by identifying claim-holders (and their entitlements) and corresponding duty-holders (and their obligations). In this regard, they look both at the positive obligations of duty-holders (to protect, promote and provide) and at their negative obligations (to abstain from violations). They take into account the duties of the full range of relevant actors, including individuals, states, local organizations and authorities, private companies, aid donors and international institutions.

Such approaches also provide for the development of adequate laws, policies, institutions, administrative procedures and practices, and mechanisms of redress and accountability that can deliver on entitlements, respond to denial and violations, and ensure accountability. They call for the translation of universal standards into locally determined benchmarks for measuring progress and enhancing accountability.[6]

---

[6] See Guidelines of the United Nations Office of the High Commissioner for Human Rights, http://www.unohchr.org.

not explicitly incorporate power analysis and rights into their approaches, are now compelled to do so, at least in their rhetoric.

This brings us to the other way in which rights go wrong: the rhetoric has assumed greater importance than the practice. Writing proposals and progress reports that are liberally sprinkled with the language of the rights-approach, viz., 'claim-holders', 'duty-bearers', 'assertion', 'violations', has become vital to mobilising resources from donors that have adopted the approach. Old approaches are often rebottled in the rights rhetoric. And the obverse of this phenomenon is the dismissal of even the most impressive empowerment strategies and movements because they do not package their work in the rights language.[7]

This is a worldwide phenomenon—one activist from an organisation that has mobilised hundreds of Kenyan women to claim their land rights from tribal councils after being widowed by AIDS put it this way:

> They tell me that I must use the 'rights-based' approach. Is not our work rights-based unless we use that term? Is our work not rights-based because we have changed only the customary inheritance system, and not some written law?[8]

There is yet another troubling dimension of the rights discourse and the way the rights-based approach is being interpreted. The experience of grassroots activists from India and other parts of the world shows that in many cultural contexts, the translation of several words at the centre of the rights approach is problematic for people and communities on the ground. In India, for instance, terms like '*haq*' and '*adhikaar*'—the most commonly used words meaning 'rights'—are loaded and can be explosive. In the more feudal contexts in which highly marginalised and oppressed people live, framing their struggles this way could trigger premature and harsh repression.

In my own experience, poor women often prefer the terminology and tools of negotiation or justice to rights (terms like '*unko*

---

[7] Personal communications with a range of grassroots activists and community-based organisations with whom the author has interacted over the past two years.

[8] Identity withheld at speaker's request.

samjhayenge', '*nyay maangenge*', '*unki zimmedari unko samjhayenge*'[9]),
because their reality involves constantly negotiating and
renegotiating their strategic interests and material conditions with
generally hostile institutions. They opt for persuasion and consensus-
building more often than confrontation. They chose carefully when
to use the language and strategies of 'claiming', 'demanding' and
'asserting'—often when they have achieved a critical mass of
mobilisation and political strength—because the terms themselves
signal readiness for confrontation. Women always move very carefully
from negotiation to confrontation, because they have to bear the
cost of possible backlash from state and non-state actors in local
power structures.

The film by Deepa Dhanraj on the Nari Adalats (Women's
Courts) of Gujarat (2002) illustrates these patient, powerful, but
negotiative strategies extremely well, and the power and legitimacy
in adjudication that the Nari Adalats have gained with the larger
community as a result. The film also illustrates that women are both
more comfortable with and more confident using a discourse of *justice
and injustice*, and the responsibility of a range of duty-holders to deliver
justice, than of rights and their assertion. This may appear a fine
distinction, but these culturally specific modes of realising formally
enshrined rights and transferring them into socially sanctioned norms
and practices are extremely powerful modes of change. They are often
derided and dismissed because their modalities appear too un-militant
for some rights advocates. The aggressive rights rhetoric in fact
alienates a number of what are in reality rights-based movements,
because it discounts their emphasis on responsibilities and negotiated
change.

Finally, and perhaps most significant of all, these culturally-
specific alternatives place a much greater degree of agency in the
change process in the hands of those most marginalised by existing
power structures. The rights approach—whether to development or
civil and political rights—has generally shifted agency into the hands

---

[9] Meaning, 'we will explain to them', 'demand justice', 'teach them their
responsibility'.

of intermediaries (such as lawyers, bureaucrats, NGO leaders and elected representatives), whose accountability to the marginalised is weak at best. These interlocutors are often not demonstrably accountable to those whose rights they are defending. And rights inevitably go wrong if those with the greatest stake in claiming those rights become dependent on external actors for interpreting, asserting and realising their claims.

Indeed, there is growing evidence that rights claimed through external agents and formal systems are not necessarily sustainable. Modes of assertion based on demanding justice and fulfilment of responsibility, which do not always use formal systems of redress, are often less visible, involve more subtle and attenuated struggles, and address a fuller range of power structures, but do not necessarily lend themselves to quick and tangible measurement. Most of all, they use local forms of engagement and articulation that are not familiar to advocates of the rights-based approach—that is, they do not look or sound like they are about the claiming of rights. But changes negotiated by oppressed communities are more likely to become sustainable shifts in power, since the processes that created them are held and owned by the claim holders rather than external champions.

The rights-based approach was devised to move development from privilege, paternalism and patronage to a more democratic, accountable process that empowers marginalised people in their struggle for social and economic justice. It was a great leap forward from the welfare-oriented or instrumentalist view of development that had held sway over the past several decades. Above all, it was built from the experience of successful movements where excluded groups, using a range of formal and informal strategies, were able to compel or negotiate for greater inclusion and access to resources. These powerful roots of the rights-based approach are unfortunately being lost as it is converted into the latest magic bullet for achieving development.

In fact, there is nothing quick or magical about it—successful rights-based interventions have been constructed through years of organising, strengthening and sustaining movements—a process for which, incidentally, donor support has virtually dried up, since it is considered too slow and hard to measure. And ironically, many of these grassroots movements regard the 'rights-based' rhetoric with the same scepticism as any other framework created by the development elite.[10] They regard donor pressure to prove that they use a rights-based approach as ludicrous. There is an urgent need, among both rights advocates and development assistance agencies embracing the approach, to move towards a more nuanced and sophisticated understanding of rights themselves and of rights-based approaches, and particularly so at the level of practice.

It has been said before but bears repetition: there are no magic bullets or fast tracks to development with social justice. It is time to move away from formulas and rhetoric that focus on fixed modes of expression and on formal governance and judicial systems. We must listen more to how people engaged in struggles for their rights— especially women—articulate and negotiate their goals and strategies. Rights are always the end goal of such struggles, but their means can look deceptively different. We must interrogate our own *mantras* about the 'right' or 'wrong' approach, and regard with greater respect the articulations and wide repertoire of means employed by marginalised women and men, exercising their own agency, that result in the actual realisation of sustainable rights.

References

Ake, Claude, 1996. 'Mistaken Identities: How Misconceptions of Relations between Democracy, Civil Society and Governance Devalue Democracy', Keynote Address, International Conference on Governance, Getulio Vargas Institute, Sao Paolo, Brazil, November.

Flynn, David. 2005. 'What's Wrong with Rights? Rethinking Human Rights and Responsibilities', *Australian Social Work*, 58 (3): 244–56.

Ljungman, Cecilia M. 2004, 'Applying a Rights-based Approach to Development: Concepts and Principles', Paper presented at the conference on 'Winners and Losers from Rights-based Approaches to Development', November, p. 10. Available at: http://www.sed.manchester.ac.uk/idpm/ (accessed 12 November 2006).

---

[10] Personal communications with the leaders of at least four transnational grassroots movements—street vendors, home-based workers, slum dwellers, and grassroots rural women—that the author has been studying over the past three years.

Mutua, Makau. 2002. *Human Rights: A Political and Cultural Critique*, Pennsylvania Studies in Human Rights Series (Philadelphia: University of Pennsylvania Press).

Moser, Caroline and Andy Norton (with Tim Conway, Clare Ferguson and Polly Vizard). 2001. *To Claim Our Rights: Livelihood Security, Human Rights and Sustainable Development* (London: Overseas Development Institute).

Rogaly, Ben. 1996. 'Micro-finance Evangelism, Destitute Women, and the Hard-selling of a New Anti-poverty Formula', *Development in Practice*, 6 (2): 100–12.

SIDA. 2000. 'Working Together: The Human Rights Approach to Development Cooperation', Report on the workshop of donors and practitioners, Stockholm, Sweden, October (Donor workshop report, p. 9, and NGO workshop report, p. 7).

12. Walk Beside Us

In this concluding chapter, it seems appropriate to reflect on some of the lessons I have learnt on the journey to understanding women's empowerment. What do I know today that I did not know when I began the journey? What have been the significant shifts in global and local contexts—social, economic and political—that compel us to think, analyse and act differently today than we did in the 1980s or 1990s? What would I do differently if I was launching a women's empowerment programme like Mahila Samakhya today? I will address these questions not only through my own views and opinions, but also through the voices of the poor women that I have had the privilege of working with in the cities and villages of India. I am not speaking for them here—I have no authority to do so—but I am including in this summary the thoughts and insights that they shared with me over many years in the field.

Empowerment is still about power!

I know that power is still at the heart of the empowerment process—and it always will be. However, our world today is rife with even more complex power structures than it was thirty years ago—we have lost some of our old allies (like a pro-poor state) and gained new ones (other social movements more committed to gender equality now than they were in the past). There are now the global edifices of the market, finance and trade that make the old binaries of 'developed and developing' and North and South seem almost simple in comparison. We have new economic actors—like the BRICS and the G20—that did not exist earlier, and we have the unfettered power of international corporations who operate by stealth, often in cahoots with governing regimes, to plunder the earth's resources, violate labour norms, and flout environmental regulations with impunity. We have a resource-rich continent like Africa beset with civil wars and rogue regimes that commit untold atrocities on women. We have fundamentalist ideologies and armed struggles built around obscurantist visions of women's subordinate place in society, and an international war on terrorism that further aggravates these backlashes against the meagre gains made by women over the past decades.

In India, even as absolute levels of poverty have supposedly declined, we have widening gaps between the rich and the poor, and a huge and burgeoning middle class that wants more malls and less corruption, but was largely uninterested in gender equality until a middle-class girl was gang-raped and killed in the heart of New Delhi. And we have the continuing and persistent struggles of women in every corner of this country—the Women's Jamaat and the women of Kudankolam fighting a state-sponsored nuclear plant in Tamilnadu; the national federation of poor urban women, Mahila Milan, going from strength to strength and mobilising their constituents in new towns and cities across the country; the women of Manipur and Nagaland and Kashmir fighting the atrocities of the armed forces; the 'green shirt' women of Odisha fighting, alongside their brothers, to protect their ancestral lands from the predatory mining companies, who want them moved so they can plunder their land.

So the contexts in which women must organise are in many ways more dangerous and restrictive than at any time in the past. The state, from being an enabler and protector of their right of struggle—as it was in the days of Mahila Samakhya—is now often their main opponent, aligning with international and national business interests, citing 'national security' interests, and constricting the democratic space and associational rights of poor women to organise and build their struggles for change. Activists involved in mobilising and supporting women's empowerment processes are increasingly becoming targets of attack and repression, often jailed for 'anti-national' activities when all they did was to stand behind women's own critique of the failure of those they elected to answer to them.

What is remarkable, though, is that no one is giving up. The empowerment process continues, in different locations and forms, prioritising different issues and interests. So even as power structures have become more complex and multilayered and draconian, even as the state abandons poor women and their communities to their fate, or even violently represses them, new forms of resistance, new movements and challenges keep emerging. It is as though women have decided there is no turning back.

What is also remarkable is that at one time, it usually required a group of external activists, committed to gender equality and women's rights, to launch the empowerment process at the grassroots level. Today, we are witnessing movements that need little or nothing by way of external catalysts—movements like the Women's Jamaat or that of Kudankolam in Tamilnadu, or in the Northeast of India, have sprung up from local leadership. They have their own approaches to the empowerment process, and do not need an activist from beyond their borders to raise their consciousness or teach them about how power operates in their situation. So overall, there has been a larger process of political awakening and awareness—the first step in the empowerment process—and hundreds of thousands of women around the country have been empowered by it, seeing themselves as both political subjects and actors in a change process. In all humility, I salute them.

If power is still at the heart of empowerment, then my understanding of power itself has grown in leaps and bounds. At one time, deeply influenced by Marxist, Freirian and Foucaultian frameworks, I saw power as stemming mainly from a material and intellectual basis, and sustained largely by ideological conditioning and institutional mechanisms. This is what I laid out in the first women's empowerment concept paper (Chapter 3). But over the past decade, I have learnt to see many other 'faces' of power—especially the hidden and invisible ones—and the other realms in which it operates, particularly the intimate realm. Most of all, I have come to appreciate the inexplicable and enigmatic role of the self in the empowerment process—the conundrum of why some women, living lives in abject poverty and oppressive relationships, can be so bafflingly strong, confident, clear and sure of their paths, while others, far more privileged, are insecure and oppressive in their own practice of power. These insights find reflection in the feminist leadership paper (Chapter 8). So I have moved from a somewhat flat and materialist understanding to a more multidimensional and nuanced grasp of power. This means that today, when I speak of empowerment, and of key steps in the process of empowerment, I always start with the self—the inner transformations that must occur—as well as the external engagements for a more collective form of empowerment. And I will pay more attention to resourcing and supporting these internal transformations—in both women and men—as much as I would focus on organising women to struggle for the resources, services, rights and entitlements essential to rearranging the social power structures in which they transact their lives. I know now that only then will we achieve true empowerment—and a truly just social order.

Another tectonic shift in my view of empowerment has been my growing awareness of intersectionality—of how multiple forms of power intersect with each other. I am far more aware now of the multiple other marginalities and social exclusions—apart from gender—that I paid little attention to in my activist life, focused as I was on women disempowered by their poverty, caste and ethnicity. But today, I see how even progressive feminist movements failed to ally themselves with the struggles of other groups of women acutely marginalised by their identities—because they were lesbian, or disabled, or occupied in sex work. I realise how unthinkingly we had framed the empowerment process around the traditional gender binary of male and female, and around a heteronormative social norm.

However, in more recent writings—such as 'The Feminist and the Sex Worker—Lessons from the Indian Experience' (Batliwala 2010) and 'Unpacking Social Exclusion—A Primer for Marginalized Women' (Batliwala 2011)—I broke out of this box, and tried to apply my understanding of empowerment and movement-building to support the struggles of constituencies traditionally omitted from the feminist mainstream. And my interactions with these constituencies—in contexts like CREA's 'Count Me In' project and the conference it culminated in—has indelibly changed the way I think about both power and powerlessness. I see that even though we thought we were addressing the poorest and the most marginalised women of all in our empowerment work and conceptual framework, we were in fact leaving out many others even more marginalised because they were in sex work, or because they were lesbian, or disabled, or several of these at once. I have been similarly sensitised to the hierarchies—and marginalisations—of age that are so rampant, particularly in South Asian cultures, so that today, I examine different women's locations in terms of power and disempowerment through a much sharper and variegated prism than was at my disposal in the early 1990s. I see power now much more in terms of Gayle Rubin's 'Charmed Circle' (1984), and have adapted this tool to look for who is inside the innermost circle and who in the outermost in any given context that engages me.

What I learnt from women

The lessons learnt from the women I have worked with are too numerous to list, and in any case, the chapters in this book are studded with them. Instead, I will highlight a few of the most dramatic and important ones, those that led to the blinding revelations that completely altered my way of seeing my work and the world of social change that I occupied. I should hasten to add that most of these gems of wisdom came from women who had reached a high level of political maturity and astuteness in their own journeys of empowerment.

The first flash of insight came from how differently women define what they consider 'women's issues' and what they consider 'community issues'. A group of feminist activists from an autonomous women's group asked a group of Mahila Milan women—all pavement dwellers living on the streets of central Mumbai—what the women's issues they were dealing with were. Their response was astonishing: steady, secure income and employment, they said; safe and decent housing and habitats, decent toilets, adequate and safe water, a greater voice in family and community decision-making; an end to the constant demolition of their homes; land with secure tenure where they could resettle safely and permanently. And what did they consider 'community issues' or larger social issues, that the entire community, the government and society at large must take responsibility for: childcare, care of the elderly and the sick, all kinds of violence against women and girls (rape and other forms of sexual violence, wife-beating, dowry deaths), the ill-treatment of girls, and the demand for sons. Why, the feminists asked—shouldn't it be the other way around? No, the women said—housing, water, toilets, secure land for our homes, control over our income—these are things that affect women far worse than men. Men can sleep anywhere, defecate anywhere; we are the ones who cannot, who are responsible for making sure there is water for washing and cooking, for producing a hot meal, for earning enough to feed the children, whether the men have work or not. So decent housing, water, toilets, livelihood— these are women's issues. But the violence committed against us, the injustices against women—that is not something we can solve because we are not the ones who commit the crimes—the whole community has to be involved in tackling these, in ending these injustices. So those are community issues, not women's issues. There is an elegant, if baffling, logic behind this argument, if one can step out of one's mental box long enough to consider it.

Extending the same logic, women taught me that women's organisations should not assume sole responsibility for crimes against women, even if they take the lead. In the classic words of Madina, one of the Mahila Milan leaders,

> If a mad dog is running amok in the neighbourhood and biting lots of people, do we say it is the responsibility of those who were bitten and their families to end this scourge? NO! In the same way, when there are crimes against women, why should people ask what the women are doing about it? It's everyone's responsibility, not just ours!

And indeed, I have used this argument multiple times when challenged—usually by slightly hostile groups of men—'What are the women's organisations doing about _____?' You could fill in the blank with any major problem affecting women—child marriage, rape, dowry harassment, sexual harassment in the workplace or on the street, or what have you. I have always turned it back to them and asked, 'What are you doing about it? Does this problem not concern you?'

For the same reason, women have humbled me when it comes

to the importance of respecting their priorities in the empowerment process, which are often at odds with ours as external activists. This tension would inevitably arise when the consciousness raising process had advanced reasonably well, but the issues the women wanted to focus on always seemed to be around their poverty, or access to water, fuel, or common grazing lands, or improving the quality of education or healthcare delivery, or dealing with caste or ethnic violence—rather than internal issues like domestic violence, the early marriage of their daughters, or the lack of any equity in the division of labour in their own households. Over time, though, I came to understand that when women live in such immensely vulnerable situations, their instinct is to turn the focus of their rising consciousness on external targets—they do not want to interrogate and destabilise the more intimate and immediate spaces of their lives because these are their only safety nets, precarious and inadequate as they may seem. I grew more sensitive to how heavy the cost of every change they made was, of how they had to bear those costs in their lives every day. But I also learnt that over time, as their confidence and belief in their mission grows, they do begin to look within, and tackle the inequities of their intimate spheres.

I also grew sceptical about the great hopes and emphasis placed on new laws and better laws for women. Women taught me that the law was very remote for them, and that even the best legislation we advocated would not give them a few more gallons of water, kerosene for their lamps and stoves, or a decent meal every day—nor would they change the patriarchal biases of the customary laws and traditions that governed their lives. I saw how the opportunity cost of accessing or seeking redress through the formal judicial system was simply too high for poor women—and that they had to jump over so many barriers (as described in Chapter 2) to reach even the most basic services. And finally, I saw their generosity, when we told them about those laws, in saying how happy they were to know that such laws existed, so that maybe, someday, they might make a difference in the lives of their daughters or granddaughters. Laws do not change social realities, but people can and do.

I had always understood poverty unidimensionally, as being about material deprivation—the lack of land, livelihoods, income, assets, resources. From these women, I learnt that poverty is much more multifaceted—that they experienced as acutely a poverty of words and ideas, of new ways of understanding and analysing the world, of ways of organising themselves to change their reality. This is why they would gladly give up a day's wages to attend our periodic 'information fairs', where they would learn about a new smokeless stove, herbal remedies for common health problems, or how to compose songs or poems to express their feelings and dreams. They liked the idea of dreams, of being able to have them at all.

Most important of all, I learnt that we, as external change agents, must keep shifting our own role and location in the change process. Women taught me that we must not compete with them or feel threatened when they grew, became organised, politically articulate and analytical, and learnt to speak for themselves. I saw how many NGOs and women's organisations take all the space, and continue to speak for poor women even when the latter have found their own voices. We then need to learn to work *with* them, not *for* them. They do not want to be our 'beneficiaries' and 'target groups' and 'victims'.

They are the most important agents of change in the struggle for all forms of equality, not just gender equality. They do not wish to be romanticised or essentialised, either, as 'the all knowing ones', nor do they want to be tokenised.

I therefore choose to end this book on my journey of learning about women's empowerment with the words of Sundaramma, a women's collective leader from Bidar district in north Karnataka. I had asked her, 'What is our role in your empowerment?' Without the slightest hesitation, she responded:

> Work with us, not for us; don't tell us what to do to change our lives but expand our knowledge and skills so we can make those choices; help us eradicate the poverty of our ideas and dreams, show us new ways of understanding the world. Help us be heard by those who don't listen to us. At first, when we are still looking for the path we wish to tread, walk in front of us, help us find the way; then, as we grow surer, walk beside us; and finally, when we are truly strong, you must learn to walk behind us. We will still need you, in case we stumble and fall— but you must finally learn to walk behind us.

References

Batliwala, Srilatha. 2010. 'The Feminist and the Sex Worker—Lessons from the Indian Experience', *Himal South Asia*, August. Available at http://www.himalmag.com/component/content/article/241-.html.

———. 2011. 'Unpacking Social Exclusion—A Primer for Marginalized Women', in CREA, 'Count Me In Conference Papers'. Available at *web.creaworld.org/files/cmi/Conference%20Papers.pdf*.

Rubin, Gayle, 1984. 'Thinking Sex: Notes for a Radical Theory of the Politics of Sexuality', in Carole Vance (ed.), *Pleasure and Danger* (Boston and London: Routledge & Kegan Paul).